SAYINGS of the
ANCESTORS

I0130268

SAYINGS of the ANCESTORS

The Spiritual Life of the Sibundoy Indians

JOHN HOLMES McDOWELL

THE UNIVERSITY PRESS OF KENTUCKY

Copyright ©1989 by The University Press of Kentucky

Scholarly publisher for the Commonwealth,
serving Bellarmine College, Berea College, Centre
College of Kentucky, Eastern Kentucky University,
The Filson Club, Georgetown College, Kentucky
Historical Society, Kentucky State University,
Morehead State University, Murray State University,
Northern Kentucky University, Transylvania University,
University of Kentucky, University of Louisville,
and Western Kentucky University.

Editorial and Sales Offices: Lexington, Kentucky 40506-0336

Library of Congress Cataloging-in-Publication Data

McDowell, John Holmes, 1946-
  Sayings of the ancestors : the spiritual life of the Sibundoy Indians
/ John Holmes McDowell.
    p.   cm.
  Includes index.
  Bibliography: p.
  ISBN: 978-0-8131-5383-4
    1. Ingano Indians—Religion and mythology.   2. Camsa Indians—
Religion and mythology.   3. Indians of South America—Columbia—
Sibundoy Valley Region—Religion and mythology.   I. Title.
F2270.2.I53M33   1989
299'.8—dc19   89-5435
                                                               CIP

This book is printed on acid-free paper meeting
the requirements of the American National Standard
for Permanence of Paper for Printed Library Materials. ⊛

Contents

Illustrations follow page 86.

Preface

The Sibundoy Valley of Colombia is a South American microcosm, an indigenous cradle and crossroads, that has so far eluded thorough ethnographic description. In the following pages I offer an account of the spiritual life of its native peoples, a life marked by the unflagging quest for spiritual indemnity. The story is told primarily in the words of the Sibundoy peoples themselves, in their "sayings of the ancestors," in their glosses on the sayings, and in a parallel corpus of mythic narrative that provides the conceptual scaffolding for this spiritual edifice.

The perspective adopted here shuns the esoteric kennings of the ritual specialist (an important topic in its own right) in favor of a basic spiritual competence lodged within the minds of "ordinary" members of the community. It fastens on a system of everyday divination, on a set of folk medicinal practices originating in "home remedies," and on a spiritual sensibility distributed throughout the community. The dramatic techniques of the native doctors are indeed relevant as they enter into people's calculations, but this treatise remains firmly grounded in a pervasive spiritual orientation that lies very close to the heart of Sibundoy ethnicity.

One enters the domain of popular religious expression with some trepidation, out of respect for the inherent complexity of its phenomena and in awe of the extensive body of previous scholarship. In these pages I seek to fathom one additional matrix of human spirituality, by locating a corpus of traditional belief statements within its sustaining cosmological field. It will be readily apparent that I part company with those who merely catalogue atomistic beliefs, or worse, dismiss them as "idle" or "empty" superstition. To some extent this book should be received as a tract *against* the presumption of superstition; it construes the spiritual life of Sibundoy natives as a rational and coherent system, indeed as a folk religion. I suggest we explore the advantages of an approach that perceives "the spiritual phenomena of folklore as truth or possible truth and not as illusion or superstition" (Carvalho Neto 1983: 54).

This project, like every labor of love, imposed its own dimensions and logic as it evolved. My initial appreciation of the sayings as verbal art miniatures yielded to a recognition of their deep resonance within the indigenous worldview; what began as ethnopoetics came to encompass folk medicine, folk psychology, and folk religion. Exegesis of the Sibundoy materials pivots on an inherent duality of expressive forms, which are at once a 'collective' possession of the community and a factor in the life dramas of its individual members. As a storehouse of traditional wisdom, the sayings conserve portions of a "brute" ancestral spirituality by capturing associations between dream images and other experiences and their spiritual implications. As a form of "equipment for living," they foster some comprehension of the hand of fate as it operates within a particular web of circumstance.

The sayings of the ancestors emerge in this study as elements in an abstract code that acquires force as it is creatively adapted to the needs of people in turmoil. The mysteries of the ancestral world and its modern residue, the spirit realm, invest dream images and wakeful experiences with a special immanence; the play of imagination on the wrenching circumstances of actual lives finds causality and necessity in the capricious paths of human destiny. The ensuing chapters illuminate this dialectic linking traditional resources and idiosyncratic strategies in the folkloristic process.

For Latin Americanists, the Sibundoy Valley is one of those neglected peripheries with the potential to refine our understanding of cultural evolution in the South American context. As a region that is transitional on two axes—it lies just beyond the northern fringe of Incan expansion and at the eastern rim of the Andes—the Sibundoy Valley is a virtual laboratory of South American ethnohistory, witness to the encounter and accommodation of various cultural prototypes. The diversity of its heritage is evident in the two native languages of its peoples: Inga (from the Quechuan stock), brought to the valley by migrants from the adjacent lowlands; and Kamsá (from the Quillasinga stock), the only living remnant of the local pre-Incan linguistic substrate. Two prominent features of South American ethnohistory are brought into especially clear focus: the hybridization of highland and lowland antecedents, and the living web of social and economic interaction that binds these contrastive zones into an organic entity.

As a consequence, the Sibundoy materials lend themselves to an inspection of the very lenses used to view South American Indians.

There is much that tallies with the extensive ethnohistorical and ethnographic record for the central and southern Andes; there are unmistakable affinities with the societies of the Upper Amazon; and parallels with the Chibchan peoples to the north are easily identified. Inspection of Sibundoy Valley materials complicates the facile use of handy labels such as "Andean" and "Amazonian", "highland" and "lowland," "Incan," and even "northern," "central," or "southern" Andes. This book portrays the Sibundoy complex as a unique cultural formation, one that incorporates multiple influences from a variety of human environments and combines them into a distinctive pattern of civilization.

A work of this nature accumulates many debts and I can only begin to acknowledge them here. My first debt is to my compadre, Professor Francisco Tandioy Jansasoy, who played an important role in the collection and initial processing of field data. His patient, good-humored explanations finally alerted me to the full outlines of spirituality embedded in the sayings. Naturally, Professor Tandioy must be absolved from any flaws that have crept into the analysis, which is entirely of my own making. As I retouch this preface I am pleased to report the arrival of *Muscuycuna y Tapiacuna: Sueños y Agüeros en inga y castellano* (Colombia, 1987), a compilation of sayings and commentaries from Francisco's mother, Margarita Jansasoy, containing some of the same texts that appear in this study.

Apart from this primary debt, I owe a word of appreciation to the many Sibundoy friends, Ingano and Kamsá alike, who received me in their homes, most often with a "drop" of *chicha* and often with a "taste" of cuy, and tolerated my curious penchant for asking questions and taking notes. I would like to recognize in particular don Justo Jacanamijoy, his wife doña María Juajibioy, and their children, who provided me with a secure and stimulating homelife in the vereda of San Felix during a year's sojourn in the Sibundoy Valley.

Acknowledgment is also due those who helped nourish this manuscript to completion. I thank my colleagues and students at Indiana University's Folklore Institute for their curiosity and interest. My mother and father and each of my three sisters have lent a helping hand at various moments along the way. Patricia Glushko has been an angel of support throughout, and she is responsible for preparing from my negatives a set of excellent prints for the photographs included with the text. I thank Professor Frank Salomon for his useful comments on an earlier draft of this manuscript. I have enjoyed working with the resourceful Jerome Crouch of the University Press of Kentucky, who showed enthusiasm for this project when it was still only an idea. Lastly, I include a tribute to the patience of my two children, Juan and Sofía; they often held the fort while their father sat riveted to the word processor.

1

Introduction

Tucked away in its mountain fastness, the Sibundoy Valley of Colombia houses a fertile plain that has nourished the evolution of a remarkable South American civilization. The Sibundoy natives are renowned for their agriculture and weaving, for their colorful indigenous carnival, and for the prowess of their native doctors. This inquiry examines the spiritual life of these peoples, which enters into all facets of the daily routine and imposes a distinctive orientation to reality. The natives of the valley inhabit a world charged with spiritual presence, where the intervention of *animas* (souls of the departed) and *sacha huayra* (spirits of the forest) settles the fortunes of individuals and families. The conventional beliefs associated with this pugnacious spirit realm are codified in traditional sayings that circulate throughout the indigenous communities, surfacing in conversational settings as people strive to forecast their futures and to account for events already witnessed.

The following chapters make available an annotated collection of one corpus of sayings, gathered from members of the Santiago Ingano community, and locate this corpus within the context of Sibundoy cosmology, so that the prescriptions and proscriptions of the sayings acquire a plausible heritage and logic. In addition, we will explore the process of implementation, which inserts the wisdom of the sayings into the day-to-day affairs of Sibundoy natives. Fulfillment of these objectives entails a systematic presentation of texts and commentaries, in conjunction with a discussion of mythology and folk medicine as these contribute to a clearer understanding of the sayings.

The *sayings of the ancestors* are proverb-like belief statements that capture the spiritual connotations of empirical signs, thereby casting light on a pervasive cosmic order underlying all human experience. They bespeak a world saturated with spiritual agency, conceived as a dynamic interiority to the surfaces of ordinary experience. They alert people to the insistent activity in the spirit realm, which constantly threatens to wreak havoc in the fragile course of human lives. Directly or indirectly the sayings warn of *huayra*, or 'spirit sickness', and they provide an irreplaceable guide to the maintenance of spiritual health, a blessed condition conferring invulnerability to the ravages of misfortune. Those who possess spiritual health are said to be 'strong,' and the Inga word denoting this quality, *sinchi*, is also one of the terms used to name the native doctors, whose principal mission is conveyed by the term, *sinchiyachiy*, literally 'to make strong'.

The central thesis of this study is that the sayings are the practical component of a folk religion localized in the Sibundoy Valley but with analogues in many parts of indigenous South America. I use the term *folk religion* to designate a religious system conserved in the everyday practices of a community rather than in the canonic forms of organized worship. Don Yoder (1974: 11) provides (among several alternatives) a definition amenable to the Sibundoy case, invoking "the totality of all those views and practices of religion that exist among the people apart from and alongside the strictly theological and liturgical forms of the official religion."

Following this line of reasoning, the religiosity of the sayings stems from their preoccupation with the place of humanity in the cosmic design rather than from some association with an established church. The sayings conserve fidelity to the example of the first people, who established for all time the guidelines for a civilized life. They encourage the pursuit of spiritual health by aligning the contemporary frame of events with this eternal ancestral model. The American philosopher and poet George Santayana (1922) defines religion as that which "tunes human actions to an envisioned cosmic order and projects images of cosmic order onto the plane of human experience." The sayings of the ancestors, in their roles as signifiers of spiritual reality and harbingers of individual and collective spiritual health, promote just such an integration of the cosmic and the human.

The aboriginal Sibundoy religion survived the Spanish conquest and colonization by working out an intricate accommodation of indigenous America to folk and institutional Europe. The emergent folk religion displays elements widely distributed throughout indigenous South America: a pan-Andean cosmological bedrock, featuring the celestial deities, the actions of the culture hero, and the displacement of a previous race of "heathens"; a tropical forest charismatic shamanism, featuring the use of visionary hallucinogens, the dramatic performances of native doctors, and a reciprocity between human societies and the "masters" or "owners" of the natural world; and an infusion of elements taken from orthodox and folk Catholicism, especially beliefs concerning the wandering souls of purgatory. The sayings activate a syncretic consciousness, enlisting the Catholic rosary and cross, as well as signs drawn from dreams and the natural world, in the struggle to monitor the spirit realm for evidence of deteriorating spiritual health.

The sayings of the ancestors are a multipurpose genre, and their connection to an underlying folk religion is not immediately obvious. Perhaps their most apparent function is the enculturation of children into the traditional native lifeways. Some of the sayings are strictly pedagogical in character and are used to instruct or reprimand children. Consider saying 167 and a rationale provided for it:

If you stick your head into a jar,
your breathing will be obstructed,
and you will not be able to run.

"We tell the children not to be drinking from the earthen jar. 'If you drink sticking your head into the jar, when it is time to run you will not be able to; like a dog with its tongue sticking out you will be running, trying in vain to climb a hill.' "

In this manner children are deterred from the unseemly (and unhygienic) practice of drinking directly from the large jars housing the family's water supply. At the same time they are being initiated into the proper way of doing things, a balanced and harmonious way of life chartered by the example of the ancestors.

The pedagogical function of the sayings is prominent in some native accounts of the genre, especially accounts that are directed to an outside audience. Consider the following introduction to the tradition provided by Domingo Tandioy Chasoy, a native of the Santiago Ingano community who has assembled and published a small compendium of the sayings (Tandioy Chasoy, n.d.):

The sayings, proverbs, and recipes of the indigenous Ingas of Santiago that are presented here are still conserved in the tradition of the old folks. The young people are influenced more and more by modern civilization, and because of this we have already forgotten many of our traditions.

As far as many of these sayings and proverbs are concerned, it seems that they do not actually reflect the beliefs of the ancestors, but rather that they used them to educate or to form a mentality of respect among young people, since they had no other method than actual illustration.

Domingo Chasoy's commentary highlights the pedagogical intent of the sayings and plays down the belief element. There can be no doubt that the corpus of sayings plays a major enculturative role, one that is not limited to the instruction of children. There are sayings in circulation addressing concerns and problems endemic to all stages of the life cycle. A great many sayings move beyond the parent-to-child framework and offer assistance to parents in raising their children, as in saying 162: "It is bad to tickle the bottom of a child's foot, because he will not be able to cross over the bridges." Foot travel within and between the native settlements entails crossing numerous log bridges, so this piece of advice deals with a topic that is important in the making of a competent adult.

Other sayings leave behind the period of childhood and deal with all manner of subjects, for instance the care of a pregnant woman, the planting of crops, or the proper times and places for bathing. For example, saying 173 warns against placing a basket on the head of a pregnant woman ("it will be as if the baby in the mother's stomach were held in a basket"), and saying 136 warns against bathing on the day after the full moon ("the rainbow will urinate on you, and leave you covered with warts"). Once a substantial corpus of sayings is assembled, it becomes clear that the tradition indexes beliefs and practices active in every domain of human experience. Its scope and breadth is such that it amounts to a comprehensive guide to native lifeways. In a style that is unselfconscious and practical, the sayings encode attitudes, values, and recipes for action defining the indigenous ethos in the Sibundoy Valley.

It would be a mistake, however, to view the sayings as mere tools of enculturation or as quaint curios of a South American ethnic life style. Nor can they be dismissed as sheer superstition, as empty holdovers from a previous belief system. One indication of a greater significance is their preoccupation with dream images and dream interpretation. When the large inventory of sayings focused on dream images is scrutinized, it becomes apparent that dreaming is valued as a direct channel of communication with the spirit realm. Moreover, the majority of sayings implicate a superhuman agency in some fashion, and most of them are concerned with divination as a means of insight into human destiny. A great many of the sayings center on the pivotal concept of *huayra*, the Inga word literally meaning 'wind' but signifying 'spirit' and 'spirit sickness'. As I have already intimated, even those sayings dedicated to apparently mundane goals (such as raising children to behave properly) impose the prevailing moral order and draw implicitly on the wisdom of the ancestors.

Tandioy Chasoy's downplaying of the belief component simply does not wash in view of the many proclamations to the contrary by members of the native communities. Characteristic is the following kind of statement: "What is foretold in the sayings generally comes to pass, if not right away then within a few days or weeks. Here in the valley we live by the proverbs." Statements like these indicate a pattern of belief in the accuracy and validity of the tradition. In view of these considerations, I contend that the sayings, along with the surrounding complex of belief and practice, must be viewed as elements in a thriving folk religion whose overriding concern is the spiritual health of the individual, the family, and ultimately the entire indigenous community.

It will be apparent that this study is decidedly synchronic in character, assessing the place of the sayings within a conceptual and pragmatic system. This approach necessarily slights the important issue of the worldwide distribution of comparable beliefs and sayings. At the outer limit, the Sibundoy corpus of sayings possesses a universality, for it would be difficult to imagine a human society that did not share at least a few of these beliefs. Many of the sayings strike a familiar chord in Western thinking, and are common to numerous folk cultures around the world: among them, the idea that a pregnant woman must eat whatever food she craves, that the call of an owl foretells a death, or that the loss of a tooth warns of the death of a parent. This last belief, for example, is attested in Asia, indigenous America, and Europe (Seligman 1923: 188). To a considerable degree, this corpus of sayings captures a "natural" mode of human consciousness, a way of thinking that surfaces readily and quickly becomes reified as canonic folk belief.

At the same time, the sayings of the ancestors exhibit the peculiar stamp of their physical and cultural environment, of Amerindian, and most particularly, Sibundoy ethnicity. Tzvetan Todorov (1984) attributes to Amerindian societies a mastery in "the art of ritual discourse," premised on the notion that "prophecy is memory." He sees the preoccupation of Moctezuma and his priests with the interpretation of codified signs as a major factor in their inability to deal effectively with the Spanish presence. The central elements in the Sibundoy folk religion—the utilization of signs and portents from the dreamworld and from naturalistic observation, and an overwhelming concern with individual and collective spiritual health—are surely cornerstones of Amerindian consciousness (Kroeber 1902; Morgan 1932; Wallace 1958; Eggan 1966; Myerhoff 1974; Bruce 1975; Whitten 1976; Gregor 1981; Conrad & Demarest 1984; Marzal 1985; B. Tedlook 1987).

If we look for close parallels to the Sibundoy system, we find them in other indigenous communities of the Andes and the nearby lowlands, and in a more diluted form, among mestizos residing in the towns and cities of the Andean region. From this base, these orientations have flavored the cultural life of the Andean polity generally, as can be evidenced in the current wave of literary fiction emerging from the Andean republics. The closest parallels to the Sibundoy tradition are found, not surprisingly, in Indian societies of the Andes and their eastern foothills, where a preoccupation with the spiritual effects of *huayra*, and the reliance on dream images and wakeful signs to combat them, seems to be a commonplace feature, both currently and historically (Whitten 1976; Bastien 1978; Isbell 1978; Flores-Ochoa 1979; Conrad & Demarest 1984; Mannheim 1987). To cite only one example, the Canelos Quichua of Ecuador, who inhabit the eastern periphery of the Andes, maintain a system of dream interpretation that appears to replicate many features of the Sibundoy system. As in the Sibundoy Valley, these people arise each morning to discuss their dreams and formulate plans for the coming day on the basis of a traditional code of dream interpretation (Whitten 1976).

Compilations of similar, in some cases identical, folk beliefs in mestizo provinces such as Nariño, Colombia (Cabrera Rodriguez 1986), Cajamarca, Peru (Ibérico Mas 1971), and Santiago de Estero, Argentina (Lullo 1944), demonstrate a considerable spillover of indigenous thought patterns in the formulation of a composite Andean popular culture. But certain key differences between mestizo and indigenous systems emerge: the mestizo systems often encode different values, and the folk beliefs persist largely outside of a validating cosmological framework. For example, in Cajamarca (as in Sibundoy) the dream of riding a horse is significant, but the polarity of connotation is reversed: whereas in Sibundoy this dream warns of spirit sickness (saying 45), in Cajamarca it foretells "the realization of a pleasant event" (Ibérico Mas 1971: 140). These differences correlate to a contrasting value accorded the horse in these two settings (in the Sibundoy Valley, the horse is considered an alien beast). Moreover, the mestizo traditions appear to exist apart from an operative cosmology; in the absence of a cohesive mythical consciousness, these folk beliefs acquire the aura of *superstitions*, that is, beliefs held without any decisive rational foundation.

What is special about the Sibundoy case is that it favors the inspection of a corpus of traditional sayings within a cohesive framework of ideology and praxis. By relating the sayings of the ancestors to the cosmology enshrined in Sibundoy mythology and to the everyday quest for spiritual health, we can appreciate them as dynamic components of a living folk religion. The Sibundoy natives have indeed absorbed much from the European and mestizo cultures that have so profoundly altered their historical destiny; witness the presence of Catholic icons, such as the rosary, cross, and altar, in the corpus of sayings. At the same time, the Sibundoy peoples have retained a distinctively "native" orientation to the cosmos, an orientation that has infiltrated the thinking of their non-Indian neighbors. The story of the Spanish impact on the native peoples of the Andes has been told and retold; the story of the indigenous foundation of the modern Latin American worldview is only beginning to be understood. Investigation of the sayings of the ancestors opens up the possibility of juxtaposing, and reevaluating, these two stories in the cultural laboratory of the Sibundoy Valley.

THE SANTIAGUEÑOS

The Sibundoy Valley houses four major human populations coexisting in an uneasy state of mutual dependency. Three of these are indigenous groups: the Inganos of Santiago and San Andrés, Quechua-speaking communities of some 4000 and 1000 individuals respectively; and the Kamsá, some 3500 speakers of a language isolate that has been related to the language of the archaic Quillasinga federation. The other major group in the valley, numbering perhaps some 20,000, is the *colono* population, Spanish-speaking Colombian nationals who migrated into the valley in this century for the most part. The colonos are in many ways the dominant population, controlling the regional economy and providing the link to external institutions of the nation. Nonetheless, it is probably accurate to say that the indigenous lifestyle still sets the tone in the valley, and the colono population is perceived to have only a tentative foothold in this territorial preserve of the Kamsá and Ingano.

In spite of their distinct languages and origins, the native peoples of the valley participate in a standardized indigenous culture, characterized by identical modes of subsistence and social organization, and by a common life style and worldview. The Kamsá and Santiago Ingano peoples have shared the Sibundoy Valley for at least half a millenium, and under the influence of their legendary *cacique* (native chieftain) Carlos Tamoabioy, they forged in the eighteenth century a political unification that has endured into the present (Bonilla 1972). Furthermore, Kamsá and Santiagueño alike have been subjected to the autocratic control of one Catholic mission after another, each striving to mold a homogeneous indigenous population. The San Andrés Inganos appear to have adapted to these conventions shortly after their arrival in the Sibundoy Valley, perhaps toward the middle of the eighteenth century (Levinsohn 1976). Melvin Lee Bristol, who spent a considerable amount of time investigating Sibundoy ethnobotany, came to the conclusion that the native communities of the valley are "culturally similar and in many ways identical . . . excepting the profound language distinction" (1965: 20).

This is not to deny the separate identities of these peoples, nor to suggest that every trace of cultural diversity among the native enclaves has vanished. Alberto Juajibioy, the distinguished Kamsá ethnolinguist, asserts that the Inganos and Kamsá differ with regard to language, mythology, and origin (1987: 18). Moreover, members of each group recognize oddities in the speech, foodways, and dress of their neighbors. The Santiagueños refer to the phonologically complex speech of the Kamsá as *coche* or 'pig-language'; the Kamsá find it amusing that the Inganos reprocess the dregs to squeeze a second round of chicha from them, and that they eat their meat with the skin on the animal. In Santiago, when a youngster mispronounces a word, he may be chided for being a "San Andresiño". But these fine-grained discrepancies pale in comparison with the manifest convergence of social, economic, political and expressive forms. A concerted inquiry might reveal systematic differences in the cultural heritage of the valley's prinicipal groups, but for the purposes of this study the term *Sibundoy natives* refers collectively to the indigenous peoples of the valley, and I draw freely on the mythologies and other traditions of Kamsá and Ingano alike, even though the primary corpus of sayings was collected among the Inganos of Santiago.

The Sibundoy Valley is a highland preserve of some 21,000 acres, situated at approximately 7000 feet above sea level and just over one degree north of the equator. The provincial city of Pasto lies across the continental divide, some 20 miles to the west; to the east, beyond the last vertical thrust of the Andes, is the town of Mocoa at western edge of the Amazonian basin. The valley is a scene of captivating beauty, a verdant expanse hedged on all sides by stately mountains rising to an elevation of some 10,000 feet above sea level. The valley floor is dissected at every turn by cool, sparkling waters, emerging from the adjacent foothills and eventually joining forces to form the highland origin of the Putumayo river, a major tributary to the Amazon. As one walks the footpaths connecting the native settlements, the senses are pleasantly accosted with the sights, sounds, and aromas of the place: the bright, many-hued flowers marking the boundaries of human residences; the rustling stalks of corn standing guard about the edges of the houses; the musky aroma of smoke seeping through the thatch roofs of the cottages; the endless panorama of sunlight and shade moving across the face of the mountain walls visible on all sides; and the calm sonority of voices emanating from the kitchen areas, as people gather in the evening to drink chicha and converse.

The Sibundoy Valley, as noted, is the ancestral and actual home of the Ingano and Kamsá peoples. The Kamsá community, referred to in the scholarly literature as the Coche, Sibundoy, Mocoa, or Camsa, speaks the Kamsá language and resides in the towns of Sibundoy and Colon and in the open stretches of the valley south of these two towns. The Kamsá language is an isolate and appears to be the sole surviving dialect of the language spoken by the prehistorical and early historical Quillasingas (Sañudo 1938), who shared control over the region around Pasto with the Pasto Indians at the time of the Spanish conquest. One scholar characterizes the Kamsá as "the prototype in the Andes sector of the most archaic culture on the South American continent" (Oviedo Zambrano 1978).

The Sibundoy Ingano communities reside principally in and around the town of Santiago and also around the smaller village of San Andrés, located across the Quinchoa River just under two miles from Santiago. Inganos are also found in the town of Aponte, in the state of Nariño, a day's walk out of the Sibundoy Valley, and in the Lower Putumayo area, where they live along the large rivers that fan out across the Amazonian basin. These Inganos of the Lower Putumayo are known by Kamsá and Ingano alike as *amigos*, and they are perceived as a friendly extension of the native communities of the Putumayo highlands.

The indigenous groups of the Sibundoy Valley have participated from time immemorial in a complex network of horizontal and vertical trade, encompassing an extensive domain ranging from the

Pacific Ocean to the Amazonian basin, and from the Carchi plateau
in the north of present-day Ecuador to the northern reaches of the
modern Colombian province of Nariño (Uribe n.d.). Involvement
in this trade network, and not a Polynesian origin as some commentators have suggested (but see Juajibioy 1987), probably explains the presence of conch shells in the valley, used as musical
instruments in association with the indigenous carnival. Ethnohistorical documents depict the Sibundoy natives as an eastern
adjunct of the Quillasinga federation, which appears to have been
a political amalgam of several diverse ethnic groups. The native
peoples of the valley are portrayed in these documents in generally
favorable terms, as in the following citation from a Spanish royal
inspector who visited the valley in 1574 (Lopez de Velazco 1894):
"The province of Sibundoy is cool, and its people dress with distinction. There is abundance of all kinds of foods, and it is rich in
gold mines worked by the Indians of that place." Other sources
attest to the autonomy of the Sibundoy natives, who are said to
have "neither dealings nor contracts with other Indians because
they are surrounded by mountains" (Vollmer R. 1978). These early
documents characterize the native peoples of the valley as excellent
farmers, as miners of affluvial gold, and perhaps most significantly
for our purposes, as powerful spiritual healers (Salomon 1983;
Taussig 1980).

The Santiagueño Ingano community, the source of our present
corpus of sayings, lives in the town of Santiago and in the surrounding *veredas* (native hamlets). A significant portion of the
community resides in displaced migrant and immigrant colonies
in the major cities of Colombia, Venezuela, Panama, and Costa
Rica. With the harsh regimen established by the Capuchin mission
around the turn of the century, a pattern of external migration was
established, and to this day almost every Santiagueño family has
one or more relatives seeking their fortunes in these faraway places.
By far the largest group of expatriates resides in Caracas, Venezuela,
drawn there by the purchasing power of the *bolivar*, the Venezuelan
currency. Santiagueños living in Bogotá, Caracas, Panama City, or
San José, Costa Rica, make every effort to return to the Sibundoy
Valley for carnival season, which falls every year just before Lent,
usually in the month of February.

The origin of the native peoples of the Sibundoy Valley remains
uncertain. The prehistory of the Santiagueños has been the subject
of a good deal of speculation. The known pieces in the puzzle are
these: they reside in the northwestern corner of the Sibundoy Valley; they share the life-style of their Kamsá neighbors; their lan-

guage is Quechua, in a dialect related to the Quechua of Imperial Cuzco; their family names are predominantly Kamsá in origin. This cluster of vital facts leaves open a number of possible interpretations. One view holds that the Santiagueños are a Peruvian people resettled by the Incas at the fringe of their territory (Bonilla 1972). It is well known that the Incas sometimes exported subject peoples to serve as a human buffer for their empire, and also that they inserted Inca-instructed bureaucrats to govern newly acquired populations. These practices affected peoples as far north as Quito, Ecuador (Salomon 1986).

However, in spite of claims to the contrary in some ethno-historical documents, there is no compelling evidence that the Incas ever founded any significant settlements as far north as the domain of the Santiagueños. It is possible that some of the confusion on this point derives from the existence of two segments of the Pasto Indians, the Pastos of Ecuador, who were partly conquered by the Incas, and the Pastos of Colombia, who were not (Romoli de Avery 1978: 15). If we discard the theory of Inca implantation, there remain at least two additional options. In one scenario, they are a remnant of a *yanacona* group, an 'indigenous bureaucratic order' brought into the south of Colombia by Spanish soldiers and settlers rather than by the Inca lords. Kathleen Romoli de Avery (1978: 15) accounts for the diffusion of Quechua place names in southern Colombia thus: "The Spanish conquistadores brought with them from Quito many hundreds of Quechua-speaking Indians, a good many of them *yanaconas* of high caste. These were the interpreters, intermediaries, and informants of the explorers and settlers." It is conceivable that some portion of this population might have settled voluntarily or through coercion in this niche of the Sibundoy Valley.

Another scenario has the Santiagueños entering the valley from the Amazonian lowlands via a route leading westward up the slopes of the Andes some time prior to the arrival of the Spaniards in the early sixteenth century. The San Andrés Inganos relate that they ascended into the valley in this fashion in comparatively recent times, perhaps the eighteenth century (Levinsohn 1976), and it is possible that the Santiagueños derive from this same lowland Inga stock. In this case they would represent one of the western-most population thrusts from the Upper Amazonian region with its tumultuous history of migratory peoples (Lathrap 1970; Reichel-Dolmatoff 1975; Jackson 1983).

Whatever their origin, it is certain that the Santiagueños have lived in the Sibundoy valley for some centuries, and over this period they have worked out a polite but distant relationship with their Kamsá co-residents of the valley. Today the Santiagueños reside in some twenty-seven *veredas* located in and around the town of Santiago. Most of these settlements are perched on the lower slopes of the mountains rising above the western perimeter of the Sibundoy Valley; a few of them lie at the edge of the valley along the national highway as it runs eastward toward the towns of Colón and Sibundoy. The vereda is a geographical and social entity, each separated from its neighbor by natural features such as cliffs, woods, rivers, or streams. A large vereda might contain as many as fifty houses, a small one fifteen or twenty. Within each vereda, the majority of families are related. Frequently, a number of sisters and their families reside in a cluster within the vereda, each having received from her father a plot of land on which to raise her family.

The vereda is the focus of much of the individual's social and economic life. Most of one's friends and relatives live in the vereda, and marriage partners are often sought from one's own or a neighboring vereda. The Santiagueño vereda can be compared to the well-documented Andean social unit known as the *ayllu*, even though this term does not occur in the Inga of the Sibundoy Valley. According to oral tradition, the veredas were once designated as matrilocal clan residences, but historical events have altered their original character. Through the intervention of the missionaries, indigenous families have been forced to relocate, so that contemporary vereda residents do not trace their origin back to a common ancestor. Moreover, in the present climate there is a good deal of buying and selling of land, and this process has further diluted the social composition of the veredas.

In recent years, a great deal of local initiative has been generated by the vereda-based *junta de acción comunal*, or 'committee of community action', sponsored by the territorial government operating out of Mocoa in the Lower Putumayo. The vereda is emerging as a key political unit in the interaction between external authorities and the native peoples of the valley. In addition to the juntas, elementary schools and job training programs are now operating at the level of the vereda. These progressive, vereda-based elements are taking a leading role in bringing amenities such as roads, potable water, and electricity to the Santiagueño veredas.

As important as the vereda is in the life of the Santiagueños, there are a number of occasions and institutions that operate at a communitywide level. People from all the veredas come together for mass at the Catholic church in Santiago each Sunday, and they gather in the plaza of Santiago for music and dancing during the carnival period. The Santiago *cabildo* is the traditional organ of communitywide self government, charged with maintaining the peace in all the veredas, and procuring justice for all Santiagueños. Its domain extends to all legal proceedings short of serious felonies, and it represents the Santiagueño community before the church and state bureaucracies. The cabildo deals most frequently with issues such as children's attendance at school, monetary disputes, quarrels over land, accusations of thievery, and marital problems.

Another prominent source of extra-vereda contact is the social institution of fictive kinship associated with the rite of passage ceremonies. A number of stages in the individual's life cycle are marked by these ceremonies, including baptism, confirmation, first communion, marriage, and death. These observances occur in two phases: an initial visit to town for the ministration of the parish priest; and a subsequent ceremony in the vereda, featuring traditional expressions such as ritual language speeches, ritual consumption of chicha, and dancing to the music of flute and drum.

Sponsors are named for each rite of passage, and these people become *compadres* ('coparents') and incur continuing responsibilities toward the family or individual undergoing the change of status. They are generally chosen from other veredas, as people seek to cement productive social alliances. This process creates networks of fictive kinship binding the different veredas into a single political community. The notion of community is foregrounded in the ritual language speeches, which accomplish all personal reference and address through the use of kinship terms associated with the immediate family (McDowell 1983).

Within the vereda, the household is the focus of activities for the nuclear family. In the more remote veredas, many families still reside in the old-fashioned thatch-roofed cottages. In the veredas closer to Santiago and the national highway, the native cottage has given way to the cement-floored, ceramic-tiled house, based on prototypes taken from the national culture. In either case, the conceptualization and utilization of space remains much the same. The houses consist of two principal rooms, a kitchen area dominated by the wood-burning hearth and flanked by native wooden stools of various sizes, and a kind of parlor with long benches lining the walls, where visitors are received and treated to a bowl of soup or a "drop" of chicha.

Each house stands with its back to the wind, and on the lee side shelters a patio, with a clean-swept earthen surface. Beyond the patio looms the lush garden, known as the *chagra*, with its sprawl of corn stalks, flowering bean vines, and other flowering bushes and trees, and its perimeters marked by lines of sheltering eucalyptus trees. The native peoples of the Sibundoy Valley are famous for their horticultural skills. Early Spanish documents report that an expedition under the command of Sebastian de Benalcazar's lieutenants was nourished back to life in the Sibundoy Valley after a harsh campaign to the north (Bonilla 1972). The biosphere of the valley is auspicious for agriculture. The climate is moderate, and water is abundant in the frequent rainfall that hits the valley itself and in the many streams that descend from the surrounding mountains to wander across the floor of the valley. The soil is rich, partly because of an accumulation of silt during an earlier period when the valley apparently held the waters of a large intermontane lake, and partly because of the minerals that have filtered into it from volcanic eruptions around its periphery.

Several centuries of human elaboration of this promising ecological niche has resulted in a diversified flora. Melvin Lee Bristol (1965: 35) characterizes the region as "more a refugium than one of active speciation." He observes (1968: 577) that "several plants known nowhere else in the world have evolved in the valley under the complex influences of civilization." There has been considerable propagation of fruit-bearing trees native to the valley, but the real mark of Sibundoy horticulture is the cultivation of introduced plant species. Bristol (1968) identifies 23 "endemic cultivars," that is, local varieties now confined to the Sibundoy Valley, in an inventory of some 240 plant taxa associated with the native gardens. He found that the Sibundoy Valley is the primary center of varietal diversity of two plant species, *Arracacia xanthorrhiza*, which produces an edible root, and *Datura candida* (Schultes & Hofmann 1979 propose a reclassification of these daturas within the genus *Brugmansia*), with varieties used for a number of medicinal purposes including the preparation of a hallucinogenic substance known locally as *borrachero*, important in the practice of the native doctors.

The intimate tie of the Sibundoy natives to their ecological niche can be measured in the extensive inventory of cultivated plants and their wide range of uses. In addition to sources of food and beverage, and kindling for the cooking fires, the plants in the native gardens serve a wide range of medicinal purposes, as antiseptics, anesthetics, aphrodisiacs, purgatives and narcotics, and treatments for disorders associated with virtually every aspect of human physiology. Apart from these major uses, they provide raw materials for a great many purposes: the construction of houses, bridges, fences, baskets, brooms, sleeping mats, musical instruments, dyes, detergents, and bags; the curing and feeding of domesticated animals; the expression of religious and ceremonial sentiment; and the adornment and beautification of house, garden, and human body.

The mainstay of the native diet is corn, which is consumed on a daily basis in a great variety of liquid and solid forms, ranging from soups to the roasted grain to breads prepared from a corn flour. The maize plant (*Zea mays*) appears in several varieties: *pintado sara*, the descendant of the original seed introduced to the valley, with its black, blue, and red grain; *quillu moruchu*, a yellow hybrid introduced some fifty years ago; *yura sara*, a white hybrid valued for its large grain; and *capia sara*, an older variety with a small grain that never hardens, whose cobs are greatly valued for roasting by the side of the fire.

Corn is a reliable source of food in and around the Sibundoy Valley. Those Santiagueños maintaining plots on the valley floor can plant corn all year around, but most families have their chagras on the slopes of the mountains and are limited by the natural cycle to one or two plantings per year. The planting season runs from February to August; it is said that plantings outside of this period will not produce a good harvest. Corn is planted by the women, who are thought to have a better hand for it than the men (see sayings 128 and 129), perhaps because of their association with Mama Quilla, the moon deity, closely tied to the agricultural cycle in Sibundoy thought. Seed is retained from the previous year's harvest. By planting corn of different kinds at different elevations in and around the valley, the Santiagueño family assures a continuous supply of fresh corn for a period of two months or more. Moreover, most of the corn is harvested after the grains have hardened, allowing for an additional few months of storage. The grains on the cobs harden through a series of stages known as as *sarasu*, *shuna*, and finally *tusta sara*, or 'dry corn'. Corn harvested while the grains are still soft is known as *chugllu* and must be consumed within a few days of picking. In spite of these strategies to prolong the availability of corn, the three months just before harvest are referred to by the label *yarcay quilla*, or 'hunger moon', and they are characterized by lean living and thin soups. In early October the first fresh corn becomes available, ushering in a period of plenty (known as *alli timpo* or 'good times') that culminates in the abundance and extravagance of the carnival season.

In addition to this mainstay, Santiagueño chagras produce beans (*Phaseolus vulgaris*), a number of greens and edible seeds, and an extensive inventory of ground roots. These vegetables are consumed primarily in soups. The gardens abound in delicious fruit bushes and trees, including the native berry known as *motilón* in Spanish (*Physalis peruviana*), a favorite among children; the *naranjillo* (*Solanum quitoense*), a delicious fruit found only in the central Andes; the *chilacuan* (*Carica candamarcensis*), a cool-climate relative of the papaya; as well as European-derived relatives of the apple, lime, and peach.

Formerly the Santiagueños supplemented their vegetable and fruit diet with a considerable amount of wild game meat, especially that of the deer, tapir, wild pig, and duck. Large numbers of trout were also found in the streams and rivers of the valley. Today most of the forest cover is gone, and the major sources of animal protein are domesticated beasts and fowl. Hens are kept for eggs and meat, and pigs and cattle are slaughtered and eaten in association with special festivities in the vereda or beyond. The Andean guinea pig, known in Spanish as the *cuy* (*Cavia porcellus*), scuttles about in the kitchen areas, feeding on discarded leaves and such, until it is caught, roasted, and served on a plate, usually in recognition of some important visitor or social event.

Perhaps the most celebrated utilization of corn is in *chicha* (known to the Santiagueños as *asua*), the corn beer brewed by the women, and consumed as a routine source of nourishment and refreshment, as well as in the ritual drinking sessions associated with all major social ceremonies. Not all chicha is made from corn; virtually all the other vegetable crops (excepting beans, cabbage, and onions) can be used for this purpose. But the great majority of chicha production in the valley involves the use of corn. Different kinds of chicha are prepared from the different types of corn, by several related processes: *chugllu asua*, made from the fresh soft grain, is considered refreshing and nourishing, but not very potent; *sarasu asua* has the flavor of hard corn, and is slightly more intoxicating; *jura asua* is a very potent chicha made from hardened grains, which are soaked and set out to sprout; *yanga asua* is another mild chicha prepared from cooked grains of corn.

All of these chichas are prepared through the same general process, which begins with the removal of the grains from the corncob. They are then soaked or cooked and ground into as fine a mash as possible. This mash is brought to a near-boil (for chugllu asua) or a complete boil (for jura asua) on the wood fire, and then set aside to cool slowly. Once cooled, the liquid is poured into large wooden barrels, and the fermentation process is started by bacterial residue in the wood of the barrel. To enhance the process, either *panela*, a lightly-processed cane sugar, or *guarapo*, sugar-cane juice, is introduced (previously, in the days of *chicha mascada*, or 'chewed chicha', human saliva performed this function). After four or five days, the brew begins to bubble and produce a sizzling sound. It is now ready to drink, and the contents of the barrel must be consumed in its entirety, since refrigeration is lacking.

The consumption of chicha is often associated with significant veredawide or communitywide events such as rites of passage, the collective labor parties known as *mingas*, and festivals such as Saint John's Day and carnival. It is a necessary part of the compensation made by property owners to the roving work crews employed for the day on their lands. The chicha parties associated with these moments in the social life of the community activate a rigorous etiquette in the distribution and consumption of chicha. Large quantities of the brew circulate in an orderly fashion, as the hosts on these occasions recognize their guests in order of social rank and importance.

The chicha party begins with a series of ritual speeches in which the hosts show deference to their guests, and the guests in turn express gratitude. The owner takes the first quantity of chicha out of the barrel but then often appoints a younger man, known as the *huisidor* or 'tapper', to help him distribute the chicha. The first portion, a large bowl containing three or four gallons, goes to the most highly respected person among those present, often a former governor of the community. After a brief toasting ritual, a dramatization of refusal and insistence, this most honored guest requests a smaller cup that he uses to scoop out a manageable serving. He is held responsible for finishing his portion of chicha, but he does so with the help of all present, whom he calls forward one by one to partake of his allotment. Over the course of the evening, each adult will eventually be entrusted in this fashion with a large bowl of chicha.

As the intoxicating effect of the chicha takes hold, the men begin to make music on wooden flutes and drums, and there is dancing and revelry "as long as the chicha lasts," often for some three days and nights. Even as the chicha begins to slosh over the edges of the well-routed containers, the public enactment of sharing persists, and the setting is said to be "full of caring." In view of its role in fostering social solidarity and the reverence with which it is regarded (it is referred to as "God's work" in ritual language speeches), chicha is nothing less than the fluid of life in the native communities of the Sibundoy Valley.

Some sense of the importance of corn and its celebrated derivative, chicha, can be grasped from a mythic narrative, "The Tale of

the Shulupsi Bird," which is popular among Kamsá and Ingano
people alike. The following telling of this story was performed in
Inga by my research associate Francisco Tandioy; as in all tran-
scriptions from Sibundoy mythic narrative cited in this study, I
have made use of poetic line breaks to capture the phrasing of
utterance in the original performance:

In the old days, it is said, there was a very beautiful woman.
This woman went to the home of a young man, it is said,
to live with him in order to become his wife.
At that time the one who would become her mother-in-law
liked to order her, it is said,
to do everything that had to be done.
Sometimes, it is said, she would order her to bring wood;
sometimes, to work in the fields;
and sometimes to make chicha.

One day the one who was to become her husband went out,
it is said, to work in the fields.
And at that time her future mother-in-law
brought down from the attic, it is said,
three bushels of corn,
and then she told her, it is said:
    "Please prepare three earthen pots of chicha
    with these three bushels of corn."
And then that one who was to become her mother-in-law went
    out,
it is said, to work in the fields.

And at that time, that young woman, with only one grain of
    corn,
it is said, prepared three earthen pots full of chicha.
When her mother-in-law returned, the young woman, it is said,
was sitting in the patio combing her hair.
And at that time the one who would be her mother-in-law
came running, it is said, into the house,
to see if she had already made the chicha for her.

And when she came in, the same three bushels were full,
it is said, and seeing that, she went to scold her,
it is said, quite harshly,
plenty, plenty, it is said, she scolded her.

And at that time the young woman, crying, became angry,
and showing her the full earthen pots, she said:
    "And from this time on, with three bushels

you will make only one earthen pot of chicha.
In my time, I was used to making chicha
with only three grains of corn for one earthen pot."

And saying that, she turned into a shulupsi bird, it is said,
and flying right into the same chicha she had made,
bathing herself, she flew off.
As she flew away, the three earthen pots split apart.
And at that time the ants, it is said, came to drink it all up.

This mythic narrative accounts for the harsh realities of the human condition by relating a prototypical incident of conflict between an elderly woman and her prospective daughter-in-law over the availability of chicha. It occurs within the framework of what has been referred to as "trial marriage," a courtship arrangement still practiced today, allowing the family to test the merits of the proposed match. Another contemporary social institution depicted in the story is the *minga* or collective labor party; the older woman's anxiety derives from the obligation to provide chicha to the workers, part of the unwritten contract in this precapitalist economic system.

In the Sibundoy interpretation, there was a high price to pay for the mother-in-law's scolding of the young woman: they portray the latter as a messenger of the gods who was sent here to teach women how to make chicha with relatively little effort. Taking umbrage at the undeserved rough treatment she receives from the older woman, the messenger decides not to convey this vital piece of information but instead transforms into a shulupsi bird, a common sparrow-like resident of the valley, and flies off, leaving the delicious chicha she has prepared to the ants.

In the evenings around the fire, or in the early phases of a chicha party, this story is told to explain why men and women must labor so hard to find a living in this world. It was meant to be otherwise, but as a consequence of human frailty displayed by the mother-in-law, extensive plots of corn must be planted, weeded, trimmed, and harvested and large piles of grain must be ground and cooked, for people to survive. Sibundoy Indians find confirmation of this mythological episode in the appearance of the modern shulupsi bird, which has ruffled body feathers (the result of the dive into the chicha) but very smooth head feathers (the result of the combing that infuriated the older woman).

This popular narrative affords a glimpse into the spiritual life of Sibundoy natives, implicated at every turn in the sayings of the ancestors. The shulupsi bird story falls into the category of myth rather than folktale (Thompson 1966), since the Sibundoy natives do not treat it as a suggestive fable, but rather accord it a literal truth value. Faith in a transcendental reality, established during the times of the first people but persisting into the present, colors the native understanding of the everyday world. The story of the shulupsi bird evokes the ancestral world and its derivative, the contemporary spirit realm. It activates the same mythic consciousness that underlies the sayings of the ancestors, which often feature birds as spiritual messengers.

SAYINGS OF THE ANCESTORS

The study of traditional verbal expressions may lead into the heart of a people's cosmology, once the researcher is allowed or compelled to penetrate beyond the surface layer of spoken representation to the sustaining groundwork of belief and practice. The folklorist may find that the verbal text proffered by native friends in the casual exchange of conversation is merely the tip of the iceberg, as in the case of these brief allusions to sign and consequence. At the outset of a year's residence among the Kamsá Indians in Colombia's Sibundoy Valley, I took note of what appeared to be a flourishing proverb-like genre of verbal art. Thus when doña Maria, doña Brigida, or one of their children, announced upon seeing me arrive in the valley for a visit, "So that's why I dreamed you last night," I toyed with the idea that such statements might implicate a residual belief in dream prophecy but preferred viewing them instead as mere poetic conceits, politeness formulas smoothing over that moment of uncertainty attending greetings of this sort.

But my curiosity was aroused, and over time I became aware of the pervasive influence of the interpretation of dreams and other portents in the lives of my Kamsá hosts. The domain of these "dream proverbs," as I first called them, is intensely private. They lie within the cloistered realm of family interaction and could easily escape the notice of a casual visitor. Since I had been adopted into the Jacanamijoy family as their "eldest son," I began to gain access to this traditional system of everyday divination. The first formal research I conducted in this area involved a listing procedure: I requested that my hosts (or should I say my "foster family") simply recite all those traditional statements tied to the interpretation of dreams they could recall. They seemed slightly embarrassed by the request, as if I had stumbled upon a cherished private possession, but as the session progressed I detected a rising surge of pride, accompanied by an unflinching affirmation of these interpretive precepts.

The harvest of Kamsá dream proverbs that first evening included a substantial quantity of traditional associations, all couched in routine formulae like this one:

bokoy tkojotjena
chicha you dreamed

> If you dream of chicha

ibsana wabtena jabinynam
tomorrow rain to dawn

> you will see rain at dawn

Here is a listing (in English translation) of the seventeen interpretive phrases articulated by my Kamsá hosts that evening, my first exposure to the traditional code of sign interpretation:

If you dream of a friar in habit,
    it means spirit sickness.

If you dream of an orange, or lulo, or mako [fruits], or
        chontaduro [a local palm],
    it means that you will receive a
    punch or see somebody throw one.

If you dream of the drum, flute, guitar or seed rattle,
    you will witness an argument or fight.

If you dream of a plane passing overhead, or of a
        car, helicopter, or radio,
    you will happen on problems among the white people.

If you dream of a snake or dog,
    you will run into an evil doctor on the path.

If a young woman dreams of a ring,
    she will soon marry.

If a man dreams of a crucifix, staff, bamboo, or
        sugar cane stalk,
    he will be named a member of of the cabildo.

If you dream that people are dragging a long pole
        to make a bridge, or gathering a bundle of
        shorter sticks,

it means that a relative will die,
for these are the candles at a wake.

If you dream that you are losing a tooth,
it means that your father or mother will die.

If you dream of chicha,
you will see rain at dawn.

If you dream that you are crossing a river, or
that you see showers of water,
or that you almost drown,
it means that you will come down with a serious illness.

If you dream of beans, corn, or bread,
it means that you will find money.

If you dream of plantains, or of a machete or comb,
it means that you will come across some meat
in the next few days.

If you dream of the weasel, cat, cuy, rat, or mouse,
then thieves will come to your house.

If you dream that you are killing a hen,
or cooking a large quantity of meat,
or shredding meat,
it means that you will lose a child.

If a girl dreams of a red shawl,
it means that she will soon bleed.

If a man dreams of a red shawl,
it means that he will cut himself or see blood.

The seventeen items (actually indexing some forty-three associations) take as their signs the mundane activities, objects, and experiences of everyday living, and they monitor the realm of generic fortune that is of concern to people everywhere: health, prosperity, success, and happiness. This recitation of sayings was not accompanied by much in the way of explanation; for the most part, the sayings appeared to stand for and by themselves. However, some ancillary information did emerge; for example, my Kamsá host, don Justo, recalled that he once dreamed of a fine wooden staff, and sure enough, the next morning, they came to advise him that he had been named *alguacil*, a position in the cabildo roughly equivalent to constable.

In my early work with the sayings, I noted that my Kamsá friends were little given to speculation on two issues of great interest to me: the rationale linking sign to consequence, and the mechanisms bringing dream images into the consciousness of the dreamer. Only on occasion would they freely provide this kind of information, as they did in reference to one of the items just listed, when they explained that the poles or sticks seen in the dream were equivalent to the candles at a wake. These dimensions of the system of every-day divination are not so immediately accessible; they must be teased out of the surrounding cultural matrix, especially from expressive traditions like mythology and ritual that run parallel to the sayings of the ancestors.

It was not difficult to amass evidence for the importance of dream interpretation in the traditional culture. For instance, dreams figure prominently in the mythic narrative corpus, where they constitute an invaluable window on cosmic reality. In what appears to be the most ancient layer of mythic narrative, dreams are clearly accorded a prophetic character, perhaps even a *genera-tive* power, the ability to "beget" reality. Consider the case of the primordial miner, one of the first people: after setting a trap, he dreams first a parrot and then a woman caught there, and on successive mornings finds these nocturnal visions fulfilled. The woman so unceremoniously snared turns out to be Our Mother the Moon, and their encounter culminates in the birth of the culture hero, Wangetsmuna. At this early moment in mythological time, the agency of dream vision plays a critical role in moving the world toward its present condition. The mythic narrative of the valley establishes dreams, along with drug-induced visions, as principal lines of communication with the spirit realm.

The dreamworld remains a vital resource to this day: people attend closely to dream images, subject them to systematic interpretation, take preventive measures to counter any unwanted events foretold in the dreams, and scan the events of coming days, weeks, or months for confirmation of the prophesied occurrences. As one Ingano informant told me, "Every day we are living our dreams." Each morning consultations take place within the immediate family circle: dream images are recalled, their meanings are discussed, and plausible courses of action are devised.

As I pursued my research into the Sibundoy system of dream interpretation, I returned to the Sibundoy Valley and shifted my attention to its manifestation among the Santiagueños, largely under the guidance of my research associate, Francisco Tandioy. The Ingano refer to the dream sayings as *muscuycunamanda*, or 'concerning dreams'. In Spanish they use the term *de los sueños*, or 'about dreams'. Delving further into the matter, I found that the code of dream interpretation is only one component (the major one) of a larger code, a comprehensive system of everyday divination, taking as its meaning-laden portents almost any chance, or seemingly unmotivated, occurrence in the natural world. Observations and experiences as diverse as the twitching of a muscle, the tic of an eye, or the intrusion of a field animal on the home domain, could be taken as signs of a future event. In such a system nothing is left to chance—any event can possess transcendental meaning, and every misfortune is preceded by its telltale signs.

Many of the people I talked to used the labels signifying "about dreams" as a cover term for the entire code of interpretation. However, on reflection some members of the community would produce more comprehensive terminology, such as the Ingano phrase, *ñugpamandacuna imasa rimascacuna*, which can be parsed and translated as follows:

nugpa-manda-cuna imasa rima-sca-cuna
first-ablative-plural how to speak-historical-plural

Literally, "How the first people used to speak", or more freely, "Sayings of the ancestors".

This label invokes the exemplary model of the first ancestors and defines this code of interpretation as an inheritance, a cultural treasure, passed from one generation to another since the beginning. The ancestral prototype permeates the worldview of the native peoples of the Sibundoy Valley. In spite of the devout efforts of many generations of Catholic missionaries, these Andean Indians continue to believe that a timeless truth was established by the first ancestors. At every turn the sayings exalt the example of the ancestors, who are viewed as spiritually far superior to the modern people. The underlying notion can be conceived of as a Sibundoy equivalent to the big-bang theory, premised on a pivotal instant in cosmic history that determines for all time the shape and meaning of things to come. This pivotal moment is the dawn of human civilization, when the celestial bodies interacted directly with the first people, when the line between animals and people was yet to be drawn, and when the coalescence of brute spiritual power set in motion the forces that created the natural and social universes of contemporary human experience.

The Sibundoy ancestors are not literally consanguine or affinal forebears, actual predecesors to be traced meticulously through the generations, as encountered in Asian or African systems of ancestor worship or in the state religion of the Incan period (Conrad & Demarest 1984). Instead, these are figurative or conceptual ancestors, conceived as the first people, the designers of Sibundoy civilization; consanguinity with them is postulated in general terms, not reckoned in precise tabulations.

This reverence for the example and the knowledge of the ancestors is prevalent in many spheres of indigenous life today. It haunts discourse in the Kamsá ritual language, a speech variety used in public rituals and occasionally in private conversations, for example, in this constant refrain stitching together the models of Christ and the ancestors: *chabe mundo tsjiyetsashekwastona*, "In His world I am following in the footsteps of the ancestors". The same reverence prevails in the mythic narrative tradition preserved in the storytelling of the elders, and can be discerned in the traditional weaving designs of the women, depicting the animal familiars of ancestral spirits in striking geometrical patterns. The ancestors "come out" during the indigenous carnival, when the men wear feathered crowns in remembrance of the first ancestors who triumphed over mute heathens to establish social mores as they are practiced today.

When asked to identify the origin of the sayings, people formulate statements like this one:

God left us the dreams, the dreams don't only originate in nature. God left them to us, that's why we dream like this, and each person, the smart ones, take them as a warning. The dream proverbs are inherited from the elders, from the very first ancestors. You see, the old people told of their dreams, and the young people listened and took it to be true. Our mother also told us about them: we dreamed of a thief, and our parents would tell us, if something was missing, they would tell us: "You see, it's true what we dreamed."

Here the Christian God (perhaps cognate with the Andean creator god) oversees a method of everyday divination inaugurated during the period of the ancestors. An unbroken chain of transmission brings this system into the modern period, making it available to those who are clever enough to profit from its warnings. In addition, people often mention hallucinogenic vision experiences, primarily those associated with *yagé* or *ayahuasca*, as a means of recovering "lost" sayings: "My deceased father, after drinking of the medicine vine, used to speak like this."

In these accounts, the sayings are guaranteed by three authori-

ties: the indigenous ancestors, the vision experiences associated
with dreaming and with hallucinogenic substances, and the Christian God. These assignations correspond to the principal roots of
Andean folk religion: a pan-Andean cosmology, a shamanism influenced by tropical forest spirituality, and Christian elements absorbed into this precolumbian substrate. The convergence of these
ultimate sources of authority reflects the cultural saliency of the
sayings complex, and it exhibits the capacity of Sibundoy thought
to weave diverse cultural resources into a cohesive whole.

2

Muscuycunamanda

The sayings of the ancestors occupy a position of modest respect in the canon of traditional verbal art cultivated by speakers of the Inga language. Among the Santiagueños, the sayings are savored as pithy allusions that tumble off the tongue in an agreeable fashion and capture the spiritual implications of mundane human experience. Lacking the phonological intensity of ritual language speeches and the drama of sustained narrative discourse, these short statements of belief possess instead the beauty of the miniature: they draw together in their brief compass phenomena that are normally encountered separately and thereby perform the miracle of the trope, rendering congruent the incongruent. In the classic manner of the proverb, they balance their divergent references in parallel constructions: "if you dream of chicha/you will see rain at dawn." The principle of congruence here is the pan-Andean concept of the circulation of fluids (see Bastien 1978), coupled with the Sibundoy postulate that chicha, as God's "work", is a kind of "celestial water" under the control of the thunder deity.

A selection of the sayings of the ancestors circulating among members of the Santiago Ingano community will be introduced here and highlighted to bring out their artistry and their resonance in the lives of Sibundoy natives. This placement of the primary corpus of data reflects my perception that this field evidence is too crucial to the main argument (and too compelling on aesthetic and ethnographic grounds) to be consigned to an appendix. This chapter and the next divide the overall corpus into two units: *muscuycunamanda*, 'about dreams', concerning the interpretation of dream images; and *tapiacunamanda*, 'about signs', concerning the interpretation of signs and portents outside of the dreamlife. These categories reflect an approximate parity in the interest accorded dreams and wakeful signs. It is not clear, however, that Sibundoy natives insist on any discontinuity between these two domains.

As noted in the preceding chapter, dreams are a vital resource in the spiritual life of Sibundoy Valley natives. For the Kamsá or Ingano person, to state that something happened "as if in a dream" carries perhaps the opposite force that it would carry in Western thinking. Dream images (along with drug-induced visions) are regarded as manifestations of an ultimate reality. The following corpus of sayings revolving around dreams should be construed, then, as an impeccable avenue of insight into the spiritual foundation of the events that constitute the everyday lifeworld.

It is safe to say that there is no finite limit to the number of sayings circulating among members of the native communities in Colombia's Sibundoy Valley. Even if every traditional saying could be tracked down and collected, this would still leave at large the sayings that are temporarily "lost" and those that are for the moment merely potential, awaiting coinage or refurbishing as the proper circumstances arise. Although the sayings of the ancestors hark back to venerable example, the modern corpus, like all living folklore traditions, continues to evolve in keeping with the experiences and needs of the host community. One sign of the innovative capacity of the genre is the subset of sayings centered on the problematic relationships with "whites" (Spanish priests and Colombian nationals) and the incorporation of mechanical devices associated with them (like the airplane, heliocopter, and radio) as signs. A considerable inventory of sayings will be presented in these two chapters, but it should be stressed that this compilation likely represents only the tip of the iceberg: further fieldwork could surely snare many additional items. What I present here is simply a "working vocabulary" of sayings, a sampling of items in general circulation, of the kind that could be readily produced by members of one vereda or one extended family.

The Santiagueño corpus derives from fieldwork that I carried out in the Santiago Ingano community during most of 1985 with the assistance of Francisco Tandioy, professor of Inga and English at the University of Nariño in Pasto, and a native of the Santiago Ingano community, from the vereda of Vichoy. We made use of both direct elicitation and casual observation in gathering the sayings. Additional texts were culled from the pamphlet assembled by Domingo Tandioy Chasoy, who does not tell us exactly how he assembled his corpus. Selections from this publication are marked with an asterisk; all commentary appended to the texts is original to the present study.

It is the efforts and connections of Professor Tandioy (henceforth Francisco) that have made possible this collection of sayings and commentary in Inga. His mother and her friends were kind enough to provide valuable information, and they constitute a primary resource, one that was supplemented by visits to the houses of relatives and friends in other veredas. I recall with pleasure a journey to the home of Francisco's aunt, who lives high on a hillside above the town of Santiago. Taking leave of friends at the edge of Santiago, we walked along the footpaths and gradually gained a beautiful perspective over the valley. After perhaps an hour's walk we approached a traditional thatch cottage, to the standard greeting of yapping dogs at the boundary of habitation marked by the rustling stalks of the cornfield.

Francisco had not visited these people since his childhood, and we had barely walked in the door when his elderly aunt exclaimed (as if on cue), "No wonder the cuys were coughing this morning" (see sayings 105 and 106). After the obligatory (and after our walk, most welcome) rounds of chicha, we were able to initiate a discussion of the sayings that netted us a good number of traditional items in addition to the one spoken by the old lady, in a purely natural vein, at the moment of our arrival. The kindness and generosity displayed by this family marked all of our transactions with the Ingano people of Santiago, a tendency that I attribute to their natural delicacy and also to their high regard for Francisco Tandioy.

The total inventory of sayings amounts to just over 200 items, after eliminating numerous variants of items already represented in the corpus. It wasn't always easy to decide whether to include a saying that shared nuances with other sayings. As a rule of thumb, I opted to include all those sayings possessing some unique and significant detail. It should be noted that the 203 items in the corpus actually index a rather larger number of sign-consequence associations, because several of the sayings present multiple connections.

In an effort like this one some thought must be devoted to the presentation of the materials. The techniques developed here foster two simultaneous lines of appreciation: of the sayings as exemplars of traditional verbal artistry, and of the sayings as practical recipes within a specific cultural nexus. But it must be conceded that among the many possible formats for arranging a collection of this nature, none seems especially compelling. The very act of compiling a list imposes an alien intent on these items, a necessary sundering of their bond to natural discourse and situational habitats. Clearly, these traditional sayings reside most naturally in the discourse surrounding the actual events to which they are applied.

The requirement that this inventory of sayings be arranged in some plausible order introduces a number of nagging complexities. The sayings contain two parts, a precondition and a consequence. Each part contains a theme or major referent, or in some cases, a plurality of themes. It makes sense to use one of these stated themes as a handle for locating each saying within the total inventory. But giving preference to one theme forces the neglect of others in the saying.

The dilemma can be appreciated with reference to any of the sayings. Consider saying 79:

huevos muscugpica, pelea tiangapa

If you dream eggs, there will be a fight.

Dreams, *eggs*, or *fighting* could serve as the topical handle for this saying. There is logic in keeping together all those sayings involving the dream faculty, all those sayings that name food items or refer to foodways, and all those sayings dealing with social relations and altercations. Should we proceed using elements from the precondition or elements from the consequence? And when there are multiple elements within either of these portions, which one should be selected as the dominant one?

It should be clear that there is no perfect solution to this problem. I have tried to preserve the native patterns of thought in arranging the present corpus, by recognizing for the most part named thematic categories of considerable reach within the Santiagueño worldview. The use of subcategories such as 'thievery' within the overall category 'about dreams' has facilitated a more sensitive grouping of the sayings. In the end, I decided to group the dream sayings according to their *consequences* and the sayings founded on wakeful observations according to their *signs*, a tactic that highlights the practical and empirical foundations of the tradition. And so the sample item, "if you dream of eggs, there will be a.fight," finds itself within the broad category 'about dreams', and in a subcategory pertaining to 'social relations'.

I selected a presentational format that gives each saying the chance to sing out in its original Inga phrasing, accompanied by a grammatical parsing (whose key is presented in the appendix, p. 194) and lexemic translation, as well as a rather free English translation. This procedure allows the reader to grapple with the original sound, syntax, and diction of the traditional item, instead of having to rely exclusively on my finished translations. Oral performance of the Inga originals should heighten the perception of their canonic bipartite structure by counterposing a rising and falling intonation, and by inserting a brief caesura between these component segments.

The free translations stay rather close to the original texts, though admittedly only one option among many was chosen for the phrasing in English. Generally, I strive for an informal, colloquial tone, which I think best captures the spirit of the Inga original. Thus you will find, "if you dream eggs, there will be a fight," rather than the more formal but equally possible, "should one dream eggs, there will be a fight." Significant semantic nuances, such as the detail "you *are made* to dream" (signalled by the causative morpheme, -*chi*) are preserved in the free translations.

One feature of the Inga language requires further discussion, the evidentiary system obligating the speaker to adopt a stance toward the truth value of each utterance. Every proposition in Inga speech must be accompanied by one of the following morphemes: -*mi*, the affirmative, linking the statement to the speaker's first-hand experience; -*si*, the reportative, assigning the utterance to the category of hearsay; -*chu*, expressing uncertainty concerning the statement's truth. Ingano mythic narrative characteristically makes use of the reportative morpheme, which I render as "it is said," signifying that the stories have been passed along through community tradition. I have opted not to translate every occurrence of this morpheme to avoid the cumbersome effect this produces in English. Most of the sayings make use of the affirmative, which I believe is best left untranslated. The prevalence of the affirmative -*mi* in the sayings texts is a linguistic indicator of faith in the system: the predictions have been confirmed through personal experience.

The sayings occur naturally in a number of phrasings, each statement preserving the kernel association between sign and consequence. The briefest statements, mere abbreviations ("corn, money"), capture the bare essence of the matter and tend to occur in artificial "listing" discourse, with the framework "if you dream" already provided or understood. Another likely product of listing discourse, perhaps evincing a movement toward the reflective stance, is the phrasing that lumps together a large number of signs pointing to the same consequence. Only the occasional saying makes direct reference to the ancestors, using clauses like *ñugpamandacuna nincuna,* ' . . . the first people used to say . . . ' . Some phrasings are quite elaborate, even discursive, with considerable peripheral or explanatory detail, but these strike the ear as aberrations. In general, I have opted for phrasings that are complete but not unnecessarily wordy, as these seem to best embody the discourse aesthetic of this genre.

Along with the texts of the sayings, I provide commentary of two sorts. The passages enclosed between quotation marks derive from from indigenous glossing of the tradition, primarily the astute comments of Francisco and his mother. In addition, I have occasionally inserted brief ethnographic observations as these aid in the comprehension of particular sayings in the corpus. These commentaries are designed to promote a level of understanding beyond that obtainable from texts in isolation. I have sought to preserve these materials from the fate befalling folklore consigned to indices and lists: burial in a stale and inanimate crypt so unlike their natural habitats. It is hoped that the format used in this chapter will make it possible for the reader to acquire some feeling for the vitality this tradition possesses within its actual cultural setting. A sketch of Inga phonology and a key to the grammatical parsings used in this study are provided in the appendix, p. 194.

The sampling of sayings relating to dreams (muscuycunamanda) is organized according to the following topical scheme: Death; Sadness; Sickness; Spirit Sickness; Thievery; Social Relations; Fortune.

HUAÑUYMANDA

The first group of sayings under this rubric concerns omens of death (in Inga *huañuy*). The presence of death is unrelenting in this community that enjoys only sporadic and incomplete medical services (Seijas 1969). The dream images include objects associated with the Catholic mass, evoking the funereal rites; physiological processes such as the loss of teeth; perceptions such as that of flying through the air; the breaking of a ring or machete; and routine daily activities. Those projected to die are primarily members of the immediate family, though prominent social figures such as native doctors and house builders are sometimes named.

1   **altar muscu-chi-mi huahua huañu-pu-ngapa,**
    altar to dream [*caus-aff*] child to die [*ben-purp*]

    huahua yuca-gpi-ca.
    child to have [*cond-foc*]

You are made to dream the altar,
a child will die for you,
if you have a child.

2* **altar muscu-gpi-ca,**
    altar to dream [*cond-foc*]

    maycan huamra o familia huañu-ngapa.
    some child or relative to die [*purp*]

    If you dream the altar,
    a child or close relative is to die.

"The person indicated in this saying is a child of the one who has
the dream; or if not a child, then a close relative such as the father,
mother, or a brother or sister of the dreamer."

3   **atahualpa huañu-sca huarcu-chi-cu-gta muscu-chi-mi,**
    hen to die [*hist*] to hang [*caus-prog-sub*] to dream [*caus-aff*]

    huamra-cuna yuca-spa-ca, huamra-cuna huañu-pu-ngapa.
    child [*pl*] to have [*ger-foc*] child [*pl*] to die [*ben-purp*]

    You are made to dream that you are hanging out a dead hen;
    if you have children, your children will die for you.

The hens are kept for eggs and also slaughtered and prepared in
soups. Part of this process involves hanging the plucked carcass to
allow the blood to run out. It may be that the appearance of the
carcass at this stage provides the basis for this association.

4* **rosario o santo cristo-ta muscu-gpi-ca**
    rosary or crucifix [*acc*] to dream [*cond-foc*]

    marca-sca huahua o confirma-sca huahua huañu-ngapa.
    to carry [*hist*] child or to confirm [*hist*] child to die [*purp*]

    If you dream a rosary or a crucifix,
    a godchild, either from baptism or confirmation,
    is to die.

The Catholic rites of passage are extremely important events
within the community, and every time a child is baptized, confirmed, or goes through first communion, the parents must enlist
a male and a female sponsor, who then become the godfather and
godmother of the child, and the *compadre* and *comadre* of the
parents. The accumulation of godchildren is a mark of prestige,
and the death of a godchild is taken as a serious loss.

5   **atun yuca-spa, atun huañu-ngapa,**
     grandparent to have [ger] grandparent to die [purp]

marca-sca tayta o marca-sca mama ima yuca-spa-ca,
to carry [hist] father or to carry [hist] mother also to have [ger-foc]

chi atun-cuna huañu-ngapa,
that old one [pl] to die [purp]

chi-manda-mi quiru pila-ri-sca ca-gta muscu-chí.
that [abl-aff] tooth to pull [ref-hist] to be [sub] to dream [caus]

Having a grandparent, that old one will die,
also having a godfather or godmother,
those old people are to die;
because of that you are made to dream
that you are losing a tooth.

"But not just any tooth. If you dream that it is a back tooth, for example the one we call *mamquiru*, then they say that your parents are going to die. But they say that this is when they still have a year or two left, at a considerable distance in time."

The Inga word *atun* means literally, 'large' or 'tall', but it can take on the idiomatic meaning of 'old person' and can refer to a person's parents or grandparents.

6*   **vola-spa puri-cu-gta muscu-gpi-ca,**
     to fly [ger] to travel [prog-sub] to dream [cond-foc]

atun-cuna huañu-ngapa.
old one [pl] to die [purp]

quiru-cuna pela-ri-gta muscu-gpi-ca, chasa-lla-ta.
tooth [pl] to pull [ref-sub] to dream [cond-foc] same [del-acc]

If you dream that you are flying through the air,
your parents are to die.
If you dream that your teeth are pulled,
it means the same thing.

"Imagine that you dream that like a bird you are flying over the mountains, then it may be that your parents are going to die."

7   **cachi, aycha, u cancha-ta limpia-cu-gta muscu-chi-mi,**
     salt meat or patio [acc] to clean [prog-sub] to dream [caus-aff]

atun huañu-ngapa.
old one to die [*purp*]

You are made to dream salt, meat,
or that you are cleaning the patio,
an old one is to die.

"When my poor father was dying, we were dreaming of sad things
like salt, or meat, or that they were sweeping the patio very, very
clean; and when my father-in-law died, the same thing happened.
Both of them passed away."

Abstinence from the consumption of salt or salty foods is frequently associated with ritual fasting in the Andes (Molina 1883,
Rappaport 1978). Cleaning the patio takes place in preparation for
rites of passage such as the funeral.

8   **surtija paqui-ri-gta muscu-spa-ca, huarmi huañu-pu-ngapa.**
     ring to break [*ref-sub*] to dream [*ger-foc*] woman to die [*ben-
         purp*]

     o huarmi chasa muscu-spa-ca, cusa huañu-pu-ngapa.
     or woman thus to dream [*ger-foc*] husband to die [*ben-purp*]

     chi-ca chasa muscu-chí.
     that [*foc*] thus to dream [*caus*]

     You are dreaming that a ring breaks,
     your wife is to die for you.
     Or, a woman is dreaming this,
     her husband is to die for her.
     For that you are made thus to dream.

     The breaking of the ring here is symbolic of the sundering of the
     conjugal union.

9*   **machete o sorteja paqui-ri-gta muscu-gpi-ca,**
     machete or ring to break [*ref-sub*] to dream [*cond-foc*]

     casado-pura pipas huañu-ngapa.
     spouse [*reci*] whoever to die [*purp*]

     If you dream that a machete or a ring breaks,
     your spouse is the one to die.

10   **machiti paqui-ri-gta muscu-chi-mi,**
     machete to break [*ref-sub*] to dream [*caus-aff*]

sinchi huañu-ngapa,
doctor to die [*purp*]

nuca-nchi-ta ambi-dur huañu-ngapa.
I [*pl-acc*] to cure [*agt*] to die [*purp*]

You are made to dream that a machete breaks,
a native doctor is to die,
one of our curers is to die.

The machete is the principal instrument of the Ingano cultivator.
Here the machete as a tool is symbolic of the native doctor, also
an instrument—in this case, an instrument of spiritual intervention. The breaking of one instrument foretells the demise of the
other.

11   **huasi vuiltia-gta muscu-spa-ca,**
      house to turn [*sub*] to dream [*ger-foc*]

      chi-ca yuya-cu-ngui huasi-chi-dur huañu-ngapa,
      that [*foc*] to think [*prog-2nd*] house [*caus-agt*] to die [*purp*]

      o mana ca-gpi-ca, huasi propio dueño huañu-ngapa,
      or not to be [*cond-foc*] house actual owner to die [*purp*]

      ña propio dueño pues.
      already actual owner so

      Dreaming that the house turns,
      you will think that the builder is to die;
      otherwise, the actual owner is to die,
      the owner himself.

The machete is the principal instrument of the Ingano cultivator. Those who have the skill to lay out the basic structures of the new
houses are highly valued in the community. Along with skilled
flute players, they are known by the Spanish word *maestro*.

LLAQUIYMANDA

The consequence of the next set of sayings is sadness (in Inga
llaquiy). The sadness may derive from any number of sources: the
loss of a loved one or of some property, illness in the family, or
some other misfortune. The dream images that foretell sadness
include meat, salt, experiences such as dancing, and a set of root
crops of American origin, *arracacha* (*Aracarica xanthorhiza*),
achira (*Canna edulis*), and *cumala* (*Ipomoea batatas*). The consis-
tent association of root crops with sadness may derive from their

isolation in the earth, so far from Our Father the Sun (see the final chapter).

12* **papa o cachi muscu-gpi-ca, llaqui-y tucu-ngapa.**
potato or salt to dream [*cond-foc*] to be sad [*nom*] to become
  [*purp*]

If you dream potatoes or salt,
you are to become sad.

"So they say that salt and potatoes mean that you are going to have sadness. You are going to receive some bad news. Maybe you will be sad because you lost something, they stole something from you, or somebody dies on you."

13 **duci, cachi, papa, chi-cuna-ca llaqui-y-mi muscu-chí.**
candy salt potato that [*pl-foc*] to be sad [*nom-aff*] to dream
  [*caus*]

Candy, salt, potatoes,
these mean sadness,
when you are made to dream them.

"If you dream these things, you will be thinking that something might go wrong, or that someone in your house might die."

14 **racacha muscu-chi-mi llaqui-y yuca-nga-hura.**
arracacha to dream [*caus-aff*] to be sad [*nom*] to have [*3,f-temp*]

You are made to dream arracacha
when you are to have sadness.

Arracacha (*Arracacia xanthorhiza*) is a root crop native to the Americas, with perhaps more cultivars in the Sibundoy Valley than anywhere else in the world (Bristol 1968). It is planted from cuttings and matures in 5 to 6 months. The root is used primarily in soups and occasionally in the making of chicha; the leaves provide fodder for the domesticated animals.

15 **achira muscu-chi-mi llaqui-y yuca-nga-hura.**
achira to dream [*caus-aff*] to be sad [*nom*] to have [*3,f-temp*]

You are made to dream achira
when you are to have sadness.

Achira (*Canna edulis*) is a bulb used for a number of purposes. The bulb is edible and prepared in soups; it can also serve as pig fodder; it can be worked into a cotton-like substance used in weaving; its leaves are broad and serve as a natural container for food and other objects.

16   **cumala muscu-chi-mi, llaqui-y.**
sweet potato to dream [*caus-aff*] to be sad [*nom*]

You are made to dream sweet potatoes, sadness.

Cumala (*Ipomoea batatas*) is not grown in the Sibundoy Valley but brought in from the lowlands. It is a sweet potato used in soups, and also renowned as the source of a delicious and very intoxicating chicha.

17   **baila-cu-gta muscu-chi-mi chi-ca llaqui-y-ca.**
to dance [*prog-sub*] to dream [*caus-aff*] that [*foc*] to be sad [*nom-foc*]

You are made to dream that you are dancing,
that is sadness.

Here the dream image conveys its opposite. But the association of dancing and sadness emerges very clearly during the carnival season, when the elders express the fear that they will not live to dance another carnival, using the phrase *wataskama*, 'until next year', a kind of nostalgic farewell to carnival.

UNGUYMANDA

The following set relates to sickness, physical sickness indicated by the Inga root *unguy*. Some sayings refer to a general condition of illness, whereas others pinpoint the problem in the stomach or head, or else predict a fever. The dream images include meat, salt, bathing, stones, filth, and spilled bowls of lard. The association of spilled fat and sickness recalls pan-Andean concepts relating the accumulation of fat to physical health (Bastien 1978; Gose 1986).

18* **huasi-pi achca aycha tia-gta muscu-gpi-ca,**
house [*loc*] plenty meat to be [*sub*] to dream [*cond-foc*]

ungu-y chi huasi-ma chaya-mu-ngapa.
to be sick [*nom*] that house [*dat*] to arrive [*cis-purp*]

If you dream that there is plenty of meat in the house,
then sickness will arrive at your house.

19   **aycha-ca ungu-y-mi muscu-chí,**
      meat [*foc*] to be sick [*nom-aff*] to dream [*caus*]

      ima ungu-y-pasi grave pia-nga-hura-mi, chasa muscu-chí.
      some sickness [*add*] grave to strike [*3,f-temp-aff*] thus to dream
          [*caus*]

      You are made to dream of meat, sickness;
      when some grave sickness will strike,
      thus you are made to dream.

      "If you dream meat, or plenty of meat, it depends often on what
      kind of meat it is. If it's horsemeat they say the sickness will be
      very grave. The person will arrive at the house and they will be-
      come very sick. So they are wondering: 'Who is going to get sick?'
      It can be any kind of sickness. When you dream the meat, not the
      animal, they say that some kind of sickness will arrive at the house,
      or that someone will fall sick. They say that meat is very harmful."

20   **ungu-y-cuna**
      to be sick [*nom-pl*]

      muscu-chi-mi ajay aycha chi-cuna-ta micu-cu-gta
      to dream [*caus-aff*] lots meat that [*pl-acc*] to eat [*prog-sub*]

      u macha-sca diltudu tia-cu-gta.
      or to drink [*hist*] completely to be (seated) [*prog-sub*]

      Sickness:
      you are made to dream that you are eating lots of meat,
      or that you are sitting around completely drunk.

      The association of meat with sickness may reflect an awareness
      of the dangers of spoiled meat, but it may also relate to the notion
      of the animal's loss of vital substance in the process of slaughtering.
      The immobility of the drunk is reminiscent of the sequestered sick
      person.

21   **purutu muscu-chi-mi huigsa nana-y.**
      bean to dream [*caus-aff*] stomach to hurt [*nom*]

      You are made to dream beans,
      a stomach ache.

"It may be your own stomach that will hurt, or else you may see someone else's stomach turn on them. With that dream I am very sad, I know I will be seeing, like it just happened with my sister from over there, the stomach will be hurting, all the way to the ribs, a terrible pain. Its because of that I am made to dream of beans."

22   **uma huangu-spa puri-cu-gta muscu-chi-mi,**
      head to tie [*ger*] to travel [*prog-sub*] to dream [*caus-aff*]

      uma nana-y tucu-ngapa.
      head to hurt [*nom*] to become [*purp*]

      You are made to dream
      that you are walking with a band around your head,
      you will end up with a headache.

23   **culqui cunchulli-cu-gta muscu-chi-mi quiru nana-ngapa.**
      money to stuff [*prog-sub*] to dream [*caus-aff*] tooth to hurt
          [*purp*]

      You are made to dream
      that you are carrying money about the waist,
      a tooth will be aching.

      "You are dreaming that you are gathering some loose coins, then you will think: 'I am going to have a tooth ache, its going to hurt me for a day or two.' "

      The verb *cunchulli* refers to the *cunchulla*, a space created between the *cusma*, the man's skirt, and the body around the midriff. It is customary to use this space for carrying small objects such as money.

24   **istera muscu-chi-mi ungu-y pia-ngapa,**
      straw mat to dream [*caus-aff*] to be sick [*nom*] to strike [*purp*]

      o sura-ca muscu-chi-mi chasa huiru huaglli-ngapa.
      or again [*foc*] to dream [*caus-aff*] thus cornfield to damage
          [*purp*]

      You are made to dream a straw mat,
      sickness is to strike;
      or else, you are made to dream like this,
      your cornfield will be ruined.

      "You will become toasted like the totora, you will turn yellow."

      The straw mat is the traditional sleeping pallet for the Ingano people; the mats are made from *totora*, a local reed; they are laid out at night for sleepers, then set aside during the day.

It may be significant that the totora reed grows wild in the swampy areas toward the center of the valley, whereas corn (with its positive associations in the sayings) is the major domesticated food crop, and it is carefully planted and tended in fields at the periphery of the valley.

25   **limpu mapa ca-gta muscu-chi-mi,**
     entirely filthy to be [sub] to dream [caus-aff]

     ungu-y chaya-ngapa ca-hura.
     to be sick [nom] to arrive [purp] to be [temp]

     You are made to dream that you are quite filthy,
     it is time for sickness to arrive.

     "When a person is sick, he should not bathe himself."

26   **chaqui malla-ri-cu-gta muscu-chi-mi ungu-y-lla-ta-ta.**
     foot to wash [ref-prog-sub] to dream [caus-aff] to be sick [nom-del-acc-acc]

     You are made to dream that you are washing your feet,
     it is only sickness.

     The Sibundoy Valley offers a temperate mountain climate, with only occasional warm interludes. This saying may reflect an awareness of the health dangers of bathing, or it may derive from a violation of ritual prescriptions concerning bathing, several of which are presented in the sayings (see the section titled *armaycunamanda* in the next chapter).

27   **ungu-y chaya-ngapa ca-hura,**
     to be sick [nom] to arrive [purp] to be [temp]

     arma-cu-gta-mi muscu-chí.
     to bathe [prog-sub-foc] to dream [caus]

     When sickness is to arrive,
     you are made to dream that you are bathing.

28   **rumi muscu-chi-mi chiri tucu-ngapa.**
     stone to dream [caus-aff] cold to become [purp]

     You are made to dream of stones,
     you will become cold.

"This 'coldness' has to do with a chill in the bones akin to the effects of rheumatism." The salience of this complaint is demonstrated by the large number of herbs used to treat it (Bristol 1968).

29   **misa-ma yaycu-cu-gta muscu-chi-mi,**
     mass [*dat*] to enter [*prog-sub*] to dream [*caus-aff*]

     ungu-y pia-ngapa.
     to be sick [*nom*] to strike [*purp*]

     You are made to dream that you are entering the mass,
     sickness is to strike.

     "When you are about to die, when you are with very little time,
     then you will dream this, you will be made to dream that you are
     going to hear mass in the church."

30   **isma muscu-chi-mi ungu-y pia-ngapa.**
     feces to dream [*caus-aff*] to be sick [*nom*] to strike [*purp*]

     You are made to dream of feces,
     sickness is to strike.

31   **quinquin isma-ri-sca ca-gta muscu-chi-mi,**
     self to defecate [*ref-hist*] to be [*sub*] to dream [*caus-aff*]

     quinquin-ta ungu-y pia-ngapa.
     self [*acc*] to be sick [*nom*] to strike [*purp*]

     You are made to dream
     that you are soiled with your own feces,
     sickness is to strike you.

32   **ispa-ri-sca paca-ri-gta muscu-chi-mi,**
     to urinate [*ref-hist*] to dawn [*ref-sub*] to dream [*caus-aff*]

     ungu-y pia-ngapa.
     to be sick [*nom*] to strike [*purp*]

     You are made to dream
     that you awake wet with urine:
     sickness is to strike.

33   **ispa-ri-sca puri-cu-gta muscu-nga,**
     to urinate [*ref-hist*] to walk [*prog-sub*] to dream [*3,f*]

     ña atari-nga mana pudi-gta-mi,
     already to arise [*3,f*] not to be able [*sub-aff*]

ungu-y pia-ngapa sinchi.
to be sick [*nom*] to strike [*purp*] strong

You will dream that you are walking, wet with urine,
a sickness will strike you,
so strong that you cannot get out of bed.

34 **huira muscu-chi-mi sinchi ungu-y.**
grease to dream [*caus-aff*] strong to be sick [*nom*]

You are made to dream of fat,
a strong sickness.

35 **huira batia-pi urma-gta muscu-spa-ca,**
grease bowl [*loc*] to fall [*sub*] to dream [*ger-foc*]

mana alia-ngapa,
not to improve [*purp*]

yapa sinchi ungu-y pia-spa.
very strong to be sick [*nom*] to strike [*ger*]

Dreaming that you fall into a bowl of grease,
you will not improve,
a very strong sickness is striking you.

"Right away you will not get better, when you dream that you fall
into the bowl of fat."

The *batia* is a wooden bowl carved out of a single section of log.

36 **huira batia ladu-pi siri-cu-gta muscu-chi-mi,**
grease bowl side [*loc*] to lie [*prog-sub*] to dream [*caus-aff*]

sinchi ungu-y pia-ngapa ca-hura.
strong to be sick [*nom*] to strike [*purp*] to be [*temp*]

You are made to dream
a bowl of grease lying on its side,
when a strong sickness is to strike you.

HUAYRAMANDA

This set of sayings relates to spiritual sickness, designated by
the Inga word *huayra*, literally meaning 'wind' and the medicinal
practices of those who treat this condition, the *sinchicuna* or native
doctors. These sayings warn of encounters with good (curing) and
evil (bewitching) doctors, and they alert the dreamer to the onset

of spiritual sickness. White often signifies the curing doctor, whereas black signifies the harming doctor. Dream images include animals and artifacts associated with the non-Indian lifestyle, as well as animals like snakes and birds associated with the practice of shamanism in the valley.

37 **yana alcu muscu-chi-mi maycan curinti sinchi tupa-ngapa.**
    black dog to dream [*caus-aff*] some very doctor to encounter
    [*purp*]

You are made to dream a black dog:
you are to encounter a very powerful native doctor.

The dog occupies a position of importance in Sibundoy mythology: in different mythic narratives the dogs of the volcano composed of rock come to life and aid hunters in snaring the tapirs; a white dog stands guard over a vein of affluvial gold; and two magnificent hunting dogs possess spiritual powers that allow them to procure food without fail for their masters.

38 **yana alcu muscu-chi-mi dañu-dur sinchi tupa-ngapa.**
    black dog to dream [*caus-aff*] to harm [*agt*] doctor to encounter
    [*purp*]

You are made to dream a black dog,
you are to encounter a harmful doctor.

"If someone has the dream of the black dog, he will say: 'So, today I will encounter the one who is witching me, the one that doesn't love me, the one who is not a good healer.' And many people, that day, rub their hands with red pepper, and they say that the first person you meet is the witch. But only an indigenous person, not a white person. And only a man, not a woman. My mother, when she dreamed a black dog, would generally say: 'I am going to run into Esteban Tisoy.' She always said that he was witching her. And she always would run into him. Since he had had some problems with my father, he didn't like my father to get ahead, because my father liked to work a lot. And so she said that because of that Esteban was witching him, and that's why my father became a wanderer."

39 **yura alcu muscu-chi-mi ambi-dur sinchi tupa-ngapa.**
    white dog to dream [*caus-aff*] to cure [*agt*] doctor to meet [*purp*]

one has witched them. If you dream this, you should go see a doctor; otherwise, you will travel far off and never return."

The Ingano are a very mobile people, travelling great distances in order to earn a living or to avoid the harsh dominion of the Catholic missionaries. They use this saying to explain the absence of those members of the community who move away and never return.

6   **oso muscu-chi-mi pinu lagrun yaycu-nga-hura.**
     bear to dream [caus-aff] fine thief to enter [3,f-temp]

     You are made to dream a bear
     when a fine thief will enter.

"When you dream a bear the thief will not only carry off things, but in addition to carrying them off, he will go doing harm. He steals and does harm. He leaves you open to witchery."

There are no longer any bears in the Sibundoy Valley, but the elders still remember seeing them there, and what is more, the bear has left behind quite a presence in the lore of the native communities of the valley. In mythic narrative among the Kamsá and Ingano people, the bear figures as a somewhat oafish character, often the blundering victim of tricksters like the rabbit and the squirrel. In another guise, known generally as the "Juan Oso" tale, the bear as an animal-person shows an unwarranted interest in human females.

SISAYCUNAMANDA

This next set of sayings centers on thievery (Inga *sisay*, 'to steal'), a constant problem in a setting where people spend lengthy periods of time away from their homes, attending chicha parties or working far-flung fields. The institution of the *huasikama*, or 'house-watcher', is a traditional response to this problem. The sayings specify the origin of the thief, whether from far away, from among the 'whites', or a member of the extended family, and some of them indicate whether or not the thief will be caught. The dream images are mostly insects and animals, from the domain of either home or forest.

7   **taruca muscu-chi-mi pinu lagrun.**
     deer to dream [caus-aff] fine thief

You are made to dream a deer:
a fine thief.

The phrase *pinu lagrun,* of Spanish origin, indicates "a very professional thief, one who will clean you out without leaving a trace".

58   **conejo muscu-chi-mi lagrun-cuna.**
     rabbit to dream [*caus-aff*] thief [*pl*]

You are made to dream a rabbit:
thieves.

This saying invokes the actual rabbit as well as the mythological rabbit. The rabbit is the primary trickster figure in the mythic narrative of the Sibundoy Valley. In the Ingano version of the "Tar Baby Story," rabbit is a boy in a home where there is a garden, and it is his job to spread the refuse from dinner around the bean plants after dinner. He rolls about in the dirt to take on the form of a rabbit, and in this form he munches on the bean plants. Eventually, of course, he is pinned to the sticky doll left by the owners to catch the thief who is eating their beans.

59* **mono-ta muscu-gpi-ca, chagra-pi sara sisa-y palla-ngapa.**
     monkey [*acc*] to dream [*cond-foc*] field [*loc*] corn thief [*nom*]
         to harvest [*purp*]

     mono-ta api-cu-gta muscu-spa-ca,
     monkey [*acc*] to catch [*prog-sub*] to dream [*ger-foc*]

     sara sisa-y-ta api-ngapa.
     corn to steal [*nom-acc*] to catch [*purp*]

If you dream a monkey,
in the field a thief will be harvesting your corn.
Dreaming that you are catching the monkey,
you are to catch the corn thief.

"We say that when you dream the monkey, not only in the field they are going to rob you. And the monkey also means that the thief is going to be a witch. As he robs you, he might leave your luck ruined."

60* **tigre muscu-gpi-ca, huagra sisa-y tucu-ngapa.**
     tiger to dream [*cond-foc*] cattle to steal [*nom*] to become [*purp*]

     tigre-ta api-cu-gta muscu-spa-ca,
     tiger [*acc*] to catch [*prog-sub*] to dream [*ger-foc*]

huagra sisa-y-ta shachi-ngapa.
cattle to steal [*nom-acc*] to discover [*purp*]

If you dream a tiger,
cattle thieves will appear.
Dreaming that you are catching the tiger,
you will surprise the cattle thief.

"The tiger, especially, means white people, not indigenous people because they rarely steal cattle. The tiger means a first-class thief."

The Spanish word *tigre* is used to refer to the puma, an animal that was formerly present in the Sibundoy Valley, and is still found in the Lower Putumayo, in the territory of the *amigos*, or lowland Inganos.

61*   **misitu muscu-gpi-ca, huasi ucu-ma sisa-y yaycu-ngapa.**
cat to dream [*cond-foc*] house inside [*dat*] thief to enter [*purp*]

misitu-ta api-cu-gta muscu-spa-ca, sisa-y-ta api-ngapa.
cat [*acc*] to catch [*prog-sub*] to dream [*ger-foc*] thief [*acc*] to catch [*purp*]

If you dream a cat,
a thief is to enter your house.
Dreaming that you are catching the cat,
you are to catch the thief.

"So they say if you dream a cat, you will be on the lookout for a thief entering the house. They always say that the cat has long claws, so they make the comparison there."

The cat is not a notable presence in Sibundoy myth, though Alberto Juajibioy (Juajibioy & Wheeler 1973) records one story from his father in which the devil in the form of a cat creates discord within a household.

62   **misitu muscu-spa-ca huagra ima ruba-ngapa.**
cat to dream [*ger-foc*] cattle what to rob [*purp*]

Dreaming a cat,
they are to rob your cattle.

63   **usa pamilia lagrun-mi muscu-chí.**
louse family thief [*aff*] to dream [*caus*]

You are made to dream lice:
a thief from within the family.

The notion of a "thief from within the family" points to an area
of stress in social relations in the community, the problem of ri-
valry and competition among members of the immediate and extended family. Lice, as parasites carried on the body, seems an
especially appropriate dream image for this kind of thief.

64* **usa-cuna api-cu-gta muscu-spa-ca,**
louse [*pl*] to catch [*prog-sub*] to dream [*ger-foc*]

ucu-pi chinga-pu-ngapa.
inside [*loc*] to lose [*ben-purp*]

Dreaming that you are catching lice,
from inside something is to be lost for you.

"If you dream that you are catching lice, killing lice, then they say
that they are going to rob from your house. The louse after all is
something that they have in the house, something that one carries,
right? Along these lines, they say that they will come and remove
the things that you have there in the house."

65 **cuchi usa muscu-chi-mi lancu lagrun.**
pig louse to dream [*caus-aff*] white person thief

You are made to dream of pig lice:
a thief from among the white people.

The color of the pig plays a role here, for the Ingano perceive white
people to have the same pinkish coloring.

66 **cuy muscu-chi-mi pamilia lagrun yaycu-ngapa ca-hura.**
cuy to dream [*caus-aff*] family thief to enter [*purp*] to be [*temp*]

You are made to dream cuy
when a thief from within the family is to enter.

"When you dream a cuy, they say that the thief will be from
the household, one of the family members connected to the
house. Not the children: it could be a nephew or some more
distant relative of the household members."

The cuy (*Cavia porcellus*) or Andean guinea pig is also a resident of the house, one that scampers about eating leaves and
other vegetable rubbish until its time comes. Then it is slaughtered and roasted on a stick, usually in connection with special
occasions.

The Ingano commentary presented above pinpoints the source
of much intrafamilial trouble: those kin falling into the category of distant relatives (beyond the immediate family).

67   **cuy muscu-spa-ca ca-nca pamilia, vecino lagrun.**
     cuy to dream [*ger-foc*] to be [*3,f*] family neighbor thief

     Dreaming a cuy,
     the thief is a close relative, or neighbor.

68   **ajinu lagrun yaycu-nga-hura,**
     stranger thief to enter [*3,f-temp*]

     muscu-chi-mi ucucha, michichin,
     to dream [*caus-aff*] mouse porcupine

     ubi mana ca-gpi-ca, chucha.
     or not to be [*cond-foc*] opossum

     When a thief from afar is to enter,
     you are made to dream a mouse, a porcupine,
     or if not that, an opossum.

69   **chugllu lagrun-ca chi-ca muscu-chi-nca ardilla.**
     corncob thief [*foc*] that [*foc*] to dream [*caus-3f*] squirrel

     A thief of your ripe corncobs,
     for that you are made to dream a squirrel.

The squirrel is another trickster figure in the mythic narrative of
the valley. In one much relished episode, after causing the bear
(who is portrayed as *gobernador* or governor of the community) to
crush his own testicles with a rock, the squirrel organizes an army
of ants and wasps to fight off the soldiers sent by *el señor gobernador.*

SOCIAL RELATIONS

    This set of sayings features people in their social rounds, trying
to get along with one another. They make reference to encounters
with whites, showing the urgency of this particular social tie, and
to legal processes in the court and cabildo, to arguments and fights,
and to marriage. Dream images include a cresting or subsiding river,
as well as food items such as eggs, root crops, and chicha. The set
relating to the "behavior" of the river suggests the intervention of

the pan-Andean thunder god, who reigns over the skies and controls
the levels of rainfall (see the final chapter).

70   **pato huahua-cuna lanco-mi muscu-chí.**
      duck child [*pl*] white person [*aff*] to dream [*caus*]

      You are made to dream ducklings:
      white people.

71*   **yacu muscu-gpi-ca,**
      river to dream [*cond-foc*]

      mana rigsi-sca lanco-cuna cahua-ngapa.
      not to know [*hist*] white person [*pl*] to see [*purp*]

      If you dream a river,
      you are to see unknown white people.

      "If you dream a river it means that you are going to see people that
      you don't know, especially white people. So all of a sudden they
      will visit you or something."

72   **yacu arca-y tucu-sca muscu-gpi-ca,**
      river to restrain [*nom*] to become [*hist*] to dream [*cond-foc*]

      pleito yuca-ngapa.
      argument to have [*purp*]

      If you dream an unfordable river,
      you are to have an argument.

      "If you dream a large river that you cannot cross, they say that you
      will have to go to the court and to the mayor's office. For whatever
      problem, you will have to go to these places. If you can get across
      the river quickly, you have no problem getting across, then they
      say that you will have no trouble in court. Easily you will resolve
      whatever difficulty you might have. But if you can't ford the river,
      then you are going to have problems there. With the judge or with
      the mayor, you are not going to be able to disentangle yourself
      easily, and they might trap you there."

73*   **yacu arca-y tucu-spa ca-spa tusta-gpi-ca,**
      river to restrain [*nom*] to become [*ger*] to be [*ger*] to dry [*cond-
      foc*]

      imapipas lanco-cuna-hua alli ri-ngapa.
      whoever white person [*pl-inst*] well to go [*purp*]

If the river that you cannot ford dries up,
things will go well with any whites.

74   **mana yacu-pi yali-ngapa pudi-cu-gta muscu-chi-mi,**
     not river [*loc*] to cross [*purp*] to be able [*prog-sub*] to dream
     [*caus-aff*]

     justicia-pi mana pudi-ngapa rima-ngapa.
     court [*loc*] not to be able [*purp*] to speak [*purp*]

     sug-ni-manda-mi vinci-ngacuna.
     other [*conn-abl-aff*] to win [*3,f,pl*]

     You are made to dream that you cannot cross a river,
     at court you will not be able to speak well.
     The others will prevail.

     "When you are made to dream that a river prevents you from cross-
     ing, you are thinking that you will have to go to the cabildo. But
     you can't go; you just leave the complaint pending. In the mean-
     while, the others will prevail over you. Your case remains forgot-
     ten."

75   **mana sinti-glla yacu-pi yali-spa muscu-spa-ca,**
     not to feel [*post*] river [*loc*] to cross [*ger*] to dream [*ger-foc*]

     chi-ca yuya-nga: dimandu imapasi caya-hua-chu-cuna,
     that [*foc*] to think [*3,f*] complaint whatever to call [*1ob-int-pl*]

     chi-hura-ca nuca-pa parti-mi vinci-spa paci-lla-mi,
     that [*time-foc*] I [*poss*] part [*aff*] to win [*ger*] easy [*del-aff*]

     yali-ngapa ca-ni.
     to cross [*purp*] to be [*lst*]

     Dreaming that you cross a river without trouble,
     you will think: "Perhaps they will bring me a complaint.
     Then my side will win easily,
     I am to prevail."

76   **huasi-ca, justicia-ma ima dimandu-cuna yuca-hura,**
     house [*foc*] court [*dat*] what complaint [*pl*] to have [*temp*]

     presentia-ri-nacu-hura, chi-cuna-manda-mi muscu-chí.
     to present [*ref-prog-temp*] that [*pl-abl-aff*] to dream [*caus*]

     When there are complaints before the court,
     when they are presenting themselves,
     because of those things they are made to dream the house.

77*   **achira muscu-gpi-ca, puñiti tantea-ngapa.**
      achira to dream [*cond-foc*] fist to feel [*purp*]

      If you dream achira,
      you are to feel a fist.

      The root of this plant is hard and cylindrical, something like a fist.

78   **palabra-cuna, muscu-chi-mi sangu sangu jura asua.**
      word [*pl*] to dream [*caus-aff*] thick thick jura chicha

      There will be words,
      when you are made to dream of thick, thick jura chicha.

      "Thick, thick jura chicha. God preserve us, but very delicious chi-
      cha. When I see that in my dream I am thinking, 'words,' when I
      am made to dream that."

      Jura chicha is made by letting the corn grains soak for a few days
      until they begin to sprout. This kind of chicha is very intoxicating.

79*   **huevos muscu-gpi-ca, pelea tia-ngapa.**
      eggs to dream [*cond-foc*] fight to exist [*purp*]

      If you dream eggs,
      there will be a fight.

80   **puñiti livia-ngapa ca-hura,**
      fisticuff to receive [*purp*] to be [*temp*]

      huarmi-cuna-ta huevos-mi muscu-chí.
      woman [*pl-acc*] eggs [*aff*] to dream [*caus*]

      When they are to receive a beating,
      women are made to dream eggs.

      "When a woman dreams eggs then her husband is going to hit her.
      So they are anxious when they go to a party: 'Maybe this is where
      he is going to hit me.' This dream is mostly for women. Sometimes
      I would tell my mother: 'I dreamed eggs.' But she told me: 'Are
      you a woman so that your husband can hit you?' So this one is
      generally for women."

81   **cari-pura maycan maca-nacu-ngapa ca-hura,**
      man [*reci*] someone to hit [*prog-purp*] to be [*temp*]

      huivos-mi muscu-chí.
      eggs [*aff*] to dream [*caus*]

When men are to fight among themselves,
they are made to dream eggs.

"After having such a dream, a man will ask himself: 'I wonder who
I am going to fight with. Maybe I shouldn't go to the fiesta.' This
dream applies to those who wander about drinking, or else they
might come to your house to strike you."

82 **pichi bayta muscu-chi-mi, yahuar cahua-ngapa.**
red shawl to dream [caus-aff] blood to see [purp]

You are made to dream a red shawl:
you are to see blood.

The women in the Ingano community customarily wear shawls
made of very bright colored cloth, and red (along with green) is one
of the preferred colors. This saying refers to a woman's first men-
strual cycle as well as to other kinds of bleeding.

83* **sapa-lla ca-spa, sorteja chura-ri-cu-gta muscu-gpi-ca,**
only [del] to be [ger] ring to put on [ref-prog-sub] to dream [cond-
foc]

casara-ngapa.
to marry [purp]

Being single,
if you dream that you are putting on a ring,
you are to marry.

84 **surtija muscu-chi-mi casara-ngapa.**
ring to dream [caus-aff] to marry [purp]

You are made to dream a ring,
you are to marry.

ALLI HUASAMANDA

This last set of sayings decoding the dreamworld brings together
a miscellany whose common thread is the prediction of good luck
(in Inga *alli huasa*, literally 'good back'). The fortunes indexed here
include the acquisition of valuable items such as money, clothes,
yagé, or a godchild; also included are a few instances of adverse
fortune, such as having a snake appear while working in the fields.
I have also thrown in a sampling of weather predictions in this set.

85* **tanda, habas o sara muscu-gpi-ca,**
bread lima beans or corn to dream [cond-foc]

culqui chaya-ngapa o tari-ngapa.
money to arrive [purp] or to find [purp]

If you dream bread, lima beans, or corn,
money will come to you or you will find it.

"If you dream bread or corn, not so much beans, because we say
that means a stomachache, but bread and corn, yes, it means that
you can earn some money somehow. But not without working.
Often one says for example: 'Well, maybe I'm going to do some
business. Maybe they are going to give me some work. Or maybe
I am going to sell corn or sell something else, maybe a hen.' And
so they sell the hen: 'Ah, so this is what it meant when I dreamed
bread or corn.' Sometimes you just find money, but that is very
rare."

86 **rosario santo cristo-hua muscu-chi-mi,**
rosary saintly Christ [inst] to dream [caus-aff]

huahua yuca-chi-ngapa.
child to have [caus-purp]

You are made to dream a crucifix:
a godchild you are to receive.

The dream image may bring to mind the Catholic services for first
communion and confirmation, occasions when godparents are so-
licited by the parents of the children.

87 **culqui rosario muscu-chi-mi,**
silver rosary to dream [caus-aff]

maycan compadre rura-ngapa nombra-nacu-gmanda.
someone compadre to do [purp] to name [prog-hab]

You are made to dream a silver rosary:
someone will be naming you a compadre.

88 **buitsaja panga muscu-spa-ca,**
palm leaves to dream [ger-foc]

catanga yuca-ngapa.
clothes to have [purp]

Dreaming the leaves of the buitsaja palm,
you are to have clothes.

"If you dream these leaves, the leaves used for thatching houses, especially that you are carrying a bundle of them, then you will be thinking: 'I don't know, I am going to have a chance to buy some clothes.' "

The palm in question (*Prestoea*) is a small palm cultivated in the gardens. Its ample leaves are used for roofing, basket making, and religious ceremony; its trunk provides material for the construction of houses and bridges; the inner core makes a delicious snack.

89 **calabazo muscu-chi-mi llatan ca-gmanda.**
squash to dream [*caus-aff*] unclothed to be [*hab*]

You are made to dream squash:
you will be without clothes.

"The squash has a very thin skin. This dream means that you will not buy new clothes, that all of your clothing is old and you will not be able to buy any new clothes soon."

90 **yuyu muscu-chi-mi, aycha,**
cabbage to dream [*caus-aff*] meat

cahua-y o micu-nga-hura-mi.
to see [*inf*] or to eat [*3,f-temp-aff*]

You are made to dream cabbage, meat:
to see it, or when you are to eat it.

91 **tragu muscu-chi-mi indi-ngapa ca-hura.**
aguardiente to dream [*caus-aff*] to be sunny [*purp*] to be [*temp*]

You are made to dream aguardiente
when the day is to be sunny.

The Spanish word *aguardiente* labels the distilled beverage made from sugar cane juice. It is a potent brew that has become almost as ubiquitous as chicha in the social life of the valley.

92 **tragu upia-cu-gta muscu-chi-mi,**
aguardiente to drink [*prog-sub*] to dream [*caus-aff*]

ambi huasca cara-nga-hora.
medicine vine to give [*3,f-temp*]

You are made to dream that you are drinking aguardiente
when they are to give you the medicine vine.

"When I am made to dream that I am drinking aguardiente, someone might come to sell me the good vine, so I can drink it right
then and there. When I am made to dream that, it is a very good
dream I am having. When I dream that they are giving me aguardiente, then I think: 'Perhaps my little friend is coming, even now
she is on her way to make me drink of the good vine.' Because of
that, I am made to dream aguardiente."

93   **asua muscu-gpi-ca, tamia puncha tucu-ngapa.**
      chicha to dream [cond-foc] rain day to become [purp]

      If you dream chicha,
      a rainy day will follow.

"Perhaps because people always wet their upper chest when drinking chicha, they spill it on themselves."

94   **genti-mi muscu-chi-mi,**
      person [aff] to dream [caus-aff]

      caya-ndi chi genti chaya-ngapa ca.
      tomorrow [assoc] that person to arrive [purp] to be

      You are made to dream a person,
      the next day that person will arrive.

"They say that when you dream a person it means that they will
return, that they are coming to visit you, or something like that.
With such a dream, if it is a long one, they say: 'He is thinking of
me. He is far away, maybe he is coming to visit.' My mother, when
she dreams my sister, as soon as she awakes she says: 'I wonder
what's going on with my daughter. I dreamed her like this, is she
well, is she sick? Maybe she is going to come.' There she is expecting something. It depends on the nature of the dream. Often
if the dream is sad, then the person is sick. When you dream them
very healthy, it means they are thinking of you, and some notice
of that person will arrive."

"You dream this and the next day you are thinking: 'So they will
come.' At my father's house it happened that way. 'I dreamed of
so and so,' my deceased father would say, and then truly the next
day in the evening that person would arrive. And so it was true."

95   **cinta o chumbi muscu-spa-ca,**
      small woven belt or woven belt to dream [ger-foc]

culibra trabaja-cu-sca-pi cahuari-ngapa.
snake to work [*prog-hist-loc*] to appear [*purp*]

Dreaming a woven belt,
at your work a snake will appear.

"One time I dreamt the small woven belt, that I had the woven belt tied and it came undone, in that way I used to tie it to catch my hair. Mother of mine, I was working quickly like this, preparing the earth for planting, I was working along a row, grabbing the weeds with my fist, then cutting, cutting. Again I had the grass in my hands when it rubbed me here, that rascal, the head of that damn snake. When that cold snake rubbed against me, I threw it aside, as far as I could, along with the grass and all."

3

Tapiacunamanda

This chapter presents an inventory of sayings that take notice of signs and portents residing in the wakeful experience of individuals. These sayings alert people to the underlying significance of apparently accidental or unmotivated occurrences in the natural world. Everything from the internal physiology of the body to the behavior of various animals may become a theatre of signification. Even the slightest twitch of a muscle may carry information concerning the likely path of future events. Moreover, many of these manifestations are thought to reflect on the spiritual condition of the person and her or his family. The Inga term for sign or omen, *tapia*, provides the label for this branch of the sayings corpus, and one frequently hears the exclamation, *chi tapiami ca*, "that is an omen."

Some sense of the mentality implicated in this worldview is conveyed in the following rationalization for the belief in the portentous character of tics and twitches: "It isn't natural, you know, that something begins to tremble; it only happens every once in a while. And so people think, 'That means that something is going to happen.'" The unexplained, irrepressible sensation or observation triggers the divinatory framework. Twitches and tics in various regions of the body signify coming events related to the use and function of that body part: for example, a tic in the eye signifies that one will cry or that one is to see something; a twitch in the calf muscle, that someone will pay a visit; in the back, that the person is destined to carry a weight.

The domain of *tapiacunamanda* plausibly falls into a small set of topical subcategories composed of empirical domains reflecting the prevalent orientations of Sibundoy thought. One of these, *animalcunamanda*, 'about animals', conjoins naturalistic and mythological interests. Especially prevalent are birds, the major animal-people in the mythic narrative of the valley (see Chapter 4), along with insects and snakes, likewise prominently featured in mythical tradition. Animals from the domestic arena, such as the dog and cuy, also play a role in this category of the sayings. Conspicuously absent are the European-derived animals such as cow, bull, and horse, which figure instead in the sayings concerning dream images.

Another subcategory is *quillamanda*, 'about the moon'. This celestial body is equated with the Virgin Mary in a syncretic adaptation of the traditional worldview. In mythic narrative, the moon is portrayed as a feminine deity very much involved in the affairs of humankind. The sayings pay careful attention to the phases of the celestial moon. As one informant put it: "We consider the moon important in the planting of corn, arracacha, and all other crops, and by the same token, we consider it to be important in the lives of people." In the corpus of sayings, the full moon and the new moon, as well as the waxing or waning moon, are singled out for attention.

The sayings focusing on bathing manifest a pervasive Andean concern with water and the circulation of fluids (Bastien 1978, Urton 1981, Sherbondy 1982). The famous "Inca" bath in the hills above Cuzco can still be viewed to this day, and Cristóbal de Molina, a priest in the hospital for natives of sixteenth-century Cuzco, records a number of Incaic ceremonial bathing customs, noting that bathing was conceptualized as a rite of cleansing and purification. Juan de Santacruz Pachacuti-yamqui Salcamayhua (1873: 87) includes in his remarkable narrative of Inca practices an account of the Incaic worship of sacred waters: "they did honor to the water that had been touched by Tonapa," the great Andean thunder deity. Sacred lakes and rivers figure prominently in the lore of the Chibchan peoples to the north of the Sibundoy Valley as well (Graham 1925, Triana 1951). The Sibundoy natives continue to make use of water for ritual purposes: some of their curing ceremonies require water from a large sea or lake, a requirement that Molina (1873: 23) noted in the Incaic period as well. The sayings indicate a respect for the cleansing and restorative powers of water, as well as a recognition of water as a conduit of spiritual danger (see sayings 136 and 181).

The sayings making up this second broad category are organized under the following headings: animals; the moon; tics and twitches; children; bathing; fortune.

ANIMALCUNAMANDA

Mythological and naturalistic interests are reflected in this set of sayings focusing on animals. Modern representatives of the ancestral animal-people include owls, buzzards, and centipedes. Birds and dogs are the two species singled out for special attention in this set, and this corresponds to their prominence in the traditional worldview. The events signified by the various animals include death, sadness, visits, and physical or spiritual sickness.

96   **bajna uray-cu-gpi-ca,**
     spider to descend [*prog-cond-foc*]

     maycan chaya-gri-ca imapas cara-ngapa.
     someone to visit [*disloc-foc*] something to give [*purp*]

     If the bajna spider should descend,
     someone will come to visit,
     they are to give you something.

Visits are predicted in a number of sayings, and this concentration attests to the importance of social visiting in the lifeways of the community, which makes no use of the telephone and very little use of written messages.

97   **santo piso huasi ucu-ma yaycu-mi tapia,**
     centipede house inside [*dat*] to enter [*aff*] sign

     huahua-cuna huañu-ngapa o dañu-nacu-gmanda.
     child [*pl*] to die [*purp*] or to harm [*prog-hab*]

     The centipede enters your house, it is a sign:
     the children are to die,
     or they will be harming them.

The mixing of field and house is a sign of spiritual danger. The centipede figures as a spirit familiar, or insect-person, in the mythic narrative corpus. In one story, a prospective mother-in-law asks her future daughter-in-law to accompany her to plant some seeds. The young woman refuses, saying that she will turn herself into the plant itself. While in the field, the older woman strikes a centipede with a digging stick; when she returns home, the would-be daughter-in-law is wounded around the head, and she accuses the mother of striking her while they were in the field.

98   **pulga tapia-nca pamilia huañu-ngapa-glla-ta-ta.**
     flea to signify [*3,f*] family to die [*purp-post-acc-acc*]

     Fleas will foretell that someone in the family is to die.

"When someone who formerly didn't have any suddenly finds that they have a great many."

99 **usa-pasi tapia-nca maycan pamilia huañu-ngapa-glla-ta-ta.**
louse [*conj*] to signify [*3,f*] someone family to die [*purp-post-acc-acc*]

usa junda-nca chi-ca.
louse to fill [*3,f*] that [*foc*]

Lice also signify that someone in the family is to die.
Someone will be covered with lice.

100 **anangu tapia-mi huasi-pi, maycan pamilia huañu-ngapa.**
ant to signify [*aff*] house [*loc*] someone family to die [*purp*]

Ants in the house is a sign,
someone in the family is to die.

Ants are associated with the practice of the evil doctors who use castings of footprints to cause harm.

101 **nina curu ucu-pi puri-ri-gri-gpi-ca,**
firefly inside [*loc*] to travel [*ref-disloc-cond-foc*]

maycan huasi-chi-y rura-g o ayuda-g
someone to construct [*caus-nom*] to make [*nom*] or to help [*nom*]

mana unay-lla-pi huañu-ngapa.
not long time [*del-loc*] to die [*purp*]

nina curu-ta api-spa-ca, cahua-ncuna-mi:
firefly [*acc*] to catch [*ger-foc*] to see [*3,pl-aff*]

agcha cata-sca ca-gpi-ca, huarmi;
hair to cover [*hist*] to be [*cond-foc*] woman

y chasa-lla-ta, agcha cuchu-sca ca-gpi-ca, cari.
and so [*del-acc*] hair to cut [*hist*] to be [*cond-foc*] man

If the firefly should come inside
someone who built the house, the builder or a helper,
is to die before long.
Catching the firefly, they look at it:
if it is covered with hair, a woman;
likewise, if it is without hair, a man.

"When a house is built, a great number of people take part, especially for the thatching. The women often bring straw or leaves of a palm tree, and the men often bring vines to tie the crossbeams, and often they bring the beams too. Then after the house is thatched, they all receive a meal. The owner of the house generally slaughters a pig or an ox. He usually gives each person several large pieces of meat with hominy, and then there is chicha and they dance in the new house."

"When the firefly comes in, they say it's in order to see what's there, to take its last flight. So we always catch it, we try to catch it so we can look it over, so we can see if it's a man or a woman who is going to die. And so we say that when the firefly flies around inside, someone will soon die, within a year or two, but no more than two years. And so we always try to catch it to see who it is. Then, often we will start thinking: 'It must be her, she's been kind of sick lately, or maybe that other lady who is getting up there in age. I guess someone who came to help me is going to die, maybe the one who brought straw, poor thing, maybe the one who was working over in that corner where we caught the firefly.' And people become sad over this."

102 **tuta puñu-cu-hura piqui-cuna calpa-ri-nacu-sina,**
     evening to sleep [*prog-temp*] louse [*pl*] to run [*ref-prog-comp*]

     mana puñu-ri-gpi-ca, tapia-mi niraya:
     not to sleep [*ref-cond-foc*] sign [*aff*] to signify

     maycan huañu-ngapa.
     someone to die [*purp*]

     When you are sleeping at night,
     the lice are running all about,
     if you cannot sleep, it is said to be a sign:
     someone is to die.

103 **culebra tapia-mi pinu dañu-dur-cuna huañu-nga-hura,**
     snake sign [*aff*] fine to harm [*agt-pl*] to die [*3,f-temp*]

     quinquin-ta dañu-dur-cuna huañu-ngapa,
     self [*acc*] to harm [*agt-pl*] to die [*purp*]

     chi-hua-mi chi culebra-nsi-cuna cancha-pi tapia-ri-nacu-nga.
     that [*inst-aff*] that snake [*disp-pl*] patio [*loc*] to signify [*ref-prog-3,f*]

     The snake is a sign
     when one of those fine witches will die.
     Those harmful doctors themselves are to die,
     those ugly snakes in the patio are a sign of that.

104   culebra ucu-ma yaycu-gpi-ca,
      snake inside [dat] to enter [cond-foc]

      maycan jiru yacha brujo huañu-ngapa niraya.
      some ugly doctor witch to die [purp] to signify

      If the snake should come inside,
      it means that some ugly witch doctor is to die.

      "When the snake comes in, they say: 'The one who is casting spells
      around here is going to die.' The snake rarely comes into the house.
      Mostly to the chicha barrel, or sometimes there in the hearth,
      sometimes you find him there. So they say: 'The one who is causing
      harm is going to die.' "

105   cuy chucari-cu-gpi-ca,
      cuy to choke [prog-cond-foc]

      maycan caru-ma ri-sca chaya-mu-ngapa.
      someone far [dat] to go [hist] to arrive [cisloc-purp]

      If a cuy should be choking,
      someone who had gone far away is to return.

106   cuy chucari-gpi-ca maycan caru-manda visitante samu-ngapa-
      ca.
      cuy to choke [cond-foc] someone far [abl] visitor to come [purp-
      foc]

      If the cuy chokes, someone from far off,
      a visitor, is to come.

      "Some people say that someone from far away is going to visit.
      They are thinking: 'I wonder who is coming to visit today.' Some
      say that one who has gone far off is going to return. Others say
      that a native doctor will arrive. Because the cuy rarely does this.
      And so they say that he coughs or chokes primarily when someone
      is going to visit or return or something. But not people that live
      in the same place; rather people who live in another place. This
      doesn't happen every day, but only a couple of times a year."

107   cuy chucari-mi tamia-ngapa u maycan chaya-ngapa ca-hura.
      cuy to choke [aff] to rain [purp] or someone to visit [purp] to
      be [temp]

      The cuy chokes when it is to rain,
      or someone is to visit.

108 **cuy malla-ri-mi ñahui tamia-ngapa.**
cuy to wash [*ref-aff*] eye to rain [*purp*]

The cuy washes its face,
it is going to rain.

109 **alcu-cuna ahulla-ncuna-mi genti huañu-ngapa.**
dog [*pl*] to howl [*3,pl-aff*] people to die [*purp*]

The dogs howl,
a person is to die.

"Look over here, my compadre Benito. First the dogs, saintly God, every night they would howl. Howling, howling, they would go on top of the hill above our house. Again, after that, back to the house, crying, crying. And with that, one after another they passed away: let's see, Marcelino's wife, my compadre Benito, then Miguel Jansasoy, after that my compadre Domingo, Juan Jansasoy, and then his wife the very next day."

110 **tuta alcu-cuna ahulla-nacu-gpi-ca,**
night dog [*pl*] to howl [*prog-cond-foc*]

  animas-ta-mi cahua-ncuna.
souls [*acc-aff*] to see [*3,pl*]

If the dogs are howling at night,
they see the souls of the departed.

Dogs, with their keen sense of smell and hearing, are thought to be able to detect the presence of departed souls as well.

111 **ima herramienta-cuna-ta alcu salva-spa yali-gpi-ca,**
any tool [*pl-acc*] dog to step [*ger*] to cross [*cond-foc*]

  maycan chi-hua trabaja-g-ca quilla-mi tucu.
some that [*inst*] to work [*nom-foc*] lazy [*aff*] to become

Should a dog step over some tools,
with that, the worker will become lazy.

"They say that if you leave any tools around, and the dog steps over them, you will become lazy. If you leave a machete or some other tool out, and a dog steps over it, when you go to use that tool you are going to cut yourself, your hand or some other part of your body. So people are always careful; they don't leave tools on the ground but leaning against the wall. That way the dog cannot step over them."

112 **maycan alcu huanguina micu-gpi-ca, shachina-mi.**
some dog droppings to eat [*cond-foc*] to wither [*aff*]

Should a dog eat chicken droppings,
he will become timid.

"They say that when they eat that, chicken droppings, the dog will start drying up, however fat snd handsome he might be. Little by little, until he dies. And this seems to be true, from what I have seen. Dogs that were very handsome that started eating this, they become dry and it is very difficult to cure them. We call that *shachina*, when a dog cannot walk, when it has been eating hen droppings. In order to cure him, you must squeeze some liver over his head. If you do this without getting him wet, he will recover. There is another cure, a potion made from the leaf of a particular plant."

113 **maycan alcu, purutu yanu-sca-ta micu-gpi-ca,**
any dog beans to boil [*hist-acc*] to eat [*cond-foc*]

mana valesi tucu.
not valuable to become

huasca-cuna-pi y millay-cuna-pi-si laza-ri-spa,
vine [*pl-loc*] and bog [*pl-loc-rep*] to tie [*ref-ger*]

mana ri-ngapa pudi-ncuna.
not to go [*purp*] to be able [*3,pl*]

If a dog eats cooked beans,
he will become useless.
Tying themselves down in vines and bogs, it is said,
they are unable to walk.

"They say this about hunting dogs in particular and not about dogs in general. In regard to hunting dogs, they say you shouldn't give them cooked beans. If they eat cooked beans they will no longer be good hunters. They will be tame, they won't bite anyone, they won't even protect the house. They say that the bean is not very strong, that it is mild, just the opposite of the hot pepper."

114 **cuscungu huasi-ladu-pi huaca-gpi-ca,**
owl house [*side-loc*] to call [*cond-foc*]

chaya-dur huañu-ngapa ubi sinchi huañu-ngapa,
to visit [*agt*] to die [*purp*] or doctor to die [*purp*]

ambi-ngapa ri-dur huañu-ngapa,
to cure [*purp*] to go [*agt*] to die [*purp*]

ubi dañu-dur ima huañu-ngapa,
or to harm [*agt*] also to die [*purp*]

chi-manda-mi cuscungu-ca tapia.
that [*abl-aff*] owl [*foc*] to signify

If the owl calls beside the house,
someone who comes to visit is to die,
or else a native doctor is to die,
one who goes about curing is to die,
or one who does harm is to die.
This is what the owl announces.

115 **cuscungu huasi lado-lla-pi huaca-gpi-ca,**
owl house side [*del-loc*] to call [*cond-foc*]

maycan huañu-ngapa.
someone to die [*purp*]

If the owl calls beside the house,
someone is to die.

116 **lechuza huasi ahua lado capa-ri-spa yali-gpi-ca,**
owl house back side to cry [*ref-ger*] to pass [*cond-foc*]

huañu-sca yali-chi-ngapa.
to die [*hist*] to pass [*caus-purp*]

If the owl passes behind the house, hooting, then you will see
   a corpse pass by.

"Let's say that the house is beside a path or road. There, in front
of the house, they will pass by with the corpse. You are to see a
corpse."

117 **diulpi gallinazo huasi cumbrera-pi tia-ri-chu,**
suddenly buzzard house eaves [*loc*] to be [*ref-int*]

chi-cari yapa sinchi unguy-ta-mi huilla,
that [*emp*] very strong sickness [*acc-aff*] to tell

chi-cari unguy mana-ta-mi falta.
that [*emp*] sickness not [*acc-aff*] to lack

Suddenly there is a buzzard on the eave of the house:
this tells of a very strong sickness,
indeed sickness will not be absent.

118 **maycan quindi ucu-ma yaycu-gpi-ca,**
some hummingbird inside [*dat*] to enter [*cond-foc*]

ura-manda gente chaya-mu-ngapa.
below [*abl*] people to arrive [*cisloc-purp*]

Should a hummingbird enter the house,
people from below are to arrive.

"Even though my father wasn't there at that time, because he had
left a long time before, my father was a good curer, and they knew
him, so they would still come looking for him. When the hummingbird appeared, after two weeks or a month, they would really
arrive. Then someone or my mother would say: 'You see, that's
what I was telling you, don't you see?' "

"Whenever a hummingbird appears in the house, which is only
rarely, not every week but once in a while, that is very rare. So
when they see that, whoever sees it, they say: 'Someone from the
lowlands, one of the *amigos* as we call them is coming to visit,
but one of those who drink lots of yagé, or what we call in Inga a
sinchi taita ('strong doctor'). One of those fine curers is coming to
visit.' And so that's what we say when they appear, sometimes
they fly right in the door. This saying applies only when they come
to the door, not when they appear in any other part of the house.
The hummingbirds will often fly all around the outside of the
house, but no, here we refer only to the doors. Because from time
to time they approach the door and almost come inside. Then they
say it is one of those good ones. They say that this little bird is
like a messenger of the ones who are curers, the good ones."

119 **quindi huasi-ma yaycu-mi quinquin-ta dañu-nacu-gmanda.**
hummingbird house [*dat*] to enter [*aff*] self [*acc*] to harm [*prog-hab*]

The hummingbird enters the house,
the owner himself they are harming.

120 **quindi piña-gpi-ca cuchu-ri-ngapa,**
hummingbird to scold [*cond-foc*] to cut [*ref-purp*]

ubin urmay-lla-pasi urma-ngapa nana-gta simpri.
or down [*del-add*] to fall [*purp*] to hurt [*sub*] plenty

If the hummingbird scolds you,
you are to cut yourself,
or else you are to have a fall,
and hurt yourself plenty.

121* **piscu 'cuin' quindi piña-gpi-ca,**
bird 'cuin' hummingbird to scold [cond-foc]

ima desgracia-pas pasa-ngapa.
some misfortune [conj] to happen [purp]

If the hummingbird scolds saying, "cuin,"
some misfortune will befall you.

"The hummingbird rarely does this, so when he does, we take
notice."

122 **quindi piña-gpi-ca, maycan-mi piña-spa yali-ngapa.**
hummingbird to scold [cond-foc] someone [aff] to scold [ger]
    to pass [purp]

Should the hummingbird scold you,
someone will pass by scolding.

"Perhaps a drunk will pass by, he may pass in front of the house
hurling insults."

123 **quinde u quinde huevos micha-mi micu-ngapa.**
hummingbird or hummingbird eggs bad [aff] to eat [purp]

micu-gpi-ca, quinde-sina-mi yacuna-ya-ngui ca-nguichi.
to eat [cond-foc] hummingbird [comp-aff] thirst [verb-2nd] to
    be [2,pl]

It is bad to eat the hummingbird
or the eggs of the hummingbird.
If you eat these, like the hummingbird,
you will always be thirsty.

"The hummingbird is always flying about drinking from one flower
after another. You will become thirsty like the hummingbird."

124 **golondrina huasi-pi huasi-chi-gpi-ca,**
lark house [loc] to build [caus-cond-foc]

fiestero manda-y tucu-ngapa.
fiestero to command [nom] to become [purp]

If the lark makes a nest in your house,
you are to become a fiestero.

"The lark rarely makes a nest in the thatch roofs of the houses. If
it does, then they say that they will name someone from the house

a fiestero for one of the fiestas in Santiago. So they always would name someone, and often fiestero mayor or perhaps his companion, depending on the number of larks found in the house. The lark, like the dove, is a messenger of peace; they are from God, they bring good news."

125 **golondrina huasi-pi huasi-chi-gpi-ca,**
lark house [*loc*] to build [*caus-cond-foc*]

lancu chaya-ngapa-mi huilla.
white to arrive [*purp-aff*] to tell

If the lark builds its nest in the house,
it tells that white people are going to visit.

126 **cancha-lla-pi tilili o cururu uyari-gpi-ca,**
patio [*del-loc*] tilili or cururu to hear [*cond-foc*]

maycan huañu-ngapa.
someone to die [*purp*]

If you hear the tilili or cururu in the patio,
someone is to die.

127 **tilili capa-ri-hora,**
tilili to call [*ref-temp*]

ñugpa-manda-cuna ni-ncuna: chi tapia-mi ca.
first [*abl-pl*] to say [*3,pl*] that omen [*aff*] to be

When the tilili calls,
our ancestors say: "That is an omen."

This is one of the rare texts that makes direct reference to the ancestors.

128 **sara tarpu-sca puncha micha-mi**
corn to plant [*hist*] day bad [*aff*]

sara cuta-ngapa, pullitu-cuna-ta cara-ngapa,
corn to grind [*purp*] chick [*pl-acc*] to give [*purp*]

atahualpa-ta sita-pu-ngapa, maqui-ca huaglli-mi.
hen [*acc*] to dig [*ben-purp*] hand [*foc*] to ruin [*aff*]

On corn planting day,
it is bad to grind corn,
or to give it to the chicks.

The hens will dig up the corn seed for you,
your hand is ruined.

"The women who plant corn either stay away from corn that day,
letting someone else attend to the grinding or the feeding of the
chicks, or else they will thoroughly scrub their hands with soap
after the planting. If you grind corn, you will have to break it, to
break it down into flour, and that ruins the hand."

"In the old days, they cured everything, the house, the field, the
animals, the children, the people. The doctor goes, he takes yagé,
he does the ritual blowing, he dances, he chants, like that. In order
to have good corn, my father would have my hands cured, to keep
the birds, mice, and everything else from digging up the seeds. And
so corn grows well for me, they don't dig it up when I plant. In the
old days, all of my older sisters had their hands cured. In those
days, we were all cured, we all lived by the cures."

The concept of *alli maqui*, or "a good hand," involves a gift for
planting corn that will yield a good crop. Women who are thought
to have a good hand are much sought after for planting. They perform this service in return for soup and other favors. In order to
achieve a good planting hand, girls and women visit the native
doctors, and are "cured" with the medicine vine.

129 **sara tarpu-sca puncha micha-mi sara camcha-ngapa.**
corn to plant [*hist*] day bad [*aff*] corn to toast [*purp*]

sara tarpu-sca camcha-gpi-ca, piscu surcu-ncuna.
corn to plant [*hist*] to toast [*cond-foc*] bird to remove [*3pl*]

The day corn is planted,
it is bad to toast grains of corn.
Planting corn, if you toast grains of corn,
the birds will pull out the seeds.

"When planting corn, if you toast grains of corn, the birds will
come and remove the seeds. The mice will also come around digging, digging up the seeds. Because of that it is bad to toast grains
of corn. If you toast grains of corn, if you toast them without first
washing your hands, you will have to stir the grains on the skillet,
and that is like calling the birds. And so the little birds will come
and break the small plants, the chiwako bird will be removing
them. And so by the very roots the chiwako will remove them,
and that is not good at all. In order to toast grains of corn we must

stir them while they heat up. Stirring the grains is bad, it ruins the hand."

QUILLAMANDA

The moon is viewed as an active agent in the affairs of humankind, and this set of sayings reveals her influence in the agricultural cycle and in a great many matters of fortune. The moon is a syncretic deity associated with the Catholic Virgin Mary. The phases of the moon mark periods of time that are thought to be auspicious or otherwise for a number of human endeavors.

130* **callari-y menguante,**
    to begin [nom] full moon

sipta uchulla-cuna-ta cacu-ngapa, alli-mi ca.
sipta little one [pl-acc] to rub [purp] good [aff] to be

chasa-ca, mana quihuiri-g ca-ngapa.
thus [foc] not to twist [nom] to be [purp]

On the eve of the full moon,
it is good to rub the youngsters with the sipta plant.
This way, they will not twist any muscles.

131* **callari-y menguante,**
    to begin [nom] full moon

ambi huasca upia-g-cuna-ca,
medicine vine to drink [nom-pl-foc]

sinchi alli-lla-pa yacha-y-cu-g-cuna.
doctor good [del-poss] to know [nom-prog-nom-pl]

On the eve of the full moon,
drinkers of the medicine vine:
good and powerful doctors.

"Most of them drink yagé on the eve of the full moon. This way, they say that they will become good doctors, and that they will be among the best. Most of the native doctors drink yagé with the full moon each month."

The term *ambi huasca,* "medicine vine," refers to the lianna found in the Amazonian basin, *Banisteriopsis caapi.* A potion, known most widely by the term *yagé,* is prepared from this vine and ingested to procure a powerful hallucinogenic reaction. Among the

Inganos, yagé is used to gain spiritual vision and as a purge. The
native doctors are especially proficient in its use (see Chapter 5 for
a fuller account).

132* **callari-y menguante rucuti uchu micu-g-cuna-ca,**
       to begin [nom] full moon rocoto pepper to eat [nom-pl-foc]

   ambi upia-spa, sinchi jiru yacha-mi tucu-ncuna.
   medicine to drink [ger] strong evil doctor [aff] to become [3,pl]

   On the eve of the full moon,
   those who eat the rocoto pepper,
   drinking the medicine,
   they become strong and evil doctors.

   The rocoto pepper (*Capsicum violecium*) is a hot pepper that is
   cultivated in the Sibundoy Valley. Because of its "angry" character,
   it is associated with trouble and evil.

133* **chi callari-y menguante-mi sinchi-cuna suerte cara-ncuna,**
       that to begin [nom] full moon [aff] doctor [pl] luck to give [3,pl]

   sinchi unguy-cuna-ta-pas ambi-ncuna.
   doctor sickness [pl-acc-conj] to cure [3,pl]

   On that eve of the full moon,
   the doctors give good luck,
   and the doctor cures all illnesses.

134* **callari-y menguante-cuna,**
       to begin [nom] full moon [pl]

   micu-y sacha-cuna-ta y calabazo huasca-cuna-ta,
   to eat [nom] tree [pl-acc] and squash vine [pl-acc]

   chisi-ma cuyu-chi-gpi-ca mas suma-mi apa-ri.
   afternoon [dat] to move [caus-cond-foc] more good [aff] to bear
       [ref]

   Those eves of the full moon,
   the fruit trees and squash vines,
   if you shake them in the afternoon,
   they will bear more.

135* **shibuju-cuna mana puncha-cama puñu-ngapa.**
       day after full moon [pl] not day [lim] to sleep [purp]

mana ca-gpi-ca, chupu-mi junda-y tucu-nga
not to be [*cond-foc*] pus [*aff*] to fill [*nom*] to become [*3,f*]

y quilla huangu-mi tucu-nga.
and moon tied [*aff*] (lazy) to become [*3,f*]

The days after the full moon,
you should not sleep well into the day:
otherwise, you will become full of pus,
and you will become very lazy.

136* **shibuju puncha micha-n-mi arma-ngapa;**
day after full moon day bad [*conn-aff*] to bathe [*purp*]

mana ca-gpi-ca, cuichi-mi ispa-nga
not to be [*cond-foc*] rainbow [*aff*] to urinate [*3,f*]

y tucuy-pi-mi muyu tucu-nga.
and all [*loc-aff*] wart to become [*3,f*]

chi-manda, huahua-cuna-ta ucu-lla-pi arma-chi-ngapa.
that [*abl*] child [*pl-acc*] inside [*del-loc*] to bathe [*caus-purp*]

The day after the full moon, it is bad to bathe:
if you do, the rainbow will urinate on you,
and leave you covered with warts.
For that, the children are to bathe indoors.

The rainbow is a significant figure in Andean cosmology (López-Baralt 1980), associated with "the processes of transformation, the seasonal and stellar cycles of nature, and the interaction of human beings and the agricultural systems on earth" (Harrison 1982). In the mythology of the Sibundoy Valley, the rainbow often appears as a rakish young man, who can be entreated to make a bridge over high waters.

137* **shibuju y cucu shibuju,**
day after full moon and day after day after full moon

micha-n-mi micuy sacha-cuna-ta-ca cuyu-chi-nga.
bad [*conn-aff*] food tree [*pl-acc-foc*] to move [*caus-3,f*]

mana ca-gpi-ca, chusa-mi tucu-nga.
not to be [*cond-foc*] barren [*aff*] to become [*3,f*]

The day after the full moon, and the next day,
it is bad to shake the fruit trees.
If you do, they will become barren.

The cultivation of native and introduced fruit-bearing plants has
been something of specialty in Sibundoy Valley agronomy (Bristol
1968).

138* **shibuju puncha,**
full moon day

micha-n-mi ima suma cahua-ri-y-ta-pas ñambi-pi
bad [*conn-aff*] what fine to see [*ref-nom-acc-conj*] path [*loc*]

sita-sca-ta aysa-ngapa.
to leave [*hist-acc*] to pick up [*purp*]

chi-pi-ca pudi-n-mi unguy tia-nga.
that [*loc-foc*] to be able [*conn-aff*] sickness to exist [*3,f*]

The day after the full moon,
it is bad to pick up
any fine thing seen abandoned by the path:
that way you could come down with sickness.

139* **shibuju, jiru yacha-ta ñambi-pi tupa-cu-hora,**
day after full moon evil doctor [*acc*] path [*loc*] to encounter
    [*prog-temp*]

lado-ma tucu-ngapa chaya, mana saluda-ngapa.
side [*dat*] to become [*purp*] to arrive not to greet [*purp*]

saludo ayni-ngapa-glla.
greeting to answer [*purp-post*]

saluda-gpi-ca, jiru yacha-ca suma yuya-y-ta-mi aysa.
to greet [*cond-foc*] evil doctor [*foc*] well to think [*nom-acc-aff*]
    to steal

The day after the full moon,
when you encounter an evil doctor on the path,
move to the side, do not greet him.
You may return his greeting.
If you greet him,
the evil doctor will quite rob you of your senses.

This saying illustrates the care that must be taken in all contacts
with native doctors, especially those who cause harm.

140* **huahua quilla, micha-n-mi monton sita-y,**
child moon bad [*conn-aff*] turf to clear [*nom*]

chapsi-y alma-y rura-ngapa,
to shake piles [nom] to trim [nom] to do [purp]

o ima micuy tucu-dero sacha o huasca-cuna-ta cuyu-chi-ngapa.
or what food to become [agt] tree or vine [pl-acc] to move [caus-purp]

mana ca-gpi-ca, curu-mi junda-nga.
not to be [cond-foc] worm [aff] to fill [3,f]

In the new moon, it is bad to clear the turf
or break the clods of earth, or trim the plants,
or shake any fruit trees or vines.
If you do, they will fill with worms.

This saying makes reference to the principal field activities between the planting and harvesting of corn: the *monton sitay*, 'first weeding' or 'removal of the mounds', which involves cutting away the clumps of grass that intrude on the young corn stalks some two months after planting; the *chapsiy* (from the Inga 'to shake'), a 'second weeding' in which the mounds of grass are cleared away and shaken loose; and the *almay*, or 'trimming', in which the dry leaves and branches are removed. All major agricultural tasks are carried out by the *cuadrillas*, which are roving work crews commanded by a *caporal*. They offer daytime field services in exchange for monetary remuneration and meals and chicha.

141* **huahua quilla,**
child moon

coles-cuna piti-ngapa micha,
cabbage [pl] to harvest [purp] bad

ima micuy tarpu-ngapa-pas-mi micha.
also food to plant [purp-add-aff] bad

In the new moon, .
it is bad to harvest the cabbages,
also, it is bad to plant any food crop.

142* **quimsa puncha huahua quilla-hora-manda-car,**
three day child moon [temp-abl-emp]

arracacha tarpu-ngapa tajudo tucu-ngapa alli-lla-mi ca.
arracacha to plant [purp] [?] to become [purp] good [del-aff]
    to be

Three days after the full moon,
arracacha planted will yield very well.

RAPIACUNAMANDA

   Twitches, tics and tremblings—involuntary muscle spasms referred to as *rapiacuna* in Inga—are among the curious phenomena
treated as signs of future events in the corpus of sayings. Muscle
spasms in various regions of the body announce happenings directly
associated with the function served by that part of the anatomy.

143 **chaqui rapia-gpi-ca maycan caru-manda**
     foot to twitch [*cond-foc*] someone far [*abl*]

     visita-nti-mi samu-ngapa ca ni-nga-mi.
     to visit [*asso-aff*] to come [*purp*] to be to say [*3,f-aff*]

     If your foot twitches, someone from far away
     is to come and visit with you, so they say.

144* **chaqui dedo rapia-gpi-ca,**
     foot finger to twitch [*cond-foc*]

     maycan chaya-mu-ngapa.
     someone to visit [*cisloc-purp*]

     If the toe twitches,
     someone is coming to pay you a visit.

     "It isn't natural, you know? That the toe should twitch. And so
     they say that someone is coming to visit, some friend. And so
     people are expectant: 'Who is coming to visit?' Often the visitor
     will arrive and they will say: 'So, such and such is the one!' He
     just arrives, and they say: 'So that's why this was happening to
     me.' "

145* **jinsa rapia-gpi-ca,**
     calf to twitch [*cond-foc*]

     maycan caru-manda chaya-mu-ngapa.
     someone far [*abl*] to arrive [*cisloc-purp*]

     If the calf of your leg twitches,
     someone from afar will pay a visit.

     "People are just waiting when this happens. As soon as it happens
     they say to each other: 'Who will be the one to come and visit me?

This is what happened.' And so they are waiting, and generally someone from far off will come, maybe from the Lower Putumayo or from Venezuela. What happens is that the person is still and this part of the body starts to twitch. This only happens rarely. And so they say: 'No, someone is going to come from far away to visit, perhaps a friend, one of my best friends.' "

146 **siqui rapia-mi azote livia-ngapa.**
buttocks to twitch [*aff*] whip to deliver [*purp*]

Your behind trembles,
you are to receive a whipping.

"This generally applies to adults who are fighting. Let's say that a husband hits his wife. Maybe they are at a fiesta or something and he strikes her. Then they call him before the governor and they say: 'There they are going to punish him.' They are going to give him some lashes on the buttocks, you see."

147* **huasa rapia-gpi-ca, llasa apa-ri-ngapa,**
back to twitch [*cond-foc*] load to carry [*ref-purp*]

o mana ca-gpi-ca, unguy-hua siri-ri-ngapa.
or not to be [*cond-foc*] sickness [*inst*] to lie [*ref-purp*]

If your back twitches, you are to carry a weight,
or else you are to be laid low with sickness.

"If it is your back they say you are going to have to carry a weight. That you are going to have to bear a heavy load. It might be firewood or something else. Or often they say: 'Someone is going to arrive from over there and they are going to tell me to carry all this.' Or maybe you are going to get sick, and you will be lying on your back."

148* **razo o maqui rapia-gpi-ca,**
arm or hand to twitch [*cond-foc*]

ungu-g o huanu-sca huahua marca-ngapa.
to be sick [*nom*] or to die [*hist*] child to hold [*purp*]

mana ca-gpi-ca, marca-sca huahua yuca-ngapa.
not to be [*cond-foc*] to hold [*hist*] child to have [*purp*]

If your arm or hand twitches,
you are to carry a sick or dead child.
Or else, you are to have a godchild.

This saying is unusual in that it offers both a positive and a negative consequence. Most of the sayings are unequivocal on the type of fortune to be expected, even when they allow some variation in terms of specific events.

149* **maqui dedo-cuna-huanta sigsi-chi-gpi-ca,**
hand finger [*pl-inst*] to itch [*caus-cond-foc*]

achca culqui chasqui-ngapa.
much money to receive [*purp*]

If your hand, with the the fingers, is made to itch,
you are to receive a great deal of money.

"In order to receive a lot of money, in order to count money."

The Inganos make the gesture of counting paper bills as an illustration of this saying.

150 **simi rapia-mi maycan tragu cara-ngapa.**
mouth to twitch [*aff*] someone aguardiente to give [*purp*]

Your mouth twitches,
someone is to give you a drink of aguardiente.

The Spanish-derived word *tragu* denotes the Spanish-derived sugarcane distillation known as *aguardiente*.

151 **simi rapia-gpi-ca, aycha ucha-hua micu-nga-hura.**
mouth to twitch [*cond-foc*] meat pepper [*inst*] to eat [*3,f-temp*]

Your mouth twitches
when you are to eat meat with hot pepper.

152* **simi cara rapia-gpi-ca, rabia yuca-ngapa.**
mouth face to twitch [*cond-foc*] anger to have [*purp*]

If your lips twitch,
you are to have anger.

"You are going to have problems with someone. Most likely, you are going to speak in a loud tone of voice. But not that you are going to punch anyone. Just exchange insults."

153* **ñahui rapia-gpi-ca, ima cahua-ngapa o huaca-ngapa.**
eye to twitch [*cond-foc*] what to see [*purp*] or to cry [*purp*]

If your eye twitches
you are to see something, or you are to cry.

"With the eye, what you are going to see is crying: either you
yourself are going to cry, or you will see someone else cry."

154* **ñahui rapia-gpi-ca, asi-ngapa o ima cahua-ngapa.**
   eye to twitch [*cond-foc*] to laugh [*purp*] or something to see
      [*purp*]
   If your eye twitches,
   you are to laugh or you are to see something.

155 **ñahui ura lado rapia-gpi-ca, huaca-ngapa.**
   eye under side to twitch [*cond-foc*] to cry [*purp*]
   If the inside of your eyelid twitches,
   you are going to cry.

156 **rinri rupa-ri-mi maycan huasa rima-nacu-gmanda.**
   ear to burn [*ref-aff*] someone back to speak [*prog-hab*]
   Your ear burns,
   they are speaking of you behind your back.

157* **rinri rupa-ri-gpi-ca, yuya-ri-dero-mi ca:**
   ear to burn [*ref-cond-foc*] to think [*ref-agt-aff*] to be

   maycan nuca-manda yuya-ri-hua-cu.
   someone I [*abl*] to think [*ref-1ob-prog*]

   If your ear burns, you have the thought:
   "Someone is remembering me."

158* **rinri-pi rama-y-sina uya-ri-gpi-ca,**
   ear [*loc*] to buzz [*nom-comp*] to hear [*ref-cond-foc*]

   ca-n-mi maycan rima-nacu-gpi.
   to be [*3rd-aff*] someone to speak [*prog-cond*]

   chasa-lla uya-ri-cu-gpi-lla-ca,
   thus [*del*] to hear [*ref-prog-cond-del-foc*]

   dedo-cuna-pi tuca-ri-spa, rinri-ma pia-ri-gpi,
   finger [*pl-loc*] to spit [*ref-ger*] ear [*dat*] to strike [*ref-cond*]

   upa-lla-mi.
   to silence [*del-aff*]

If you hear something like a buzzing in your ear,
it means they are talking about you.
If you continue hearing the same thing,
spitting into your hand,
and if you strike yourself on the ear,
they will just stop talking.

159 **suspira-chi-y anuncia-mi llaquiy yuca-ngapa.**
to sigh [*caus-nom*] to announce [*aff*] sadness to have [*purp*]

Sighs announce that you are to have sadness.

HUAHUITACUNAMANDA

One major function of the sayings is the instruction of children
and the instruction of parents in raising children. This set incorporates sayings directed to these purposes, along with a subset
relating to the care of pregnant women. These sayings ensure that
the newcomers in the community get off to a proper start, and that
they learn respect for the ways of their elders.

160 **atun-pa banco-pi tiari-spa siqui llasa-ri-ngapa,**
parent [*poss*] stool [*loc*] to sit [*ger*] behind to weigh [*ref-purp*]

aragan tucu-ngapa.
worthless to become [*purp*]

Sitting on the stool of your parents,
your behind will become heavy,
and you will become lazy.

"There are stools for the father, the mother, and the children. When
children get up slowly they will say: 'You see, that's why you
shouldn't sit on your father's stool; you see, you're getting stiff like
him.' My grandmother would not allow the children to sit on the
stools of their elders. She would say: 'They will become lazy, like
their parents they will rise slowly.' "

161 **uchu-lla-ta maqui-hua pia-gpi-ca,**
little [*del-acc*] hand [*inst*] to strike [*cond-foc*]

samaycu-ri-ngapa-mi.
to scare [*ref-purp-aff*]

If you strike a small child with your hand,
he will take a fright.

"If you don't have them cured right away, drying up completely they will die, if you can't have them cured. The one with fright must be taken to the native doctor. The doctor will look him over and do the ritual blowing. They will cure him with the *mishachiy*, 'a smoke-inhalation cure'. Heating shards of earthen pottery, bringing water from a large river, they will prepare a medicine before breakfast, chanting, chanting, and wishing that this sickness will go away. Speaking and thinking in this way, they will do the ritual blowing—otherwise, how will they get rid of the sickness?"

162   **uchulla huamra-ta micha-n-mi planta-pi sigsi-chi-ngapa,**
       small child [*acc*] bad [*conn-aff*] bottom of foot [*loc*] to itch [*caus-purp*]

       porqui chaca-pi mana-mi pudi-nga yali-ngapa.
       because bridge [*loc*] not [*aff*] to be able [*3,f*] to cross [*purp*]

       It is bad to tickle the bottom of a child's foot,
       because he will not be able to cross over the bridges.

       "Even when he is grown, he will not be able to cross the bridges. He will just stand there, full of fear, and he will fall and perhaps die."

       The Sibundoy Valley is crisscrossed by running water, and along its many footpaths are occasional log and plank bridges (some of them rather intimidating) that must be crossed on foot.

163* **camcha cuchulli-gpi-ca,**
       toasted corn to place in pouch [*cond-foc*]

       atun yacu-pi atari-chi tucu-spa,
       large river [*loc*] to rise [*caus*] to become [*ger*]

       mana yali-nga pudi-nga.
       not to cross [*3,f*] to be able [*3,f*]

       If you place toasted grains of corn in your pocket,
       and attempt to ford a swollen river,
       you will not make it across.

       "The old people give this advice to their children: 'I hope you aren't stuffing your pocket, if you stuff your pocket with toasted corn, when it comes time to cross a large river, if you fall, like toasted corn, you will be carried off and you will die.' "

       Children love toasted corn and will fill the space between their waist and their outer garment (equivalent to our pockets) with as many grains as they can. This saying strives for control over this

common form of excess in children, by linking it to the prevailing
spiritual and symbolic order.

164 **micha-n-mi cuy sungu cara-ngapa huamra-cuna-ta,**
bad [*conn-aff*] cuy liver to give [*purp*] child [*pl-acc*]

**porqui azoti-nga-hura cuy-sina-mi banco ucu-ma ñitri-
ngacuna.**
because to whip [*3,f-temp*] cuy [*comp-aff*] stool under [*dat*] to
hide [*3,pl,f*]

It is bad to give the cuy's liver to the children,
because when it is time to face the whip,
like the cuy they will scurry under the benches.

"This one is generally for the children, not for adults. We never
give the liver of the cuy to children. They say that they will become
like the cuy, so that when it is time to scold or punish them, they
will just run under the benches and hide themselves. The cuys also
are very timid; when you go to catch one, they hide. So the children
are going to be trembling there just like the cuy. And so if the
mayor or governor sends for them, they will go hide in the wilderness. So they say they shouldn't eat that, so that it will not
affect them when they grow up."

165 **ama cumala huahua-cuna-ta cara-ngui,**
don't sweet potato child [*pl-acc*] to give [*2nd*]

simi huata-mi tucu-ncangui.
mouth to tie [*aff*] to become [*2,f*]

Don't give sweet potato to the children:
you will tie their mouths.

"They won't be able to speak until they are grown up."

166 **micha-n-si chugllu asintu-ta castu-ngapa,**
bad [*conn-rep*] corncob silk [*acc*] to nibble [*purp*]

maycan chi-ta castu-spa micu-gpi-ca,
someone that [*acc*] to nibble [*ger*] to eat [*cond-foc*]

alcu huasa-mi ca-nga.
dog behind [*aff*] to be [*3,f*]

It is bad to nibble on the silk of the corncob.
Nibbling on it, if you eat it,
there will be a dog behind you.

"The children chew on it because it is sweet, but it isn't proper food. We tell them this so they don't ruin their teeth. If a dog bites one of them, the people say: 'Don't you see, you were eating that stuff. That's why the dogs are after you.' They say that the dogs like the silk, and so if you eat it, you will lure them, and they will always be behind you."

167* **manga-pi uma ñitiri-gpi-ca, samay arca-ri ca-ngapa.**
jar [loc] head to insert [cond-foc] breath to prevent [ref] to be [purp]

If you stick your head into a jar,
your breathing will be obstructed,
and you will not be able to run.

"We tell the children not to be drinking from the earthen jar: 'If you drink sticking your head into the jar, when it is time to run you will not be able to; like a dog with its tongue sticking out you will be running, trying in vain to climb a hill.' "

168* **alcu-pa huiqui-ta ñahui-ma cacu-ri-gpi-ca, micha-n-mi.**
dog [poss] tear [acc] eye [dat] to rub [ref-cond-foc] bad [conn-aff]

chi-ca tuta-cuna animas-mi cahuari-nga.
that [foc] night [pl] souls [aff] to appear [3,f]

It is bad to rub the tears of a dog in your eyes.
That way, at night, the souls of the departed will appear.

"Dogs are able to see the souls of the departed. If you rub the tears of the dog in your eyes, you will also see these souls, and you will be more likely to have an encounter with them."

169* **uchulla-cuna alcu-cuna-ta yapa travisia-gpi-ca,**
small [pl] dog [pl-acc] much to play [cond-foc]

michi muyu-mi junda.
rash [aff] to fill

If the children play too much with the dogs,
they will become covered with rashes.

"This is a means of protecting the pups from the rough play of the children. Also, many people believe that the urine of the dog causes warts on the foot."

170* **uchulla urma-sca-ta atari-chi-spa,**
small one to fall [*hist-acc*] to rise [*caus-ger*]

chi-hora-lla mana tuca-gpi-ca,
that [*temp-del*] not to spit [*cond-foc*]

samaycu-ri-n-mi.
to scare [*ref-conn-aff*]

Picking up a child who has fallen,
if you do not spit at that time,
the child will take a fright.

"If all of a sudden a child should fall, then you have to perform
the ritual blowing. Generally, as soon as a child falls, we blow on
him. Otherwise, he is going to take a fright, and he will be shouting
in his sleep."

The idea of 'fright' here is similar to the notion of *susto* which is
widely distributed in the folk religions of the Spanish-speaking
world and beyond.

171* **llullu huahua puñu-cu-sca-ta**
tender child to sleep [*prog-hist-acc*]

suma puñu-chi-g chaya-gri-gpi-ca,
well to sleep [*caus-nom*] to arrive [*disloc-cond-foc*]

alli huasa-mi niraya.
good luck [*aff*] to signify

maycan chaya-ngapa ri-cu-hora,
someone to visit [*purp*] to go [*prog-temp*]

llullu huahua yapa huaca-cu-gpi-ca,
tender child much to cry [*prog-cond-foc*]

mana alli huasa-mi niraya.
not good luck [*aff*] to signify

If a sleeping infant remains fast asleep
when people come and visit, it means good luck.
When someone comes to visit,
if the infant cries a lot, it means bad luck.

"When someone is about to arrive and they encounter the child
sleeping, and he continues to sleep, they say he has good luck. And
if the child is crying, and the person arrives, they say he has bad
luck. We believe that children are sensitive to certain things, like

luck, and so the child can perceive what kind of person has come to visit."

172* **cay uchulla misa-ma pusa-ni, alli huajua-pua-rca,**
that small one mass [*dat*] to take [*1st*] good to auger [*ben-3,past*]

pay-pa marca-sca tayta catanga yuca-chi-sca-manda.
he [*poss*] to carry [*hist*] father clothes to have [*caus-hist-abl*]

"The child I took to mass did well for himself:
his godfather gave him some clothes."

This saying reflects one aspect of the set of obligations associated with ritual kinship.

173* **huarmi ungu-g ca-spa,**
woman to be sick [*nom*] to be [*ger*]

saparu yamta micha-n-mi uma-pi apa-ri-nga.
basket firewood bad [*conn-aff*] head [*loc*] to carry [*ref-3,f*]

mana ca-gpi-ca, huahu(a)-ita naci-hora,
not to be [*cond-foc*] child [*dim(Sp)*] to be born [*temp*]

uma huaycu-mi naci-nga.
head hole [*aff*] to be born [*3,f*]

A woman being with child,
it is bad to carry a basket of firewood on the head.
If she does, at birth the little babe
will be born with a sunken scalp.

On the surface this saying reports on a symbolic mode of causation, whereby a force exerted on the head of the pregnant woman has the capability of causing an indentation (the fallen fontanelle) in the newborn baby. Indirectly, it warns of overburdening the pregnant woman with physical labor.

174 **saparu uma-pi chura-ri-ngapa micha-mi huarmi huamra-cuna-manda.**
basket head [*loc*] to place [*ref-purp*] bad [*aff*] woman child [*pl-abl*]

saparu chura-ri-spa-ca,
basket to place [*ref-ger-foc*]

ca-n-si imata-ca nucanchi-quin ña chasa huarmi-cuna-ca
to be [*3rd-rep*] what [*foc*] we [*ref*] already thus woman [*pl-foc*]

mana utca libre-ya-nga pudi-nga.
not fast free [*verb-3,f*] to be able [*3,f*]

It is bad to place a basket on the head
of a woman who is with child.
Placing a basket, they say that
we ourselves, that is, women,
will not be able to free themselves quickly.

"So they say that it will be as if the baby in the mother's stomach
were held in a basket. She will suffer very much in giving birth."

175* **maycan huarmi-pas huamr(a)-ito-hua ungu-g ca-spa,**
some woman [*conj*] child [*dim(Sp)-inst*] to be sick [*nom*] to be
[*ger*]

volcan pungu-cuna-ta chapa-cu-gpi-ca,
volcano door [*pl-acc*] to stare [*prog-cond-foc*]

uchulla-ca naci-spa huiña-hora-ca,
small one [*foc*] to be born [*ger*] to grow [*temp-foc*]

ñahui ladia-ma-mi cahua-nga.
eye to turn [*dat-aff*] to see [*3,f*]

And any woman being sick with child,
if she is staring at the doors of the volcano,
when it comes time for the child to be born,
he will see with his eyes crossed.

"Often when the volcano is shining, the Volcano Patascoy, especially in the afternoon hours, it seems as if there were some doors. So we say: 'Look, its going to be sunny. See, the devil's doors are open, the devil is out sunning himself.' There must be some rocks or something up there, and seeing it from a distance, it looks like some doors. And so they say that the pregnant woman should not look at the doors of the volcano."

The Volcano Patascoy is the most prominent of the mountains surrounding the Sibundoy Valley, directly across the valley from Santiago. It enters into the mythic narrative as the home of the dogs of the volcano, made from the very rock of the mountain.

176* **ungu-g ca-g huarmi,**
to be sick [*nom*] to be [*nom*] woman

pay ima muna-chi-sca-ta-mi mas yuca micu-nga.
she what to want [*caus-hist-acc-aff*] more to have to eat [*3,f*]

mana ca-gpi-ca, sullu-nga-mi.
not to be [*cond-foc*] to abort [*3,f-aff*]

A woman with child,
whatever she wants to eat, she must eat.
Otherwise, she will abort.

177* **huarmi-cuna-ta micha-n-mi**
woman [*pl-acc*] bad [*conn-aff*]

chugllu uray singa-ma cusa-spa micu-nga.
corncob down nose [*dat*] to roast [*ger*] to eat [*3,f*]

mana ca-gpi-ca, uchulla yuca-cu-hora,
not to be [*cond-foc*] small one to have [*prog-temp*]

mana-mi alli-lla unguri-ngapa pudi-nga.
not [*aff*] well [*del*] to give birth [*purp*] to be able [*3,f*]

For women, it is bad
to eat the roasted corncob from the nose down.
If she does, when she has a child,
she will not have an easy pregnancy.

"They say that women shouldn't change the position of the corn-cob, especially when they are pregnant, because if they change the position, they are eating the cob from the bottom up, then the child is going to change its position and the birthing will be very difficult. If they turn the cob around, the child will turn around in the mother's stomach."

The corncob nose is the end with the loose silk sticking out; the pregnant woman should eat the cob starting from the end where the husks originate.

178 **chugllu-ta casa uray singa-ma cusa-ngapa,**
corncob [*acc*] thus down nose [*dat*] to roast [*purp*]

chi-pasi ca-n-si mal aguero,
that [*conj*] to be [*3rd-rep*] bad omen

huarmi huamra-cuna-ta-ca yacha-n-si huahu(a)-ita dius
woman child [*pl-acc-foc*] to know [*3rd-rep*] child [*dim(Sp)*] God

cara-nga mana sinti-glla, saya-sca-lla.
to give [*3,f neg*] to feel [*post*] to stand [*hist-del*]

It is bad to roast for women the corncob nose down.
That too is a bad omen.

The woman with child will often not feel it,
she will give the little child, Lord, feet first.

179* **huarmi ungu-g ca-spa,**
woman to be sick [nom] to be [ger]

micha-n-mi aparido ca-sca-ta micu-nga.
bad [conn-aff] paired cob to be [hist-acc] to eat [3,f]

micu-gpi-ca, iscay huahu(a)-ita-mi tia-nga.
ato eat [cond-foc] two child [dim(Sp)-aff] to exist [3,f]

A woman, being with child,
it is bad for her to eat a corncob with its pair.
If she eats this, she will have two little ones.

ARMAYCUNAMANDA

Bathing had ritual significance in precolumbian times (Santacruz Pachacuti-yamqui Salcamayhua 1873; Molina 1873) and remains a key factor in modern Andean concepts of spiritual health
(Bastien 1985). The sayings deal with the virtues and hazards of
bathing; they indicate that a good bathing etiquette can bring
health, good fortune, and success with the opposite sex, whereas
the reverse can bring on illness and misfortune.

180* **chisi-ma-cuna uma tagsa-ri-gpi-ca,**
afternoon [dat-pl] head to wash [ref-cond-foc]

mana unay-lla-mi agcha yura-ya-nga.
not long [del-aff] hair white [verb-3,f]

If you bathe your head during the afternoons,
before long your hair will turn white.

"This is not so much that your hair will turn white, but rather so
you won't catch a chill. It's so people will bathe in the morning
and not at night. Our people rarely have white hair. There are some
very old people and they still don't have white hair. For those few
who do, they say: 'Don't you see, it's because they were bathing
in the evening hours.' So they use him as an example: 'So and so
isn't old yet and he has white hair. He deserves it because he was
bathing in the late afternoon hours.' Its mostly a warning to children."

181* **atun yacu-pi chaugpuncha-cuna arma-ngapa-pas micha.**
large river [loc] midday [pl] to bathe [purp-conj] bad

danta-cuna o huayta-nacu-g-sina-mi cahuari-nga.
tapir [pl] or to swim [prog-nom-comp-aff] to appear [3,f]

It is bad to bathe in a large river at midday.
Tapirs and swimming creatures will appear.

"They say that twelve noon is a bad hour, twelve noon and twelve midnight. So they say that at this hour the spirits are out bathing themselves, and generally the evil spirits. And so you will see the tapirs bathing themselves, and they have a strong spirit power, they can give you spirit sickness. That's why you shouldn't bathe at twelve noon. These animals are related to the spirit sickness of the forest, what they call *huayra sachu*. They say that they give a sickness that is very difficult to cure. If you have the spirit sickness of the forest, it is very difficult and they will have to bring a very good curer or you will die."

182 **maycan huarmi muna-ri-ngapa,**
some woman to want [ref-purp]

tutata-cuna arma-ngapa-mi chaya.
morning [pl] to bathe [purp-aff] to arrive

In order for a woman to want you,
you must bathe in the mornings.

183* **callari-y menguante chaugpi tuta atun yacu-pi arma-spa-ca,**
to begin [nom] full moon middle night large river [loc] to bathe [ger-foc]

unguy-cuna mana pia-y tucu-ngapa,
sickness [pl] not to strike [nom] to become [purp]

y yapa alli huasa ca-ngapa.
and very good luck to be [purp]

Bathing in a large river
on the eve of the full moon,
you will not be struck with sickness,
and your luck will be very good.

"I don't know if this custom exists now but previously the elders required of the young people, on the eve of the full moon, they would call them at something like four in the morning to go swim in the river, so that they would remain cleansed, purified. Some

of them enjoyed it, but those lazy ones, oh! But afterwards what
laughter! They made them bathe."

184* **callari-y menguante cuyanguilla-hua arma-spa-ca,**
   to begin [nom] full moon cuyanguilla [inst] to bathe [ger-foc]

   tucuy-cuna muna-y tucu-ngapa.
   all [pl] to want [nom] to become [purp]

   Bathing with cuyanguilla
   on the eve of the full moon,
   you will be wanted by everyone.

   The *cuyanguilla* (either *Peperomia galioides* or *Cavendishia quer-
   eme*) is used as an aphrodisiac. Its name derives from the Inga root
   cuyay, 'to love'.

   "There are two kinds of *cuyanguilla,* one for white people, another
   for indigenous people. Many people sell it in the market. A native
   doctor should prepare it if it is to work. People say that it is very
   effective."

185* **yapa chisi yacu-pi huarmi arma-gpi-ca,**
   very evening river [loc] woman to bathe [cond-foc]

   sapa-lla ca-spa, yapa rucu-hua casara-ngapa.
   alone [del] to be [ger] very old [inst] to marry [purp]

   chasa-lla-ta cari-ca, sapa-lla ca-spa,
   thus [del-acc] man [foc] alone [del] to be [ger]

   yapa ahuila huarmi-hua casara-ngapa.
   very old woman woman [inst] to marry [purp]

   If a woman bathes in a river in the late evening,
   being single, she is to marry a very old man.
   Likewise for a man, being single,
   he is to marry a very old woman.

ALLI HUASAMANDA

   This last set is a miscellany pulling together sayings treating of
good fortune and its opposite. Included here are additional warnings
of death, signs of good fortune like the possession of money, ad-
monishments to share things like chicha and aguardiente, and cautions about actions that can result in the loss of friendship.

Native doctor with curing branches and *huayra huahua* (spirit medium) in hand.

The table is set for a yagé ceremony. Below, chicha and talk as the cuys look on.

Bautista Juajibioy: "Our lands were left to us by taita Carlos Tamoabioy." Below, a cuy is roasted in preparation for a celebration.

De-graining corn: a perennial task since the flight of the shulupsi bird.

"Forever women must grind corn to make chicha."

Mother and daughter in a Kamsá kitchen: the *canoa* (wooden vessel for cooling the chicha) stands between the two women. Below, tapping into the chicha barrel.

The *caporal* (crew boss) provides a refreshing cup of chicha to one of the *peones* (workers). Below, relaxing with chicha after work in the fields.

Mariano Chicunque relates a humorous mythical episode.

A Sibundoy *bambuco* played on flute and drum.

The ritual exchange of food and speech at an *agradecimiento* (thanking ceremony).

Encounter on a vereda road.

186* **picangui-ta asipaya-gpi-ca, rupa-g tucu-ngapa.**
picangui bird [acc] to mock [cond-foc] to burn [nom] to become
[purp]

If you mock the call of the picangui bird,
you will come down with a fever.

187 **picangui-ta asipaya-gpi-ca,**
picangui bird [acc] to mock [cond-foc]

catanga-ta-mi rupa-chi-pu-nga.
clothes [acc-aff] to burn [caus-ben-3,f]

uchpa-lla-pi puñu-spa caya-ndi-ca rupa-spa pacari-nga.
ash del [loc] to sleep [ger] next day [asso-foc] to burn [ger] to
dawn [3,f]

If you mock the call of the picangui bird,
your clothing will be burnt for you.
Sleeping by the ashes,
you will awake burning the next day.

"One time I went into the forest with my aunt, and I started imitating the call of the picangui bird. My aunt scolded me, saying:
'Just wait and see, you are going to wake up burnt.' I don't know,
since we were sleeping next to the fire, I woke up the next morning
with part of my blanket burnt."

"The picangui calls 'chuy, chuy,' very much like our idiomatic
expression *achuchuy!* meaning that something is very hot."

In the mythic narrative, this bird is charged with the preparation
of chicha in the sky world, a function that further confirms its
association with heat and fire.

188 **huasi-pi ima-pas trabaja-cu-g-sina tuta uyari-gpi-ca,**
house [loc] what [conj] to work [prog-nom-comp] night to hear
[cond-foc]

huasi-chi-g huañu-ngapa.
to build [caus-nom] to die [purp]

If you hear in your house at night
something like a person working,
then the one who built your house is to die.

189 **maycan huañu-ngapa ca-hora yacha-mi tapia-nga,**
someone to die [purp] to be [temp] to know [aff] to signify [3,f]

maycan saluda-cu-g-sina-mi yacha uyari-nga.
someone to greet [*prog-nom-comp-aff*] to know to hear [*3,f*]

huarmi saluda-cu-g-sina uyari-gpi-ca,
woman to greet [*prog-nom-comp*] to hear [*cond-foc*]

maycan chaya-g huarmi huañu-ngapa.
some to visit [*nom*] woman to die [*purp*]

cari saluda-cu-g-sina uyari-gpi-ca,
man to greet [*prog-nom-comp*] to hear [*cond-foc*]

maycan chaya-g cari huañu-ngapa.
some to visit [*nom*] man to die [*purp*]

When someone is to die, there is often a sign,
you will often hear something like a greeting.
If you hear something like a woman greeting,
then some woman friend is to die.
If you hear something like a man greeting,
then some male friend is to die.

190* **huañu-sca pamba-nacu-sca-pi,**
to die [*hist*] to bury [*prog-hist-loc*]

mana alpa muru-ta tuca-spa, sita-gpi-ca,
not earth clod [*acc*] to spit [*ger*] to throw [*cond-foc*]

llaquiy-mi mana cungari-nga.
sadness [*aff*] not to forget [*3,f*]

When burying a deceased one,
if you fail to spit on a clod of earth and throw it there,
you will not forget your sadness.

"When they are burying a corpse, they say that in order to forget
your sadness, you must take a clod of earth, spit on it, and throw
it in there where they are placing the corpse. In order to forget your
sadness. And if you don't, they say that you will not sleep for a
long time, and you will not be able to forget. This applies especially
if it is a son or daughter, your mother, or some member of the
immediate family."

191* **maycan sinchi mancha-chi-spa mana tuca-gpi-ca,**
some doctor to startle [*caus-ger*] not to spit [*cond-foc*]

samaycu-ri-y unguy-mi tucu-nga.
to be frightened [*ref-nom*] sickness [*aff*] to become [*3,f*]

A native doctor, on startling someone,
if he fails to cure him by spitting,
that person will become sick with fright.

"If someone who cures, some native doctor frightens someone, they say that that person himself must do the blowing ritual so that the person will not take a fright. They say that the native doctor has the power to cause fright, and if he doesn't do the cure, it will be hard to find someone capable of doing it. That is, to effect the cure, it must be either the same one who caused the fright, or another doctor who knows even more than this person. If they don't like someone, they will bewitch them, but often it happens by accident, especially to children. When someone has taken yagé, they say that on that day he should not strike or even scold anyone, not even adults. If he strikes even an adult, they say that this person will take a fright and become very sick. Often when someone has blood coming out of his nose they say: 'Don't you see, such and such a person has given you a fright.' That same person can effect the cure right then and there. We say that such and such a person is of heavy blood, because he takes a lot of yagé, or some other remedy. And so we say that it's not a good idea to get together with him too often, or to receive him in your home."

192 **hura yacha genti huañu-nga-hura**
native doctor from Lower Putumayo to die [3,f-temp]

yacha-mi sinchi trihuina-nga,
to know [aff] strong to thunder [3,f]

mancha-chi-gta dunavez yacha sura-ca trihuina-nga.
to scare [caus-sub] right away to know sometimes [foc] to thunder [3,f]

When a native doctor from the Lower Putumayo is to die,
there is often a loud peal of thunder,
sometimes it will thunder so loud as to to frighten people.

The pan-Andean thunder god figures prominently in Sibundoy cosmology. In the Wangetsmuna cycle, he appears as the grandfather of the culture hero and the one who creates gold (through defecation). He destroys the heathens and sends his grandson to visit the world and establish proper civilization (see fuller account in Chapter 4).

193 **jiru yacha-cuna huañu-nga-hura tapia-dur-mi ca.**
evil doctor [pl] to die [3,f-temp] to signify [agt-aff] to be

alli yacha huañu-nga-hura mana tapia-dur ca-n-chu.
good doctor to die [3,f-temp] not to signify [agt] to be [3rd-int]

When the evil native doctors are to die,
there is a sign.
When a good native doctor is to die,
there is no sign.

194* **cuchillo-hua culebra-ta huañu-chi-gpi-ca,**
machete [inst] snake [acc] to die [caus-cond-foc]

quinqui-mi cuchu-ri-nga o cuchillo-mi paqui-ri-pu-nga.
self [aff] to cut [ref-3,f] or machete [aff] to break [ref-ben-3,f]

culebra-ta garrote caspi-hua-mi huañu-chi-dero ca.
snake [acc] club stick [inst-aff] to die [caus-agt] to be

If you kill a snake with your machete,
either you will cut yourself
or your machete will break for you.
The snake is to be killed with a club or stick.

"They explain that one should not kill snakes with a machete.
Most of them, when they are working, if they see a snake, they
will cut a stick and kill it with that. They say it is bad to kill it
or cut it with the machete, because one will cut oneself with the
machete or else the machete will break. You are working and all
of a sudden you strike a rock and the machete is broken. The
connection is that when you dream a snake, you are going to see
the witches, so they say that killing the snake with a machete also
witches them. And so a person might have a hard time, cutting
himself or breaking the machete so he can't work and earn money."

195* **rucu huata culqui siñidor-pi huata-gpi-ca,**
old year money belt [loc] to tie [cond-foc]

musu huata-mi pacari-ngapa,
new year [aff] to dawn [purp]

entero huata culqui mana pisi-ngapa.
entire year money not to lack [purp]

chasa-lla-ta, musu huata-pa culqui-hua ca-gta,
thus [del-acc] new year [poss] money [inst] to be [sub]

alli huajua-y-mi niraya.
good to auger [*nom-aff*] to signify

If you keep money in your belt during the old year,
and the new year begins,
you will not lack money the entire year.
Likewise, if you have money for the new year,
this signifies good fortune.

196* **iscay botella trago upia-gpi-ca,**
two bottle aguardiente to drink [*cond-foc*]

musu huasi-ta alli huaja-chi-ngapa.
new house [*acc*] good to auger [*caus-purp*]

If you drink two bottles of aguardiente,
this will bring luck to a new house.

"Since a person by himself cannot drink two bottles, this is a way
of saying that the owner should provide drinks for everyone. That
way all year he will be giving a party."

197 **paresia-y mana upia-gpi-ca,**
to pair [*nom neg*] to drink [*cond-foc*]

chingual-hua-mi chaya-nga casara-ngapa.
one eyed [*inst-aff*] to arrive [*3,f*] to marry [*purp*]

If you do not drink a pair of cups,
with a one-eyed person you will marry.

This saying emerges in the drinking rituals of the valley, which
involve much in the way of citations to consume.

198 **rumi-ta maqui-pi sug-ta cua-gpi-ca,**
stone [*acc*] hand [*loc*] another [*acc*] to give [*cond-foc*]

mana unay-lla piña-chi-ri-nacu-ngapa.
not long [*del*] to anger [*caus-ref-prog-purp*]

If a stone is passed by hand to another,
before long they will be arguing with each other.

"The stone is to be set down nearby the other person."

199 **micha-mi uchu maqui-pi yali-chi-ngapa.**
bad [*aff*] pepper hand [*loc*] to pass [*caus-purp*]

uchu maqui-pi chasqui-gpi-ca,
pepper hand [loc] to receive [cond-foc]

mana unay-lla-pi-mi cuntra-nacu-nga.
not long [del-loc-aff] to be against [prog-3,f]

It is bad to pass hot pepper in the hand.
If you receive hot pepper in the hand,
before long you will be against each other.

"Let's say the two of us are friends, right? So, being friends, we
should never pass hot pepper with our hands. If I have the hot
pepper, I should never give it to you in your hand. If you want it,
then 'Here,' and I set it on the table so you can take it. If I pass it
directly to your hand, they say that before long we won't be good
friends, our friendship will cool, and we are going to fight. We are
going to become just as hot as the pepper. For any little cause we
are going to have problems. We are going to fight. We are going to
resemble the pepper. We are going to get into difficulties, for no
reason at all. Even between children and their parents."

200 **iscay-cuna uma-ta sug-lla-pi ñagcha-gpi-ca,**
two [pl] head [acc] one [del-loc] to comb [cond-foc]

tanda-ri-spa-mi maca-ngacuna.
to meet [ref-ger-aff] to fight [3,f,pl]

If two people comb the hair of another,
on meeting each other, they will fight.

201* **chaqui dedo taca-ri-gpi-ca, yanga ri-cu-ngapa.**
foot finger to stub [ref-cond-foc] in vain to go [prog-purp]

If you stub your toe,
in vain you are travelling.

"If you are going somewhere you will say to yourself: 'Maybe I am
going in vain, or maybe things won't go well for me.' "

202* **jigra huagta-chi-gpi-ca, mana unay-lla chisiya-ngapa.**
sack to shake [caus-cond-foc] not long [del] to become late
    [purp]

If you shake your sack,
before long the evening will fall.

203 **jigra uma-pi chura-ri-gpi-ca,**
sack head [loc] to place [ref-cond-foc]

yapa-mi cungari-dur ca-ncangui o yapa ardita uma.
very [*aff*] to forget [*agt*] to be [2,*f*] or very squirrel head

If you place a sack on your head,
you will be very forgetful,
or very squirrel headed.

The expression 'squirrel headed' is used to designate people who
are remarkably absent minded or forgetful. Like the squirrel, they
run around without any apparent purpose.

4

The Ancestral World

The sayings of the ancestors conjoin two distinct temporal frames, the ancestral past and the current arena of human experience. Belief in an ancestral past, a moment of decisive beginnings and formative events, pervades the mental life of the native peoples of the Sibundoy Valley. Their traditional worldview is founded on the primacy of the ancestral model, which establishes agencies, patterns, and boundaries determining the character of all subsequent history. Contemporary events are viewed as pale reflections of their ancestral prototypes, since the spiritual forces that guided the creation of the world and the establishment of human society, and that continue to shape reality as we experience it, were active in their most dramatic form during these earlier moments in the cosmic time sequence.

The sayings of the ancestors derive validity from their encapsulation of wisdom originating in ancestral times. They are attributed to *ñugpamandacuna*, literally 'the first people', as can be seen in the formulation, *ñugpamandacuna nincuna*, Our ancestors were accustomed to saying. . . . These sayings tap into that abundant reservoir of spiritual vision possessed by the first ancestors, who witnessed and sometimes manipulated facets of an ultimate reality that has since receded behind a veil of petty circumstance. The sayings codify important domains of human experience in accordance with this profound spiritual awareness, drawing on the exemplary nature of the ancestral prototypes. While the brute transformative power that visited the earth in the days of the first ancestors is now only rarely encountered, and then only in small doses, the spiritual forces set in place by their actions continue to shape human destinies to this very day.

The sayings of the ancestors, then, forge a link across time, connecting the events of the present to the sources of power and knowledge concentrated in earlier cosmic moments. They are a latter-day conceptual aid, encoding incisive observations on the relationship between empirical signs and underlying spiritual conditions at a time when these associations are no longer readily apparent. Passed along in an unbroken chain of oral tradition and confirmed by present-day communion with the spirit realm, this storehouse of practical wisdom preserves the inalienable coupling of the experiential present and the ever-present ancestral past.

The ancestral world lies at the very foundation of the spiritual realm accessed by the sayings of the ancestors. The sayings draw on this ancestral world in a pragmatic and often cryptic fashion. They presuppose, but reveal only sporadically, a comprehensive orientation to the cosmos. In order to fully appreciate the cognitive reach of the sayings, it is necessary to inspect in some detail this underlying cosmology. Perhaps the most revealing source of information regarding the ancestral world is the extensive body of mythic narrative still produced and savored by members of the valley's indigenous communities. This body of traditional narrative defines the spiritual lineage of many actors, actions, and entities appearing in the manifest content of the sayings.

Each of the major indigenous groups in the Sibundoy Valley conserves a vibrant tradition of mythic narrative, consisting of stories whose plots revolve around the doings of the first ancestors. There is a clear differentiation of this treasury of mythic narrative, which is marked by explicit cover terms, *antwanos* in Kamsá, and *antioj parlo* in Inga. The fact that this terminology proceeds from Spanish loan words suggests that the advent of the soldiers and missionaries brought a newfound need to distinguish the indigenous stories from other kinds of stories. Only those stories centering on the exploits of the ancestors merit inclusion in this category of narrative, and these stories are especially valued. The intrusion of extraneous narrative material, for example biblical stories or folk narrative brought in from Colombian national traditions, are censured by comments such as "stick to the old ones, Brother."

The corpus of mythic narrative is performed mostly by the elders, except for the trickster stories that are told by children as young as five years of age. The elders are revered for their command of mythic narrative, and they themselves often pay homage to their elders in turn: "When I was a young boy, I heard my grandparents say these things, and I keep them in mind." A typical storytelling session involves a mixed-generation constituency, with perhaps a couple of younger generations attending to the narrative utterances of an elderly storyteller. Stories are usually told in the evenings and in the presence of chicha, which lends its ineffable aura of confidence and intimacy to the surroundings.

The possession of a corpus of mythic narrative is arguably a distinguishing feature of indigenous ethnicity in this central Andean zone, where *campesinos* or 'peasants' and members of indigenous communities are not so readily set apart. Enclaves of mestizo agriculturalists often display comparable modes of tilling the land and they may even use chicha as the preferred beverage, but they do not possess a mythic narrative corpus that is geographically bound, that recounts the origins of things, and that is believed to be true. It may well be that the presence of this kind of narrative tradition could be generalized as one of the most salient distinguishing features of indigenous ethnicity in the complex social configuration of the modern Andes.

How far back can we trace the wellsprings of the ancestral world? To date field collecting in the Sibundoy Valley has not uncovered a veritable creation myth, and it is not likely to do so, since we are faced with a process of further attrition as each older generation carries some part of the story to the grave. It is likely that the extirpation of the native religion, so assiduously sought by the Catholic missionaries, has permanently destroyed this and other components of what was previously a more comprehensive mythology. The closest approximation to a Sibundoy creation myth that has come to my attention is the following account, really a skeletal report rather than a telling (Hymes 1981), produced for me in Kamsá by the late Bautista Juajibioy, a distinguished elder and former governor of the community. It concerns the previous stages of civilization:

They tell about it, you know?
The time of darkness, *yibets tempoka.*
And then the time of light, *bingea tempoka.*
And then another one: *kaka tempoka,* the raw time,
they ate everything raw, kaka tempo.
All during the raw time, they ate everything raw,
all fruits, everything raw, raw, raw,
since previously there was no fire.
That's why its called kaka tempo, the raw time.
Later there was fire and they learned how to cook.
I used to like to hear these things,
since there were many of them,
and the elders would be conversing among themselves,

and oneself just listening to everything.
Before the arrival of the missionaries.

Taita Bautista's narrative suggests a sequence of stages in cosmic
time beginning with *yibets tempoka*, the time of darkness (*yibets*
means 'night' in Kamsá), moving to *binyea tempoka*, the time of
light (*binyea* means 'dawn' and also 'wind' and 'vision' in Kamsá),
then moving to *kaka tempoka*, the raw time (*kaka* means 'raw' in
Kamsá), and culminating in the modern period, which remains
unnamed, starting at the moment when people acquired fire and
learned how to cook their food. It is tempting to discern in the
framing commentary yet another stage, the time of the missionaries, which marks a moment of sociopolitical rather than cosmological significance.

We have evidence here of a linear progression in cosmic time
from the more remote and hostile initial phases, when light and
fire were absent, to the contemporary phase, with conditions favorable for human society as we know it today. The advent of
daylight mentioned in this account is reminiscent of poignant episodes in the South and North American mythology describing the
first dawning (Demarest 1981; Tedlock 1985), and it brings into
play the thought complex associated with the Kamsá word *binyea*,
binding the pivotal notions 'dawn', 'wind' (or 'spirit'), and 'vision'
into a powerful associative knot.

Alberto Juajibioy, the son of taita Bautista, learned Sibundoy oral
traditions from his father and provides a few details that can augment this sketch. He notes that the period referred to as *kaka
tempo* is also known by the term *ndwabain*, meaning "unbaptized"
or pre-Christian, and that the missionary period is sometimes
called *wabain*, "blessed" or "baptized." He also gives this interesting summation of kaka tempo: "In the epoch of 'raw time', the
sun, moon, stars, thunder, rainbow, plants and animals of the region possessed special powers to transform themselves into human
beings" (Juajibioy 1987).

This is all that remains of the Sibundoy version of creation,
though it seems likely that at one time a much fuller account of
these early moments may have existed. However, there is mythological narrative shedding light on some of the intermediate
moments in this cosmic progression. The primary strata of mythic
narrative from the valley depict key events taking us from the raw
time, a period just prior to the arrival of the first ancestors, into
the earliest moments of the present creation, when the first ancestors exerted their influence to make the world safe for human

civilization. One myth that can be traced back to this dawning of the modern period tells of the acquisition of fire and seed corn. I have translated into English a text that Alberto Juajibioy collected from his father, Bautista Juajibioy, in Kamsá (Juajibioy & Wheeler 1973):

In the old days when there was still no fire,
people ate their food raw.
One day as people were complaining about having no fire,
a weasel interrupted them with these words:
"I will go and get fire,
if each of you gives me a chicken in return.
If you don't agree with this,
then I won't do you this favor."
The people thought it over and agreed to the deal.
And so the weasel went to the home of Wangetsmuna,
for he was the only one who possessed fire.

Entering his house, she said:
"Sir, shall I make you laugh?"
He answered: "Let's see you please me."
Then the weasel began to dance,
dragging her tail along the ground.
Suddenly coming close to the fire,
she grabbed some cinders in her tail
and ran quickly out of there.
She went into the forest,
where she spread the cinders about.
Right away those places caught fire.
The people, on seeing this,
went right away to get some.

From that moment fire appeared in this world.
The mouse brought corn for planting.
So from that time on food also appeared in this world.

The knowledge of fire and corn cultivation, two essential ingredients in the development of human society, occurs through the agency of these two animal-people, the weasel and mouse. These animal pests, the one a thief of hens and chicks, the other a thief of corn seed, are members of a category of animals sharing human appetites and therefore thought to be especially involved in the affairs of humankind. The weasel is a celebrated figure in the mythic narrative of the valley, sometimes portrayed as a female shaman, sometimes as a companion to the culture hero, Wangets-muna. It is not surprising that Wangetsmuna has access to the knowledge of fire and corn, since he enjoys a special relation-ship to the deities, as we shall soon see. In bringing fire to the people, the weasel impels the cosmic progression into the modern period, with its eating customs focused on fire as a means of cook-ing food, and corn as the staple item in the diet.

Wangetsmuna is the key figure in Kamsá mythology (his coun-terpart among the Inga is Carustelinda Taita or 'Lord of the Car-nival') a figure that, like the Jesus Christ he is sometimes equated with, forges a direct link between the human and the divine. The etymology of his name (wangets is very close to the Kamsá for 'beak'; -muna is the verbal root "to be") suggests that he is a bird-like figure, perhaps the leader of the bird-people who populate the mythic narratives told in the valley. The narratives associated with Wangetsmuna form the cornerstone of this mythology and require sustained treatment here since they provide invaluable detail on the state of the cosmos at this critical moment of transition.

A great many episodes are reported in the four tellings of this myth in my possession, too many to enumerate or synopsize here. Instead, I concentrate on those episodes that are especially reveal-ing of the make-up of the ancestral world. Perhaps most dramatic among these is the portrayal of the sun, the moon, and the thunder as deities interacting directly with the very first human beings, two brothers in some variants, two brothers and a sister in others. The sun is referred to as "Our Father," and he is portrayed as a powerful and intimidating figure. His daughter, the moon, is much more accessible to humans and in fact becomes the wife of the primordial miner, one of the two original brothers.

The story begins with the primordial human beings, a miner, his younger brother who cooks for him, and in some variants, their sister who spins thread. The miner leaves a trap along a trail and dreams that night of a young woman caught there; sure enough, the next day he finds her entangled in the trap. She scolds him, he lets her go, and then they decide to marry. The identity of this woman, and of her father, is made very clear (in what follows, I will cite passages from two tellings of this myth, by Mariano Chic-unque and his nephew, Estanislao Chicunque, both in Kamsá):

Then she took that miner to her house.
And it turned out, so they say, to be the home of the sun.
Now this is what we call *bngabe taita,*

which means 'Our Lord', so its like saying "the Father."
"My father," she said, "my father, my father is the sun."
"*Taitana*," she said. "I am his daughter."
She is the moon, it turned out, she is the moon.

The identification of these characters as celestial beings locates
this particular phase of the Wangetsmuna myth in an early moment
in cosmic time, a moment when the supernaturals interacted directly with the very first ancestors of the modern people.
    After agreeing to marry her, the miner follows her home, and
experiences a near encounter with her solar father:

They arrived after a long time, and when they sat down,
by the edge of a large body of water, when they sat down,
truly, heaven forbid, suddenly those carts came roaring,
to the edge of the water, and that water completely dried up,
yes sir, and that beach was nothing but beads,
composed of beads, of beads was that beach.
Fine, then they hid, that woman and her husband-to-be,
for they had agreed to marry,
they hid in a large jar that was there,
and inside it they were able to sit down.
And then hen droppings were scattered all about there,
the sun's droppings were scattered all about.
There they took refuge, and as they were hiding there,
heaven forbid, the sun arrived to eat,
he stopped off there as he went on his rounds.
And inside there it was getting very hot,
inside, saintly God, it was getting very hot.

Then, in order to eat, every serving a bushel,
every serving a bushel, as much as three bushels to eat,
three bushels he ate, and three bushels he ate.
And then, then he said to her:
"Why, why does it smell of moss here?"
Then that daughter answered:
"I went to the woods, and there was moss on the tree.
I went to gather firewood. That's the odor."
Be careful. He came over to take the lid off,
but then he stopped. Aha.

Surely he sat down again and that machine roared,
and then that water there just completely dried up.
And like that, that body of water disappeared.

And the sun, as he went off to some other place,
that water came together again there.

The exemplary character of the Wangetsmuna sequence appears
at every juncture: in the episode just quoted, the sun's droppings
account for the presence of gold in the world, and the sands that
are beads reveal the origin of the colorful seed *chaquira* that are
worn with pride by members of the indigenous communities. But
returning to the plot: if the sun is portrayed as hostile to humankind, too pervasive in his fiery persona to be endured, his daughter
the moon is far more accommodating. In human form she agrees
to marry the miner, and she proposes the following arrangement:

Aha. Fine. Then that woman spoke to him,
they came to an agreement, so they could marry.
Then: "Take this wad of cotton.
This evening I will come to you."
She took out some cotton, she rubbed it back and forth,
that woman, and she gave it to him.
And in the old days they carried those sacks,
and like that he had it slung over his shoulder there,
and she stuffed it with that cotton. Fine.
And truly she remained inside there, with the older brother.

Cotton, portrayed here as the medium of spiritual communication, retains an important spiritual role in the practice of the
native doctors, as we shall see in the next chapter. In the mythical
context, this unusual mode of association triggers a seminal episode in the myth, the transformation of the younger brother into
the infant Wangetsmuna. The younger brother hears the sound of
people conversing during the night, and goes about inspecting the
older brother's gear to discover the secret:

Fine. And then he went to put out that bedding,
he began to search through it, looking all around.
And that spirit was there, but he didn't notice it.
She went to the mine to tell him about it.
That woman arrived at the mine:
"Your younger brother is looking for me.
He almost found me."
Then he said: "By Our Lord, appear to him.
I wonder what will become of him."

The next day the younger brother finds the cotton, which he rubs all about his body, including the crotch area. This action has the effect of turning him into a woman. In an attempt to return him to his original gender, the older brother has him (her) lie down beside a river and allow all the animals to approach, each one taking a lick at the vagina. The younger brother is to remain silent. All goes well until the last beast comes by, identified as one with very sharp claws, and very likely the small bear that used to be found in the vicinity of the Sibundoy Valley. The younger brother cries out in pain, and throws this beast off of him. Now all the beasts must return, this time not to take a lick but to take a bite.

Eventually, all that remains of the younger brother is a head, and this head becomes vexatious to the miner in the manner of the "rolling head" that appears in a number of American Indian mythologies (Levi-Strauss 1978; Niles 1981). The head proposes a solution: the older brother must take the wooden drum from the wall, place the head inside, tie the cover of the drum back on, and throw it into the river. The drum, with head inside, disappears downstream.

Far below, the heathen women are out washing clothes. One of them spots the drum and takes it out of the water. She opens it and finds a tender infant, the young Wangetsmuna, inside. The celestial bodies, the sun and the moon, play no further role in this myth, but their (especially the moon's) impact in bringing about the origin of Wangetsmuna is of course essential in the development of the plot. The emergence of Wangetsmuna takes us further along in cosmological time, to the predawn and dawn of the present creation. Wangetsmuna grows rapidly and becomes a pivotal force in this native American account of the movement from savagery to civilization.

The heathens lack specific faculties essential to civil society in the modern creation: they have fire, but they are without the anus, and therefore cannot eat food; and they exhibit a very odd form of sexuality, involving the mustering of a collective penis. These shortcomings are described as follows in one telling of the myth:

Then they had nothing in the way of an anus, nothing.
As for eating, they couldn't eat anything.
And they had turkeys, lots of them.
They would kill a fine turkey, pluck it, and put it in the pan.
And they would eat like this, only the steam,
that steam they would gulp.

That's how they nourished themselves.
· ·
Heaven forbid, it was by the edge of a large river,
and that long thing, that penis would pass by there.
Then the husband of those heathen women would lie there,
and so truly, to speak in a vulgar way,
that's how they would copulate.

It is possible that the inappropriate customs described in these
passages encode an ethnocentric highland perception of certain
lowland customs, such as the maintenance of separate men's and
women's quarters. In any case, Wangetsmuna sets about correcting
this state of affairs. In the place where the anus should be, the
heathens have a mark. They see Wangetsmuna enjoying the pleasure of eating and beg him to open their anuses so that they might
eat also:

And so they decided on it, they made up their minds,
and on that mark, with a knife, he opened them,
and a medicine, some medicine,
he chewed some bark and rubbed that on them.
And truly some of them did well and healed,
they began to eat well, they shat, truly.
Aha. But others died.

And so it seems that at the dawn of the modern age, people had
fire but they didn't eat properly, because of this anatomical defi-
ciency. Wangetsmuna plays the part of the first native doctor and
introduces proper eating habits among the heathens.

His attempt to correct the peculiar sexual practices of the heathens meets with less success. He sets a trap along the path where
the collective penis travels to cross the river and copulate with the
heathen women. This organ is crushed as it triggers the trap, and
the earth shakes as a loud groan is heard. Wangetsmuna is advised
to run to the house of his grandfather, who turns out to be the
thunder. And so another celestial deity enters the story. The thunder, a major figure in Andean cosmologies (Cobo 1956; Rowe 1946;
Demarest 1981), is portrayed in this myth cycle much as he appears
in classical Andean sources: a powerful deity given to spinning a
sling about and sending off destructive peals of thunder and bolts
of lightning.

At this juncture in the story he appears as a kindly grandfather

who agrees to hide his grandson and then obliterates the heathen
men when they insist on searching for the one who abused them:

That sling he picked up, he whirled it about,
and the lightning bolts completely finished them off.
Then that rock of gold, that ball of gold,
spun about and completely destroyed them.

With this episode, the expression of one important cosmological
network is complete: the miner searches for gold (the sun's droppings) in order to make balls of gold for his grandfather, the thunder.
Wangetsmuna enters the scene as a catalyst, and his caprice results
in the eradication of the heathens and the preparation of the world
for the establishment of modern human society.

The narrative shifts gears here, and Wangetsmuna is sent off
(much like his counterpart from the southern Andes, Viracocha)
to visit the world and report back to his grandfather after a year's
time. In his wandering through the world, Wangetsmuna goes
about "pronouncing judgments," giving the animals their voices
and characteristics, and eventually establishing for all time the
boundary between animals and humans:

Then the grandfather sent him into the world.
"With this trumpet you are to visit the world,
to every region you will travel.
You will be called Wangetsmuna.
Thus from this day you will go among the animals,
and you will defend yourself from the beasts
with an incantation.
And so prepare yourself, so you must travel.

In this way, you will make the weasel laugh,
Wangetsmuna, in this way the squirrel.
In this way you will make the monkey laugh.
In this way, the chkuro surely kills the hen.
And that rump is the first part eaten.
That one then squealed at her.
The weasel is like that,
like that she kills the hen,
like that she squeals at her.
There she turned out to be harmful that weasel.
So a curse you must lay on her.
The monkey, no, the monkey just on that rope,

on the vine he must hang.
Like the wind he must fly, thus he is to fly."

At the next dawn he had to sound the trumpet.
Whatever day it happened to be,
we human's became as we are in God's world,
we humans, human, and from that day on,
the animals remained animals.

Wangetsmuna travels about the world and sustains a series of rather biblical encounters with people in different places. The episode with the monkeys closely parallels a comparable episode reported in the Mayan book of creation, the *Popol Vuh* (D. Tedlock 1985). But surely of greatest cosmological significance here is the temporal line of demarcation, produced when Wangetsmuna blew the horn (a musical instrument still used in the indigenous carnival) and forever established the boundary between humans and animals. Wangetsmuna's horn has a number of uses: in an episode accounting for the introduction of death into the world, the horn has the power to call people back from the dead. A young girl is living alone after the loss of her entire family. Wangetsmuna offers to bring them back to life, on the condition that she remain silent until they are fully returned:

Truly from the patio he blew the horn,
he blew the horn, and after a time they were coming,
the little ones ahead of the others.
That little sister first, which the beast had eaten.
And then they all arrived. Damn!
Finally they were all in the middle of the room.
As they were arriving: "Father, Mother, Father, Mother,
you have come back to me."
They departed forever, and they became parrots,
in this world, forever, they flew off as parrots.
And then that Wangetsmuna, as he is called:
"Why did you do that? I told you not to."
Forever for this reason those parrots exist,
because of her disobedience. Aha.

In some tellings the Wangetsmuna cycle concludes with the culture hero returning to abide with his grandfather; in others, the unfortunate hero falls victim to ravenous beasts here on earth. Overall, the sequence of episodes included in this mythic narrative cycle spans a crucial moment in cosmic time: the transition from the preancestral period, when the proto-people interacted directly with the celestial bodies, to the dawn of the ancestral world, when the first people began to live in society according to norms that are recognized to the present day. The mythic narratives featuring Wangetsmuna make up the primary foundation myth of the Sibundoy natives, depicting the vanquishing of the heathens, whose inappropriate modes of living had to yield to civilized customs; the establishment of the boundary between people and animals; and the origin of many practices, objects, and habits constitutive of the modern-day social and natural worlds.

The other myth cycle with some claim to special prominence in the Sibundoy corpus involves the rainbow, a lesser deity portrayed as something of a rakish young man. "The Story of the Two Orphans," which I have heard in numerous Inga and Kamsá tellings, is a Sibundoy Valley narrative with notable affinity to the European "Hansel and Gretel" tale (see Taggart 1986). The story tells of the exploits of a brother and sister living in a world already prepared for human society, but still in a formative epoch. The cosmic time frame is not primordial, as in the Wangetsmuna cycle, but it is early enough to allow for numerous mythological transformations and some world-shaping events.

The story begins as two children are chased from their home by a merciless stepmother. They come across a sooty cottage deep in the wilderness. The old woman living there gives them food, but each day she measures their wrists to see if they are fat enough to be eaten. Finally one morning she sends the children to fetch water and firewood, intending to feast on them that day. An ant in the path alerts them to the danger they face and advises them to feign ignorance when the old woman asks them to blow on the fire. The ant tells them to turn the pot of water over on the witch when she bends down to show them how to blow on the fire.

All of this is accomplished, and the children flee while the old hag comes after them, holding her guts in her hands. The children arrive at the banks of a large river as the witch calls out behind them, "Wait for me, sweet things." By the edge of the river is a young man, identified as the rainbow:

When they came to that large river,
then there was the rainbow,
dressed in a *cusma*, dressed in a cusma,
with a blue woven belt around his forehead.
He was sharpening a machete,

he was sharpening an ax.
Then quickly they begged him:
"For God's sake, quickly let us pass, Father Uncle,
a witch is chasing us, a beast."
Then that father uncle, the girl was full grown,
so to speak, that father uncle said:
"Make love to me.
You come make love to me, then I will let you pass."
That's just what he said, and truly they crossed.
"For God's sake, let us pass." "Fine."
Right away the rainbow made a bridge from side to side,
as if a large log was placed there,
and those two crossed over to the other side.

When the witch arrives at the edge of the river, she makes the same plea and gets the same response. After complying with the rainbow's request, she starts across the bridge, but just as she reaches the midway point, the rainbow fades, and she falls to her death in the river below.

In an episode that is reminiscent of Wangestsmuna's 'visit' to the world, the two children are then sent by the rainbow to visit "the Santiagueños," or Inganos living in the town of Santiago. He provides them with magical balls of cotton, that spiritually-charged substance:

"You two thus will go among the Santiagueños, to Santiago.
Over there you will descend, there on a trail,
by the foot of the mountain you will go."
Then he gave that boy a ball of magic cotton,
and he also gave the girl some cotton.
The boy was to place the cotton by his head when he slept,
and the girl by her feet, that magic cotton.
Any beast that might be on the prowl, large or small,
from that beast they could protect themselves with the cotton,
they could sleep without fear.

Among the Santiagueños, the two children convert their cotton into a pair of fine hunting dogs and manage to secure plenty of food by hunting the wild pigs that abound in the vicinity. The people become envious of these dogs, and they kill the two children, hoping to keep the dogs for themselves. But the dogs return from the hunt and scratch so fervently at the graves of their slain masters that the people are forced to dig them up and rebury them, this time face-up. After this is done, the story concludes as follows:

And then surely both of them were placed face-up,
they turned them over.
Here the souls became doves,
and those dogs, a pair of doves,
they flew off, two pairs of doves, but not to heaven.

The clarification that they flew off, *but not to heaven*, appears to locate these protagonists outside of the Christian tradition, which is conceived here as a separate conceptual domain.

Another myth cycle that treats of the transitional period leading to the time of the first ancestors tells of the vanquishing of the *aucas*, a race of spirit-people, thought to have inhabited the high mountain areas in some versions and the adjacent lowlands in others, around the time of the first ancestors. In fact, from these uncouth but powerful beings the first people acquired much of their knowledge of the spirit realm. The Inga word *auca* is best translated 'heathen'; it literally signifies the 'unbaptized' and can refer to a newborn infant (Levinsohn 1976). This word evokes an important strand in Andean ethnohistorical thinking, appearing in the 'new chronicle' of Felipe Guaman Poma de Ayala, composed in the mid-sixteenth century. Here the aucas appear as the fourth generation of American people, living just prior to the time of the Incas. His portrait corresponds in many details to the auca of Sibundoy mythic narrative: a substrate people, fierce warriors, cannibals, possessed of spiritual powers that enable them to transform themselves into jaguars and other animals (see Guaman Poma de Ayala 1956).

We have already caught a glimpse of the aucas, who were presented in the Wangetsmuna cycle as mulelike residents of the lowlands, quasi-people lacking the basic principles of civilization. Another depiction of the aucas and their interaction with the first people occurs in "The Story of the Heathen's Walk," a story that I collected in Inga from Manuel Muyuy. In this account, the heathen is portrayed as a beastly spirit that walks about looking for human blood and at the same time as a powerful creature possessing direct access to the spirit realm. The narrator is clearly at a loss as to how best to describe this curious being:

The heathen rascal was a spirit, you see,
a spirit, say, a spirit:
it is a being, a person-being, Indian, you see,

so to speak, not like a real person, a heathen,
an eater of people, an eater of people.

In this rendition, an Ingano hunter tracks down this spirit being
and kills him with a poisonous arrow. He seizes the feather head-
ress of the heathen, and with it the heathen's spiritual knowledge.
As a result, the Ingano, described as an *amigo* or Quechua-speaking
Indian of the lowland Putumayo, becomes a powerful doctor. The
storyteller is at some pains to describe the precise means whereby
the knowledge of the auca is transfered to the mind of the Ingano:

He killed that heathen,
and he took the inheritance of that one,
the inheritance,
his knowledge he took for himself into his own mind.
Surely more, he took for himself his mind,
you see, that one was an owner of knowledge.

As a consequence of this conquest, the hunter becomes a doctor
who is described as the master of animals, one who is able to
transform himself into the jaguar or the bear. At this early moment
of cosmic time, there was direct access to spiritual power; the first
ancestors, in vanquishing the heathens, were able to tap into this
reservoir of knowledge.

The theme of the acquisition of spiritual power suffuses the
mythic narrative of the Sibundoy Valley. In one of these, "The Story
of the Wild Pigs," told by Mariano Chicunque in Kamsá, some
hunters follow a herd of wild pigs into a cave, and inside the cave,
the pigs turn into people. The master of the wild pigs appears to
them, cautions them about killing more than their share of wild
pigs, and then presents them with a small cup of remedy, probably
the mythical prototype of the medicine vine, that leaves them entirely senseless for days. When they return to human society, they
are great and powerful doctors, wise in the hunting of animals and
able to revive even the dead. This narrative makes explicit a connection between the acquisition of spiritual power and the accumulation of wealth, related to the current belief in the worldly
success awaiting those who possess sound spiritual health.

A major subset of Sibundoy myths tells of a peculiar category
of world-shaping events, namely events leading to a loss of the
knowledge that was intended as part of the human patrimony.
These myths are roughly comparable to the biblical theme of the
loss of paradise, though they are strikingly different from biblical

materials in all other respects. They are set in the ancestral world, at a moment when human society as we know it is already established but not perhaps as firmly set as it is today. Typically, a suitor comes to the home of a young marriageable person, to initiate a period of trial marriage. There is something uncouth about these suitors, who are actually animal-people, but the parents decide to give them a chance to prove their worth. They botch this chance, incur the wrath of the future mother-in-law, and are eventually rejected by the parents. At this point they assume their animal identities and vanish into the forest. The irony is that each of these suitors could have instilled in the human realm a valuable bit of knowledge, if only the future mother-in-law had not been so harsh with them.

As we noted in the first chapter of this book, the gift that the shulupsi bird-woman brought to the women was the ability to make a full barrel of chicha using only a single grain of corn. Responding to the future mother-in-law's unjust scolding, she pronounces the following curse on humankind:

"In my day I was used to making a barrel of chicha
with only a few grains of corn,
but from this day on,
women will have to grind much corn on the mortar
to produce only a single barrel of chicha."

The owl-person brought another, complementary gift to the people, the ability to cultivate land without the great amount of human labor it requires today. In "The Story of the Owl," as told by Francisco Tandioy in Inga, the owl is portrayed as a great owner of gardens, who simply positions himself at the top of a hill and shouts; as far as his voice carries, the wilderness is transformed into a garden:

With only a shout, it is said, he worked an entire field,
the clearing of the land, the weeding,
all that had to be done.
And when he shouted a second time,
he left everything planted.
When he shouted the third time,
the cobs of corn would appear,
and the fourth shout left the corn already harvested.

Unaware that the owl-person possesses this special power, the future mother-in-law and her daughters find that he is unkempt and lazy, not a suitable partner at all. The owl discovers his rejection, returns to the field, and shouts once more: as far as his voice carries, the mountainside is returned to wilderness. The story closes with a poignant thought: "For this reason, imagine how we would live, if the owl were still a man to this day, or if he had taught us what he knew."

This set of myths depicts these powerful animal-people in the ancestral world, spirit beings who came among people to bring important gifts, but who were frustrated by the rough treatment they received and left without imparting the priceless information they bore. Ingano and Kamsá narrators explain these spirits as messengers of the deities, who intended that people should have these powers. In a Sibundoy Valley redress of the notion of original sin, it is through tragic human error, precipitated by the uncouth appearance of these messengers, that these capabilities are lost for all time.

Another set of mythic narratives tells of encounters with spirit beings, often at the edge of the civilized world, in the intervening period between the days of the first people and the modern time. The events narrated in these myths apparently transpire after the times of the first generations of people, for society is already fixed in patterns familiar to us today, though direct spiritual manifestations appear to be more common than they currently are. In these narratives, no benefit attaches to encountering the spirit forces; in fact, the encounters are frequently devastating to the mortals who sustain them. Nor are these encounters loaded with cosmos-shaping significance. Instead, these myths tilt towards the present situation, attesting to the ever-present spirit realm, which hovers on the brink of human experience, always threatening to invade and overwhelm it.

In one subset of these myths, the central character is a master or owner figure, the Sibundoy representative of a nature guardian figure common in lowland mythologies (Reichel-Dolmatoff 1971; Whitten 1976; Brown 1985). It has been suggested that the protectors and regulators of wild game are elements in an archaic cultural pattern associated with hunting societies worldwide (Schultes & Hofmann 1979). The term used to refer to these lords of the elements in both Inga and Kamsá is based on the Spanish word *dueño*, meaning 'owner'. These awesome characters mediate between the human and nonhuman domains; they are 'bosses' within their specific element and sometimes guardians of a particular ecological niche. The master of the wild pigs, already mentioned, is pictured as follows: "And there that boss, that master of the wild pigs, as he is called, he had two tusks that were crossed, that remarkable old man, what a doctor he was!"

As intimidating as the master of the wild pigs appears to be, he is easygoing compared to the master of the river, who roams the waters at night looking to carry off lost or lingering people. In "The Story of the Master of the River," told by Mariano Chicunque in Kamsá, a hunter strays from his group and is forced to spend the night in a cave by the side of a large river:

And he sat there when suddenly,
a very clear night it was, the day after the full moon,
when suddenly there came a great shout,
there came a roaring from the river, and not far off.

And right away, the shout came from nearby.
Then he stuck his head out from there, he looked around.
Then, then he appeared on that river, large,
perched on top of those rolling boulders.
And there, yes indeed, there with the face of a bird,
something like a beak it was,
the body just like a monk's,
he was dressed in dark black,
the head like a bird's, it was a white head with a beak.
And so he passed by shouting,
and that river, great God, how it roared!
And then suddenly he was gone.
And the old ones knew him, the master of the river.

The frightened hunter manages to survive only through the agency of a sacred medallion, but when he returns to his town, he suffers from such a state of fright that he wastes away and dies. It is worth noting that this myth proposes a spiritual opposition between the forces of the natural domain and the forces of Christianity. The tidy syncretism that exists in some areas of the indigenous worldview breaks down here, as the sacred medallion (that is, an amulet blessed by the Catholic priest) defends the strayed hunter from the onslaught of the master of the river.

The presence of the spirit realm is attested in a number of mythic narratives describing the interaction of mortals in the modern world with spirit beings. In one of these, "The Story of the Water

Birds," performed by Estanislao Chicunque in Kamsá, a woman from the valley travels through the mountains to Aponte in search of corn. On her way back to the valley she hears laughter resounding in the hills. She goes to investigate and finds some young women splashing about in the water. She wonders: "What kind of creatures are these? What language might they speak?" The young women notice her and invite her to come to their home, where the following scene takes place:

And then truly they bid her enter the house.
There those young women sat down.
They began to sip on a drink,
they began to drink from a small cup.
In the old days there was a power,
they would just drink from those small cups.

She noticed a long pole
stretching all the way across the house.
And when she took a good look at it,
it was no bench at all, but a beast it was,
the one called a snake.
They were standing on top of it, those young women,
it seemed as if they were seated on it.
They drank and fell to the ground.

The young women disappear, but the woman from the valley finds herself in the presence of some familiar birds: "The picangui knew her, the sparrow knew her, and the one who made the chicha, the chiwako, also knew her. They were natives of the valley." The woman from the valley takes a bit of the potion herself: "Then the sparrow and the picangui, they went about sweeping the house. And they gave her a little portion of the drink, and she completely lost her senses." Unlike the hunters in a mythic narrative discussed earlier, this woman does not receive lasting spiritual powers from this experience. Instead, she comes to herself on an isolated cliff and must rely on a hawk to carry her back to the trail leading to the valley. This last episode is reminiscent of motives widely distributed in American Indian mythology and prominent, for example, in the "Star Husband" mythological complex (Thompson 1953; Levi-Strauss 1978).

The "Story of the Water Birds" replays themes already mentioned, like the spiritual origins of the hallucinogenic remedies and the prominence of bird-people in the spirit realm. It also brings into play an animal of major importance in the sayings of the ancestors, the snake, portrayed here as a kind of axis-mundi in the house of the spirit beings. The story is set in the ancestral world, as we can tell by the narrator's use of the phrase, "in the old days there was a power." But apart from this reference, the story has a very contemporary ring to it. The portrayal of the woman as "a poor woman from the valley" is quite in keeping with current realities and modes of living. The mortal brought into contact with the spirit beings cannot benefit from this epiphany, because of the recession of human spiritual tolerance as humanity moves away in cosmic time from the days of the first people. Myths like this one display the continuing presence of the spirit realm, which derives from the prototypical example of the ancestral world but persists in attenuated form as an underlying reality.

Let me reproduce the text of one final myth, selected from a group of myths attesting to the continuing presence of the spirit realm so pervasive in the ancestral world. "The Story of the Centipede" was told by María Juajibioy in Kamsá:

A young lady arrived at the home of a young man,
and that future mother-in-law said to her:
"Come and plant barbacuano seed."
And that would-be daughter-in-law answered her:
"I myself will turn into barbacuano."

Then: "Plant some achira for me."
Again she responded: "I myself will become achira."
For the second time she wouldn't listen,
and how could the older woman beg her?

Then the future mother-in-law went out to plant corn,
and where she was planting, she found a centipede.
And then as she began to plant,
she struck it with her digging stick.
Just calmly she continued planting.

When she finished she returned to the house.
Then she saw that future daughter-in-law in bad shape,
sitting there with her head banged up,
with her head mostly covered, she saw her.

Then that future mother-in-law questioned her:
"Why, Niece, are you like this?"
Then she responded to her:
"Didn't you, Aunt, do this to me?"

And then she said to her:
"Where did this happen to you?"
Then she responded: "In the garden,
didn't you strike me with the digging stick?"

Then she answered her:
"With this digging stick I struck a centipede.
So you are not a human being," she said to her.
That's all as I know it.

Myths like this one bespeak a spirit realm close at hand, poised
to intrude on any and all human activities. Beyond the moment
of demarcation, when animals and people received their permanent observable form, the sorting out of ambiguous animal-people
identities remains a significant project for mortals confronting the
spiritual residue of ancestral times. The centipede-woman is a conceptual double: at once a young woman and a centipede. The spiritual counterpart lurks at the fringe of routine human experience,
and at pivotal moments of transcendence, human beings properly
situated catch a glimpse of a spiritual reality persisting into the
contemporary period and determining the world of ordinary experience. The Kamsá phrase *cha ndoñe krischian*, 'he (or she) is
not a human being', has become a proverbial epithet for anyone
who can do something remarkable, such as shoot marbles with
special accuracy.

The Sibundoy mythic narratives delineate a traditional cosmo-
gony with these temporal divisions:

PRIMORDIAL EPOCH
    Time of darkness
    Time of light
        The sun rises for the first time
    Raw Time
        —Food is uncooked.
    Time of fire
        —Fire and corn are procured.

ANCESTRAL PERIOD
    Early Phase
        —Celestial bodies interact with first people.
        —Animal-people walk the earth.
        —Substrate populations are present.
        —Spiritual power is rampant.
    Formative phase

—Substrate peoples are vanquished.
—Proper mores are established.
—Animals and people are sorted out.
—Spiritual power retreats to the periphery.

MODERN PERIOD
—Spanish missionaries impose Catholicism.
—Indian land is lost to colonos.
—An elusive spirit realm persists.

This model of cosmic time, as conceived in the traditional cosmology of the Sibundoy natives, proposes an irreversible ebb of spiritual power as we move away from the ancestral period. The diminished presence of brute spiritual power can be traced in the decline of world-shaping events, in the scarcity of mythical transformations and mortal encounters with the deities, and in the relative infrequency of spirit apparitions. Still, it is remarkable that the spirit realm perseveres in covert manifestations and continues to play a part in the affairs of the modern people.

One of the windows onto the ancestral world and its persisting spiritual residue is the body of sayings of the ancestors. These belief statements, coined in the aftermath of the ancestral period and recovered through spiritual vision in the modern period, compose an imperfect but priceless compendium of practical knowledge deriving from the ancestral world. The body of mythic narrative in the Sibundoy Valley portrays, defines, and charters many of the agents and events appearing in the sayings: the celestial bodies, such as the sun, moon, thunder, and rainbow; spiritual presences that reside in cotton and that inhabit the phenomena we know as the wind and the earth's fertility; the river, with its powerful master; the animal domain, replete with animal-people and other animal spirits influencing human destiny.

The mythic narratives transport us to those early moments in cosmic time when every action left its permanent stamp on the visible form of reality and when the brute transformative power of spiritual essences coalesced to create the modern world and structure human society. The sayings of the ancestors capture a small fragment of that explosive, world-shaping ancestral power and relay it to the present moment, so that its ancient and eternal wisdom can enter into the lives of ordinary men and women bound to the present creation.

5

The Spirit Realm

According to the indigenous worldview, spirits abound in the Sibundoy Valley: "We believe that all places are full of spirits. These spirits, at certain hours, are not congenial one might say. And so when they are not in a good humor, they attack people. One can speak of the evil wind of the cemetery, of the rivers and streams, of the cliffs, one can speak of the evil wind of the forest. So the world is full of spirits, sometimes even in our houses." The object of this chapter is to provide an introduction to the domain of the "evil wind"; using the sayings of the ancestors as a mooring, I examine the composition and mechanics of the spirit realm and discuss the pattern of human interaction with its wandering souls and forest presences.

At every turn, the sayings of the ancestors implicate a realm of spiritual presences, a veiled domain of powerful agents and forces shaping the destiny of human beings. The spirit realm is a residue of the ancestral period when the generative powers of the universe, manifested in the actions of the deities and first ancestors, gave form and substance to the enduring natural world and human civilization with its appropriate manners and customs. What was manifest reality in that formative period has since receded to become immanent, underlying reality, still determining the fortunes of individuals, families, and communities but now apprehended only indirectly and intermittently.

The universe of contemporary human experience preserves coded representations of the ancestral world, in the form of insistent spiritual manifestations. Sibundoy natives strive to retain access to the spirit realm, believing that adherence to the ancestral model is the only reliable path to spiritual health. Native doctors specialize in the use of organic medicines that remove the barriers inhibiting access to the spirit realm, and locate the vision seeker in the midst of primordial spiritual forces. The elders keep alive a treasury of mythic narrative recounting the doings of the deities and first ancestors, and accounting for the way things are today. People of all ages extract salient images from their nocturnal dreams and use these to deduce alignments and influences emanating from the spirit realm. The sayings of the ancestors are the most pervasive component of this arsenal of spiritual resources; they serve as an interpretive code, readily accessible to one and all, assigning esoteric consequences to the images encountered in dreams and to many perceptions originating in wakeful experience.

The sayings, with their burden of ancestral wisdom, penetrate the facade of routine experience and establish a conduit to the spirit realm. In other words, they provide an interpretive key, allowing movement between ordinary experience and its underlying spiritual wellspring. With the help of this code, people are able to articulate far-reaching explanations of the events that engulf them and, frequently, to elaborate successful schemes of preventive or remedial action.

The spirit realm is profoundly alien in character, and yet, paradoxically, focused on the human sphere. Its denizens appear in visible and audible forms that range from the oddly anthropomorphic to the eerily fantastic. The spirit presence may be a tall young man whose feet do not touch the ground; an old toothless hag; a figure blending animal and human characteristics; a figure constantly changing form; or, at the most abstract, a mere stirring of the air. The sense of otherworldliness is captured in the phrase "he [or she] is not a human being," occurring as the denouement of so many mythic narratives involving the unmasking of animal-people figures. This phrase, uttered with awe and often some revulsion as human protagonists recognize the alien identity of beings they had taken to be people, signals a breakthrough into the spirit realm, an intrusion of spirit forces into the lives of the protagonists.

The entire domain of the spiritual falls under the term *huayra* in Inga, meaning 'wind' in its narrowest frame of reference but commonly used to signify the spirit realm. The notion of *huayra* as 'strong spiritual presence' or 'spirit sickness' haunts the sayings of the ancestors and constitutes their central (though often unstated) concern. There are a few key words in Inga for making reference to the specific classes of spirits: *cucu*, a word that has come to mean 'devil' under the influence of the Catholic priests but whose proper translation is 'natural spirit'; *sacha huayra*, 'spirit [or spirit sickness] of the forest'; and *animas huayra*, 'spirit [or spirit sickness] of the departed souls'.

The Inga word *cucu* rarely occurs in relation to the sayings, and appears to denote the grotesque side of indigenous spirituality, perhaps as filtered through the eyes of the Christian convert. It surfaces most frequently in the *cucu ahuila*, meaning 'spirit grandmother' or 'old hag', a witch-like figure appearing in several mythic narratives. In a number of adjectival constructions, this term carries the force of the English 'spiritual': *cucu huayra*, 'spirit wind' or 'evil wind'; *cucu piscu*, 'spirit bird', a bird whose night call is an omen; *cucu tuglla*, 'spirit flower', the name for a rash thought to be produced by contact with the spirit realm (see the excellent dictionary prepared by Levinsohn, Maffla Bilbao, & Tandioy Chasoy 1978).

Terminology for the two main categories of spirits is prevalent in the corpus of sayings. The spirits of the forest, *sacha huayra*, are associated with diverse natural forces and with the fauna and flora of the Sibundoy ecology; they reside in the wild spots, apart from the sphere of routine human activities. In the words of one Ingano informant: "They say that the spirits of the forest can send a very difficult sickness. They are not very friendly and people greatly fear them. The spirits of the forest, they say that they live there, that they are native to the forest. They never were human beings, but at times they must attack human beings."

This layer of the spirit realm evidently originates in a precolumbian animistic religion; it includes the powerful masters of the natural domains, spirits of animals, trees, and plants, and some menacing witch and monster figures. The spirits of the forest appear in a number of the sayings, for example saying 181: "It is bad to bathe in a large river at midday. / Tapirs and swimming creatures will appear." The apparitions mentioned are spirits of the forest, and they trigger a spirit sickness that is extremely difficult to cure.

The forest spirits appear to exist in a parallel society that abides within the natural features and living creatures of the forest domain. Something of the workings of this branch of the spirit realm can be gleaned from the following episode in "The Story of Owl," as told by Francisco Tandioy in Inga. The owl-person, a suitor in the home of a young woman, sets off to a far corner of the hillside to work the land by himself, and the other workers try to follow his progress:

And then, it is said, he went to begin working.
Looking, looking, they couldn't see his work at all.
From time to time they heard a shout, it is said,
and then they heard many trees fall,
but when they went to look,

they couldn't see anything,
everything, it is said, remained the same.

At some moments they heard what sounded like many people
    talking,
at others, something like a shout,
and what sounded like the voices of many people.
And on hearing that, it is said, they became scared:
"Could this be the spirit of the forest?
Perhaps this is an evil hour."

In this fashion the owl-person clears his section of land without
appearing to do any work and without the aid of the other workers.
The spirit realm appears here as a simultaneous, alternative reality,
whose events produce observable results even though their modus
operandi are not directly observable. In this domain the animal-
people engage in organized and purposeful activities, but beyond
the reach of direct human perception. It is a layer of ontology that
is somehow lodged within or beside the world of ordinary perception. The analogy that springs to mind is the silent, invisible work
of a termite colony, which can turn wood into powder even though
its progress through the wood may never be noticed.

The spirit sickness caused by encounters with spirits of the forest is particularly dangerous: "They say that this is a sickness of
the forest, that it has to do with the spirits of the forest. They say
that it is very difficult to cure. If you get an evil wind of the forest,
it's very difficult and you will need a very good native doctor to
cure you. Otherwise, you will waste away and die. So that's the
one they fear the most. They are just beginning to understand how
to work with that one."

The second layer of the spirit realm, involving the souls of the
departed, *animas huayra*, evinces a substantial admixture of European folk Catholicism. These wandering souls appear in a number of the sayings, for example saying 103: "If the dogs are howling
at night, / they see the souls of the departed." In certain circumstances, the souls of the departed are thought to persist after life
and to return to the places they frequented in their former lives.
Dogs, with their keen senses and their proclivity to howl at unseen
presences in the night, are thought to be sensitive to the spirits of
wandering souls as well.

The unquiet dead, especially the souls of those who met death
through violence, accident, or suicide, are said to be especially
rambunctuous. As one Ingano friend put it: "They say that when

you die, after you are dead you do not remain still, but rather, you start to wander about. It depends, if you were a good person, then you don't wander. But if you were bad then you wander about tempting people. Or often they say that you want people to pray for you, so that you can save yourself from purgatory. And so those ones too go about bothering the living."

The animas or souls of the departed tend to loiter about cemeteries or in the vicinity of cliffs, ponds, bends in the rivers, and other evil points, that is, places where human beings have met untimely deaths. They are especially aggressive at certain times of day, for example 12 noon, 12 midnight, and 7 p.m., and on certain days of the week, for example, Tuesdays, Thursdays, and Fridays. Such evil points and evil times are to be avoided if one wishes to remain free from spirit sickness. Otherwise, one might hear the moaning or howling of spirits, or encounter a white, formless bulk or a large white dog that refuses to allow the traveller to proceed, and leaves him crushed with fright.

A great many personal experience stories tell of chilling encounters with the souls of the departed. Here is one example of this genre:

I left town around seven in the evening, maybe a bit later, and then in a bad spot where there was a landslide, I almost turned back, I remembered what my mother had told me about the souls of the departed. And just then I heard a loud noise, it sounded like a large ox. Then I began to run and when I tried to run I couldn't do it. And then after that I saw it, you know, a firefly came along and then it turned into a dog, the dog turned white and it wouldn't let me pass. And that gave me even more of a fright. And so I arrived at my house, but the next day I awoke with fever. I woke up very sick. I was in bad shape. They had to go and bring a native doctor. They told me that I had received a bad wind.

I was told of many apparitions of the departed souls. Most of these stories involved people who were abroad at night, and found themselves in the wrong place (bad points) at the wrong time (bad hours). Typical anecdotes include experiences like these:

- Shaking hands with an anima, who proffered a cold hand, and passed on the warning: "Be careful, Nephew." This anima, a woman, walked with her feet not touching the ground.

- Being picked up off the ground by a passing wind current, lifted a meter or so in the air, and then deposited again.
- Coming upon some floating lights that carry you across a field.
- Finding some candles lit underneath a tree where a man had once hanged himself.
- Sensing a dark form that walks past you on the trail, the size of a dog; it walks past again, this time the size of a bull.
- Coming upon an old hag, dressed in ragged clothing, with her breasts hanging out (the *cucu ahuila*).
- Viewing a tall and slim man whose feet are just off the ground and whose head is up in the sky.

These and many other kinds of encounters await the unwary night traveller, who must confront the roused spirits with firm prayers for their salvation from purgatory.

Encounters with the departed souls provide excellent material for subsequent dramatic narration. Here is an excerpt from one such tale, as told by Bautista Juajibioy in Spanish. Two friends are camping in the woods, and one has a dream that something powerful is going to pass by there that night. His friend scoffs at him, and remains in the camp while the other climbs to safety in a tree:

Then all of a sudden he felt it.
A shout from above: "Heee heee,"
and the breeze beside him: fffftt.
After a short while it shouted again:
"Heeee heeee."
ffffffffttt.
And the breeze passed by, even closer.
And the other one from above:
"My God, what is going to happen?"

Well. And it came to shout closer:
"Heee heee."
ffffffttt.
It passed by there.
When he saw it, dressed completely in white, everything.
It came down, it put out the fire.
He saw it from above, it put out the fire.

The storyteller provides the following explanation of a similar event that once befell him:

It was the souls of purgatory,
who asked me to pray for them.
Just like that they told me that they chase people,
the ones who didn't know how to pray for them.
There were two burial mounds there,
the souls of those crushed by falling rocks.
Of course they were suffering there.
They had need of our help.

The concept of the living dead is also evident in the All Souls' Day preparations that are carried out by members of the native communities. If it rains around the first or second of November, the old people say that this is "the tears of the souls of the departed," who are getting ready to return and visit their old haunts. On the eve of All Souls', the families leave out an *ofrenda*, or 'offering' for the recently departed. A table is set, complete with the kinds of foods preferred by the person in real life, for example, with their favorite kind of chicha. Sibundoy natives exclaim, "This is the kind of chicha he [or she] loved best," echoing a phrase recorded at the time of the Spanish conquest (Molina 1873: 48). It is believed that the souls of those family members who have died within the last few years will return and be placated by these offerings of food and drink.

The frightening prospect of encountering a wandering soul colors people's lives in the valley, as the following statement illustrates:

There in my house we always talked about the dead, since we lived in a spot that was surrounded by hills and mountains. And around there they said that a number of spirits existed, and in my house they often said that we shouldn't stray, because we might encounter some spirits on the path. So there they attacked a number of people, several. They told it that they would arrive around seven in the evening. Because in those days it seemed like all of the dead, the unbaptized ones, the *aucas* as we called them, came out to carry off children. My own mother told me that she had heard some crying in the middle of a bamboo patch, in the middle of that grove she heard them crying. But many people tell of spirits, especially white spirits, they often appear in the form of dogs, and they grow larger. They often appear, as they tell it, with a rosary in their hands, they accost you, and they don't let you pass by anywhere. And when you try to run, it seems like your feet are tied, and you cannot move.

As this excerpt shows, the term *auca* retains a modern referent as well as the mythological referent discussed in the previous chapter. In Andean ethnohistory the term refers to a warlike precursor population vanquished by the first ancestors with the help of the thunder deity. In what appears to be a Christian overlay on an indigenous Andean belief system, this same term identifies those souls of the departed who perish in recent times without the benefit of a Catholic baptism, including infants who die before they are baptised and human eccentrics living beyond the pale of civilization. The modern-day aucas walk about with "a rosary in their hands": they are conceived of as wandering souls seeking release from the fires of purgatory. A surprise encounter with these wandering souls takes on the frightening tonality of a nightmare.

These two kinds of spirits, the nature spirits and the souls of the departed, populate the forests, paths, rivers, and houses of the Sibundoy Valley and endow the region with a relentless spiritual presence. In this remarkable melange of ideas, spirits drawn from medieval folk Catholicism rub their airy elbows with indigenous nature spirits, and spirits deriving from Andean prehistory coalesce into contemporary spirits of the unbaptised dead. The precise origin and identity of a particular spirit becomes important when a cure must be sought for an encounter that has sent someone into a state of fright. In order to remove the symptoms of this folk disease, the native doctor must secure a positive identification of the spiritual agent that has intruded in the life of his patient.

As we have noted, the term *huayra*, which translates as 'wind', 'evil wind', 'spirit', and 'spirit sickness', is pivotal in coming to an understanding of the spirit realm in the Sibundoy Valley. It designates the broad spiritual domain, the inhabitants of this domain, and the results of an unfortunate encounter with either forest spirit or spirit of departed souls. In Spanish, the term *mal viento* carries a similar range of meanings, though its usage in the Sibundoy Valley more closely approximates what is usually designated by the Spanish term *susto* (Seijas 1969). The comparable term in Kamsá is *binyea*, meaning 'wind', 'dawn', and 'vision'. These terms signify a strong spiritual power capable of adversely affecting human beings. The presence of the root 'wind' in each of these designations is not purely coincidental, for the spirits themselves are often portrayed as being wind-like, that is, airy presences moving around and through solid objects much in the manner of turbulent or moving air.

Although there is no certain refuge from an encounter with the evil wind, particular activities and places entail especially high levels of risk, and these should be avoided if at all possible. The cemetery or the home of a recently deceased person exposes people to the risk of *animas huayra*, the spirit sickness of the departed souls. Those who wander alone in the mountains or are abroad alone at night run the risk of contracting *sacha huayra*, the spirit sickness of the forest. Children are thought to be especially vulnerable to spirit sickness; they may succumb if they are left to sleep or play alone or if they accidentally fall into the river.

Not every incidence of spirit sickness derives from chance encounters with spirits. The highly effective services of harming native doctors may be invoked by jealous lovers, as well as by envious relatives and neighbors, to inflict spiritual sickness on those who have disturbed their tranquility. The two most common points of tension are unrequited love and disputes over property. Sorcery is often attributed to affinal kin and to neighbors sharing adjacent pieces of land. The *brujos* or sorcerers plant harmful spirit bundles (known in Spanish as *capachos*), work harm on castings of their victims' footprints, or place witchery in food in order to "ruin [the victim's] luck" and leave the person vulnerable to spirit sickness.

Those involved in an encounter with a spirit or harmful spiritual substance are likely to 'take a fright' and gradually or even abruptly slip into a mortal decline. The symptoms of fright are several and severe and may include any of the following commonly observed maladies: fever, rash, nausea, colored diarrhea, headache, dizziness, ugly cough, lack of strength, chills. Haydee Seijas, who examined the medical practices of Sibundoy natives in the 1960s, observed that these physical conditions were associated with spirit sickness only when some extraordinary aspect was present: green diarrhea, an acute cough that refuses to go away, an especially high fever, or peculiar rash (Seijas 1969). Unless treated with the appropriate spiritual medicines, those who suffer from fright are likely to perish in agony. People will often seek prescription drugs for these ailments at first, turning to the services of the native doctors only when these routine medications fail to relieve the symptoms.

Since the spirit realm lies just beyond the world of ordinary apprehension, contact with its elusive but highly influential agents requires special means of perception. Careful attention to dream images and perceptions impinging on the wakeful mind, in consultation with the sayings of the ancestors, can provide considerable insight into the spirit realm. The use of the native medicines provides further vision and, moreover, opens a passageway into this domain of effective forces and causes.

The Sibundoy cult of hallucinogenic medicines forges a tie between this Andean setting and the adjacent tropical forest cultures. The *remedio* complex involves two classes of hallucinogenic substances: *yagé*, as it is known in *lengua geral* throughout the Amazon area, or *ayahuasca*, 'vine of the soul', or 'vine of the dead', as it is known in the Andes; and *borrachera*, extracted from the tree daturas or *Brugmansias* that abound in the Sibundoy Valley. These medicines are thought to provide an entrance to the spirit realm; they are used for medicinal purposes under the supervision of the native doctors. The two kinds of hallucinogens have distinct origins, effects, and uses. They are generally consumed separately, though on occasion some juice from the tree datura will be added in to strengthen the effects of yagé.

Yagé is known locally as *ambi huasca*, 'the medicine vine', or just *huasca*, 'the vine'. It comes from two closely related species of the genus *Banisteriopsis*, *B. caapi* and *B. inebrians*, lianas or climbing vines of the Amazonian forests. The medicine is prepared by pounding into a mush chunks of wood taken from the stem and trunk of this vine. The mush is then boiled in water with a number of additives. The dark-colored, highly viscous liquid that emerges contains significant concentrations of the psychoactive alkaloid harmine (Schultes & Hofmann 1979).

The consumption of yagé has been a salient dimension of the shamanism of the Sibundoy Valley from time immemorial (Taussig 1980). Frank Salomon (1983: 416) reports on a curing ceremony directed by a Sibundoy shaman in the early part of the eighteenth century, involving the use of "a potion of a forest vine" that caused the patient to expel "through the mouth, as vomit, something like white eggs, and then lizards, bumblebees, and centipedes, which amazed everyone." Yagé remains a major component in the native doctor's practice, but as Schultes & Hofmann (1979: 122) correctly observe, it is far more than the mere tool of a shaman: "It enters into almost all aspects of the life of the people who use it, to an extent equalled by hardly any other hallucinogen. Partakers, shamans or not, see all the gods, the first human beings, and animals, and come to understand the establishment of their social order."

Although sometimes grown in the gardens of the native doctors (Bristol 1968), yagé usually reaches the Sibundoy Valley already in solution, through a vertical trade network between indigenous peoples in the lowland and highland portions of the territory of Putumayo. The native doctors of the lowlands are highly respected for their skill in preparing the medicine vine, and their visits are fondly anticipated by members of the highland communities. The lowland trading partners of the native peoples of the Sibundoy Valley are known in Inga and Kamsá alike as *amigos*. The amigos are Inga-speaking peoples living along the rivers that fan out at the base of the Andes and flow together eventually in the mighty Amazon River. They bring different varieties of yagé to the Sibundoy Valley, potions that differ in regard to source, means of preparation, additives used, and range of psychotropic effects. The two most common varieties are *culebra huasca*, 'snake vine', said to induce visions of snakes crawling about one's feet, and *tigre huasca*, 'jaguar vine', said to induce visions featuring the jaguar. These visionary effects are referred to in Spanish as *la pinta*, the "colorful" shapes laden with spiritual meanings.

Unlike yagé, borrachera is prepared by native doctors in the Sibundoy Valley from the *Brugmansia*, an ancient South American cultigen related to datura and the North American jimsonweed. The leaves and flowers of the various species of *Brugmansia* are crushed and mixed with water to make a potent juice. Richard Schultes, who carried out botanical fieldwork in the Sibundoy Valley, reports on the extensive use of borrachera there (Schultes & Hofmann 1979: 130): "Perhaps no locality can equal the Valley of Sibundoy in the Andes of Colombia for *Brugmansia* use. The Kamsá and Ingano Indians use several species and a number of local cultivars as hallucinogens. The Indians of this region, especially shamans, have a developed knowledge of the effects of these plants and grow them as private possessions."

Several distinct cultivars are recognized, only a few of them serving as hallucinogens. Thus *buyes*, with a high concentration of tropane alkaloids, is employed mainly to relieve rheumatism, and *biangan* is used by hunters and also added to the food of hunting dogs. The major cultivars used for their psychoactive properties include *quinde* ('hummingbird borrachera'), the most widely employed variety, and *munchira*, the most toxic. A closely related cultivar, *Methysticodendron amesianum*, known locally as *culebra borrachera*, is renowned for its powerful psychotropic effects. If the lowland doctors are skilled in the preparation of yagé, the Sibundoy native doctors are respected for their expertise in the handling of borrachera. Not only Ingano amigos, but also members of the far-flung Siona, Huitoto, Kofan and Kwakier indigenous groups come to the Sibundoy Valley in search of this powerful remedy, participating in what one informant called "an exchange of medicines."

The effects of borrachera can be very severe, including (as I was told) a permanent loss of memory. As a result, its use is confined primarily to the native doctors, some of whom are famous for their ability to dominate this powerful drug. Whereas yagé may be taken as often as twice a week by the native doctors, borrachera is taken only once every three or four months. Borrachera is not used for ordinary curing rituals; instead, its use is restricted to cases of strong witchery. As one Ingano friend told me:

The snake borrachera is not used for curing, but rather to add a sickness to someone. If you take it, you will just see a bunch of snakes, you will find yourself in the middle of snakes. They say that if someone has done you harm, you can take borrachera and do harm to that person so that they cannot be cured. That person will necessarily die. Or they will have to find someone who can take it stronger than the other. Those who can take borrachera are greatly respected by everyone else. People don't want problems with them. They might say: "If I have a problem with him he will send me an evil, and I won't be able to find a cure, and I will die."

Along similar lines, Michael Taussig (1987: 408) reports from his conversations with a Sibundoy native doctor that borrachera has the effect of *hardening* people, in the sense of closing them off to the danger of attack through sorcery.

The remedies, yagé and borrachera, are the stock in trade of the native doctor, who uses them in his commerce with the spirit realm. A young boy able to manage the effects of the medicine vine is thought to have promise as a potential native doctor. Apprenticeship to a practicing native doctor involves the consumption of increasingly larger doses until the apprentice has mastered the drug. This mastery allows him to freely enter the spirit realm under the influence of yagé or borrachera. As a practicing Kamsá doctor explained to me: "The training of a doctor consists in taking yagé and borrachera, which allows one to enter the spirit realm and converse with the spirits of plants and animals. If someone is doing harm, then one can discover exactly who it is." Those who master the use of hallucinogenic remedies are said to acquire the spiritual power of the aucas; they can return in spirit to the ancestral world, that moment of brute spiritual power on earth, and transform themselves into animal familiars.

Yagé is much more widely used than borrachera. Every member of the community will imbibe a small portion of yagé at least once a year, as a kind of physical purge and renewal of spiritual contact. Moreover, a number of treatments and cures performed by the native doctors involve imbibing yagé, generally by patient and doctor alike. In these ceremonies, people approach the spirit realm through yagé in order to gain vision, for example, to "see" what a distant loved one is doing or to "see" the source of a spiritual sickness that currently afflicts them or some member of their immediate family. Yagé is used in ceremonies designed to cure or strengthen the person, as in curing rituals aimed at procuring a good planting hand for women or protecting a household from spiritual danger.

The remedies are able to forge an entry to the spirit realm, and they are often cited as an additional source, along with God and the ancestors, of the wisdom packaged into the sayings of the ancestors. As one Ingano woman stated, in reference to the sayings: "My deceased father, after taking yagé, used to speak like this." In the mythic narrative of the Sibundoy Valley, the remedies are closely associated with divination and the acquisition of spiritual power. The central importance of the remedies in the traditional worldview can be appreciated in "The Story of Shaking Lake," a remarkable myth telling of the Spanish conquest and the survival of the indigenous peoples of the Sibundoy Valley. In a performance in Inga by Francisco Tandioy, the coming of the Spanish is foretold by the mortal fall of a hawk.

Our ancestors were accustomed, it is said,
to drink many remedies, even more than we drink now.
Drinking these remedies, they could see, it is said,
the shape of things to come.

And one time they were drinking yagé and borrachera,
and suddenly a hawk, it is said, flew past,
and that bird fell dead on the patio.
And then they said: "Oh my God, what will happen?"

And when they asked this,
the best drinkers of remedy among them answered:
"People from another place will arrive here,
they will arrive from another land, flying,
and they might come to deprive us of our lands."

Saying this, they began to consult among themselves,
and to consult with the native doctors of Sibundoy.
And consulting among themselves, they said:

"And now we must drink more yagé and borrachera,
in order to see why the hawk fell to its death."

And truly the best doctors of Sibundoy and of our people,
some three or four nights without rest,
began to drink yagé and borrachera, it is said,
to see why it fell this way.

This prolonged session with the remedies produces the following prophecy:

"They will come from afar to deprive us of our lands.
Those men will not be good like us.
They will speak another language.
They will come to deprive us of our language,
and we will have to learn their language.
And some of us will dress like those men."

The sessions with the remedies indicate that there is no way to prevent this turn of events from taking place. However, a partial solution is found: gold must be collected from each family, and a small golden figure must be buried in the middle of the Shaking Lake, a lake that lies in the middle of the Sibundoy Valley. The golden image is buried there to the accompaniment of the chants, spells, and dances of the native doctors, who have consumed remedies for this occasion. In a final prophetic statement, the narrator links the survival of the native peoples to the perseverance of the golden figure:

If they remove that image,
the entire valley will turn back into a lake,
and all of us will come to an end.
The valley will surely fill up with water,
and none of us will be able to escape.

We are told that many have tried to extract the image, but the remedy-induced spells left by the native doctors have created impenetrable obstacles: large snakes that prevent access to the lake, sudden violent thunderstorms, large black dogs, and ducks with eyeballs of fire.

This myth illustrates the intimate connection between the remedies and the practice of the native doctor, as well as the capacity of the remedies to produce spiritual vision and spiritual power. With the aid of the remedies, the native doctors are able not only to see, but also to act, in reference to the spirit realm. They divine the future and acquire the means of partially altering that future. The remedies place them in contact with the spirit realm, and they are able to properly interpret the falling of the hawk, and devise a solution that will guarantee the survival of their peoples after the cataclysm of the Spanish conquest.

"The Story of the Shaking Lake" provides a charter for the modern-day practice of the native doctors. The use of remedies to enter the spirit world, the visionary acts of diagnosis and prophecy, and the provision of spiritual antidotes, all remain within the expertise of the native doctors of the valley. In contrast to the portrait of the native doctors in this myth, the modern doctor of the valley serves individuals and families rather than the community as a whole. The shrinking role of the native doctor over the last few centuries corresponds to a general loss of political autonomy that has affected this indigenous enclave. Even so, as in colonial times, the curers of the Sibundoy Valley are renowned throughout a large area of the north-central Andes, and people travel many miles to the Sibundoy Valley in search of cures, just as the native doctors cover a vast territory plying their age-old trade.

In both Inga and Kamsá, the word for native doctor derives from the root 'to know', *tatxumbwa* in Kamsá, and *yacha* in Inga. The association between knowledge and power is very ancient in the Andes: the precolumbian creator god was known by the name *pachayachachi*, "knower or creator of the world" (Demarest 1981). In the Inga language, we find an extensive vocabulary naming the native doctors of the valley. The most common appellation is *yacha*, often in combination with *sinchi*, meaning 'strong', thus 'strong knower' or 'powerful doctor'. Likewise, the word *sinchi* can stand by itself as a means of referring to the native doctor. A fundamental distinction is made between the *ambidur sinchi*, 'curing doctor' (from the Inga root *ambiy*, 'to cure') and the *dañudur sinchi*, 'harmful doctor' (from the Spanish-derived Inga root, *dañuy*, 'to harm'). The latter is also known as a *jiru yacha*, 'evil doctor', from the Inga root *jiru* meaning 'ugly, evil'. Finally, the native doctors from the Lower Putumayo who bring the yagé are known as *sinchi yacha amigo*. The connection between the use of the remedies and the practice of native medicine is so strong that the native doctors can be referred to as drinkers of the remedies, in expressions like *yapa upiag*, 'one who drinks a lot', and *upiadur*, 'drinker'.

The Inga vocabulary for naming the native doctors indicates that a few broad categories are recognized: curing doctors, harmful doctors, doctors from the Sibundoy Valley, doctors from the Lower Putumayo. The Spanish vocabulary reinforces the central distinction between the curing doctor, who "does it in the proper way," and the doctor "who goes about doing harm." Members of both indigenous communities use the term *médico*, literally 'doctor', for the good doctor, and *brujo*, or 'witch', for the doctor who deals in harm.

How does one get to be a native doctor? In early childhood, the adults take note of the young boy's capacity for drinking the medicine vine. For example, Francisco Tandioy tells of his experience with the remedies as a child:

In my house there were seven of us and we all took the remedies. And I remember that they used to give me presents, the more I drank the more presents they gave me. Because the more you can handle, the stronger you are. And so at first I would drink two cups of yagé. Later I remember I would drink as many as five. And even with five they would tell me that no, I could drink more, that I must be stronger. I know that every time they increased my dosage.

There is a general notion that the future native doctor must be chosen, that is, selected by events outside of his own volition. One hurdle is the finding of a quartz crystal, the *huayra huahua*, a kind of spiritual lens used in curing ceremonies to obtain vision and knowledge. It is said that these distinctive crystals, of cylindrical shape and just large enough to fit within the palm of the hand, originate when lightning strikes the ground by the edge of a river. Such crystals are not easy to find and appear only to those who have mastered the remedies and are destined to become native doctors (Vollmer R. 1978).

Another pattern for the selection of native doctors is that of abduction by spirits of the forest. We have already discussed a number of mythic narratives involving human beings who enter the spirit realm, take a drink of a strong potion, and return to society to become powerful doctors. Here is an account given as a true story by an Ingano woman:

My deceased father used to tell it, they say that the *salvaje* spirit is something like a woman you will meet, they say that she hides people. They say that she will hide you for three days or a week just right there, you will be looking for the trail but you won't be able to find it. They say that she hides people in order to teach them how to cure.

They say that's why my father was such a good doctor, around here he was known as a very good curer. He went deep into the forest and they hid him for a week. Just in the same place he walked about. My brother-in-law Hernando also told how he was hidden. At one time he had a white dog. He went into the forest with it, that time that he was hidden. As he went into the forest, a woman kept walking just ahead of him. She had long hair down to the heel of her feet, that woman. The poor dog, feinting, jumping, barking, he chased her. Finally that poor dog just fell behind. My brother-in-law Hernando was just about half crazy, that woman fooled him like that. Since he saw a beautiful woman, he pursued her.

Good and evil doctors alike traffic in the spirit realm, the one to cure, the other to inflict harm. They make use of the remedies and heed the time of the month, week, and day. As we can learn from the sayings of the ancestors, the good doctors take the remedies on the eve of the full moon. Their practice avoids the evil times of week and the evil times of day. The witches, on the other hand, take the remedies in the waning moon or on the eve of the full moon but with the red pepper (saying 123), which has the effect of reversing the polarity of their efforts.

The curing doctors tend to specialize in certain kinds of spiritual disorders. Some of the native doctors are experts in spirit sickness resulting from encounters with spirits of the forest, whereas others are more competent to cure those who have suffered harmful encounters with the souls of the departed. Those who work with the spirits of the forest recognize different procedures depending on whether the spirit sickness derives from the *duende*, an elflike forest spirit, or the *salvaje*, a forest spirit who appears in the form of a beautiful woman. Encounters with the different masters of the natural elements, for example, with the rainbow, the master of the forest, or the master of the river, produce different symptoms and call for different curing rituals.

Perhaps the most important work of the curing native doctor is the curing ritual known as *sinchiyachiy*, 'to make strong' (from the root *sinchi*, 'strong', with a verbalizing suffix *-ya*, and the causative suffix *-chi*). This ceremony insulates the patient from the ravages of spirit sickness. It may be requested for any number of reasons, for example, to strengthen the hand of a woman who will be planting corn:

In order to have good corn, my father would have them blow on the hands, he would have the hands cured. Neither bird, nor mouse, nor any other animal would find the seed. That's what he would do. In the old days, people would have their hands cured drinking of the medicine vine. All of my older sisters had their hands cured. In those days everyone lived by the cures, everything was cured, even to avoid sickness. For all things they entreated the doctors to perform cures, for the chicks, the dogs, everything. We would ask the doctors to perform the cures. That's how things were.

Although this statement places the curing rituals in the past, I found plenty of evidence for their persistence into the present. To this day native doctors are called upon to cure all manner of things: people, animals, and property such as houses and other possessions. These cures are thought to protect the cured object from spiritual harm, resulting either from a surprise encounter with the spirits or from the work of a harming doctor. A cured hand produces good corn; a cured house admits no evil influences from the outside; a cured domestic animal will fatten well and will not be struck with sickness or lost to thieves. The process of curing involves gaining an accurate vision of the alignment of spiritual forces and then entering the spirit realm to produce a more favorable realignment. The well-cured person and his or her family are said to enjoy good fortune or "luck."

The curing rituals feature a charismatic performance by the native doctor, who must enter the spirit realm through the remedies, and carry out the appropriate rites to ensure the spiritual health of his patient. The family requiring the cure must solicit the expertise of the doctor. He must be invited to partake of a good meal, preferably with some pieces of chicken and plenty of fine chicha. Often enough the doctor expects to receive a bottle of aguardiente, the commercial sugar-cane distillation.

If the ceremony includes drinking yagé or borrachera, the doctor will prepare a table with several articles on it. It should be noted that the selection and arrangement of items on this table does not display the cosmology in a systematic fashion, as in some curing rituals reported in other parts of native America (Sharon 1978). For a yagé session, the table includes the bottle containing the dark-colored yagé; a clump of sacred branches; some pieces of bark and leaves from various plants; and some *copal*, an incense-producing resin. The sign of the cross is made by doctor and patient, a prayer to Saint Anthony or some other protective spirit is recited by the doctor, and the first portion of remedy is administered, generally to doctor and patient alike. After a while, several other small cups of the potion may be consumed. Following a brief bout with nausea, the hallucinogenic powers of the drug take hold, and the curing ceremony proper begins.

A great many activities are initiated by the doctor in the course of these curing ceremonies:

• ritual blowing, called *tucay* in Inga, a kind of cross between spitting and blowing, in which a fine spray of moisture driven by air is expelled from the mouth onto some part of the patient's body.

• the sucking out and expulsion of evil: the doctor sucks audibly at the extremities of the patient, and then walks out the nearest door and loudly expels saliva from his mouth.

• the rubbing of cotton on the body of the patient to remove a source of spiritual sickness.

• the use of the medicine branches: these are palm branches that have been blessed in the Catholic church on Palm Sunday, and the doctor performs a number of actions with them—he shakes them about the patient in a rhythmic fashion; he rubs the body of the patient with them; he strikes the patient with them; and he burns them to release evil and create a sacred smoke.

• the recitation of charms and spells: the doctor will call on the spiritual harm to leave the body of the patient and on the soul of the patient to return to his or her body.

• the whistling, chanting, and singing: the native doctor produces a thin whistle and muttered chant as he moves about the patient shaking the medicine branches.

• the dancing: as the doctor chants and sings, he moves in a circular fashion about the patient, maintaining a shuffling dance step.

• the use of the quartz crystal: the doctor will have the patient exhale on the *huayra huahua*, literally 'child of the wind', more freely, 'small spirit medium', and then examine this crystal for information concerning the presence of spiritual harm.

• the use of the bark, leaves, and stems of plants, including the *chonduro* (possibly *Piper angustifolium* or *Cyperus hermaphroditus*), eucalyptus, and the *huayrachinga*, the leaf of the guava plant; some of these substances are burned to create an aromatic smoke; others are chewed to form a poultice and applied to the patient's body; others are placed about the entrances to the house in order to ward off evil; still others are ingested by the patient.

 • the use of bathing: water figures as a cleansing element in many of the cures effected by the native doctors; often they will admonish their patients to bathe in a large river on the eve of a full moon.

 • the extraction of spirit arrows and bundles, attributed to the malice of sorcerers: such theatrical effects are regarded with some suspicion by members of the indigenous communities.

The discourse that accompanies the brushing, whistling, dancing, and other activities of the native doctor affords some insight into the conceptual foundations of his practice. In his monograph on the Inga language, Steven Levinsohn (1976) presents in Inga and in English translation the text of one representative curing chant, known generically as *taquingapa* (from the Inga *taqui*, 'to sing'), which translates here as 'chanting to the spirits', performed by Domingo Mojomboy. The performance alternates between episodes of quasi-conversational Inga, in which the native doctor establishes the framework of the curing event and interacts with his patient and others present in the room; and pivotal moments of rhythmic chanting, in which he communicates directly with the spirit realm.

The text is too long to consider in its entirety here, but a brief glance at a few key passages will convey something of its flavor. I have chosen to work from the Inga original, since my understanding of the text differs in a few particulars from that of Professor Levinsohn. The chant opens as follows:

cunahora nuca-lla-ta-ta-mi rima-cu-ni
now I [*del-acc-acc-aff*] to speak [*prog-1st*]
sinchi tigre-pa huahua
strong (doctor) tiger [*poss*] child

Now I myself am speaking,
child of the curing tiger.

At the outset the native doctor establishes his spiritual persona and lineage: the *tigre* or 'jaguar', an animal associated with shamanism throughout the western Amazonian area (Reichel-Dolmatoff 1975).

The doctor then invokes another kind of lineage, that of his father, also a recognized native doctor, whom he portrays in images reminiscent of the *aucas*, the powerful spirit beings of Andean prehistory:

yachacu-sca-mi ca-ni chasa-lla-ta
to learn [*hist-aff*] to be [*1st*] thus [*del-acc*]

imasa nuca huañu-j tayta taqui-dor
how I to die [*nom*] father to chant [*agt*]

imasa ambi upia-spa baila-dor
how medicine to drink [*ger*] to dance [*agt*]

imasa rondador-hua baila-dor
how pan pipes [*inst*] to dance [*agt*]

imasa pluma-cuna-hua baila-dor
how feather [*pl-inst*] to dance [*agt*]

I learned just the same,
how my late father used to chant,
how he used to dance, drinking the medicine,
how he used to dance with the pan pipes,
how he used to dance with the feathers.

The doctor then asserts his readiness to perform the chant, making reference to his consumption of yagé:

cunahora yuya-pi-lla
now to think [*loc-del*]

nuca-ca ambi upia-sca-mi ca-ni
I [*foc*] medicine to drink [*hist*]

y macha-sca-mi ca-ni
and to drink [*hist-aff*] to be [*1st*]

taqui-sa
to chant [*1st,f*]

So now, thinking in just this way,
I have drunk the medicine,
and I am drunk,
I will chant.

The spiritual core of the performance occurs toward the end, when the native doctor enters into a kind of trance and calls upon his allies in the spirit realm:

chondor chondor
chondor chondor

samu-y samu-y samu-y samu-y
to come [nom] to come [nom] to come [nom] to come [nom]

cucu huayra gente-cuna
spirit wind person [pl]

samu-y-cuna samu-y-cuna ja
to come [nom-pl] to come [nom-pl]

Chondor, chondor,
come spirit helper,
spirit helper come
spirit wind people
helpers, come helpers, ja!

The spiritual essence of the chondor is attested here by its association with the 'spirit wind people', a collective designation for
the spirit helpers required to effect the cure.

Each doctor must adapt these curing resources according to his
own genius and the nature of the specific curing occasion. After
the ceremony is over (and it may last several hours), the native
doctor prepares a purge that will protect the patient from any harmful aftereffects; then he makes the sign of the cross and utters a
prayer over the patient before taking his leave. Those who undergo
this treatment often exhibit a renewed sense of vitality and appear
to leave their burdens behind them.

The curing ceremony takes place at the bidding of the patient
or his or her family, in response to some perceived threat to the
family's spiritual health: perhaps someone in the family has suffered an accidental fall, the patient has been drinking and fighting
in town, or a dream has warned of some threat to the spiritual
health of the family. Other specific curing rituals occur in response
to other circumstances: for example, when a member of the family
has taken a fright from an encounter with a spirit of the forest or
a soul of the departed, or when some piece of family property has
been lost to thieves.

One important ceremony for treating spirit sickness is known
in Inga as the *mishachiy*. The root here is *mishay*, which generally
denotes a blessing ceremony for a house or for a recently departed
member of the family. As a curing ritual, it involves the following
procedure: "The one who is with fright must be taken to the doctor.
The doctor, examining, blowing, will prepare the *mishachiy*. They

must heat up some old broken pieces of earthenware, bring water from a large river, perform the cure before breaking the fast, chanting, chanting, thinking also that the illness will leave the one who is with fright. Chanting and thinking like this, they must do the ritual blowing. Otherwise, how will they get rid of the sickness?"

Another cure used to revive those who have taken a fright is the *cusnichiy*, involving the inhalation of a medicinal smoke. Here is a description of this ritual from an Ingano friend:

First the doctor goes to cut some branches from a tree called the *animas sacha* ('spirit tree'), then from the eucalyptus, and along with the sacred branches and then the copal. With all of these he makes a small fire, and when the smoke starts to emerge, he places it by the person so that the smoke falls on him. With the medicine branches he stirs up that fire and has the person inhale a good deal of that smoke. With that the doctor brushes him with the sacred branches, and works the various cures on him saying that the evil wind must leave him. Not only this, but he has him take a little bit of those ashes inside as well, he prepares a tea. And they say that if you do this several times, you will be more or less cured.

The native doctor's use of the medicine branches to effect these cures underscores the accommodation of an indigenous religious system to the state religion of the conquerors. Catholics in the Andes (as elsewhere) participate in the ritual blessing of the palms, taking their palm branches to church on Palm Sunday and having them blessed by the priest. These branches are then burned throughout the year in association with home remedies and curing ceremonies. In addition to the layman's uses, the sacred branches constitute a central curing resource in the practice of the native doctor. The following description illuminates some of these uses:

One goes to the woods to cut a branch of the palm tree. From there we take it to church on Palm Sunday and we keep it all year long. It works for all kinds of sickness, it isn't just for one kind of sickness. Often when one takes a fright, they use the branches, when they say there are bad winds about, or when there are evil hours. So when they say that you have taken a fright, they brush you with those, and they strike you with those. They strike you on different parts of the body, they do it like whipping someone, but after wrapping them into something like a broom. They say that those sacred branches have

the power to attract the sickness and remove it. Then they put
fire to it, they burn it, and with the smoke, they make the
smoke fall again on the sick person, and then they say that
with the smoke goes the sickness also.

The native doctors are frequently consulted in cases of robbery,
with the hopes of recovering the stolen goods, apprehending the
thief, or returning harm to the person that has committed the theft.
In addition, the injured party will request that the doctor cure the
house, since in entering it the thief has ruined its luck or subjected
the house and its residents to possible spirit sickness. The procedure is as follows:

The owner will have to pay someone to cure the house. In order
to bring the doctor he will have to pluck at least two hens,
provide eggs, and also make certain that there is aguardiente
and chicha on hand. They take a wad of cotton and rub it where
there are signs of the thief, they wipe the cotton there and show
it to the doctor in order to find out who the thief is, whether
the thief is from far off or nearby, whether he is a relative. And
often the doctor will be able to tell them. And he also tells
them if they are going to find their things, whether the thief
has already sold them or given them away. Sometimes the doctor tells them that they are going to find their things. But often
he says: "No, he already sold it, and he is buying drink with
the money right now. All you can do it watch him pass by,
drunk out of his mind, laughing right in front of you. You are
going to see him drunk."

The native doctor is his client's agent in the spirit realm. In
order to secure his services, you must provide him with a sump-
tuous meal and a good supply of aguardiente and chicha. Using the
remedies, yagé and borrachera, as visionary aids and timing his
journey according to the phases of the moon, he will enter the
spirit realm and rearrange the forces there to the advantage of his
client. Members of the indigenous communities of the Sibundoy
Valley evince high respect for the curing doctors, the ones who use
their spiritual powers to fend off evil, to bolster people's spiritual
health. Their attitudes toward the harming doctors stand in direct
contrast. One Ingano woman expressed this ambivalence in the
following terms:

Now we are foolish, as my father used to say. Now the doctors
don't even want to do us this favor of performing the cures
properly. You entreat the doctor at considerable expense, but
in vain, he will do nothing, as my father used to say. Starting
now, in some place, people are sure to be looking for a doctor,
but the doctors aren't good for anything. That's what he said,
and sure enough, the young doctors are only good for creating
evil spells. If you ask these doctors to do harm to someone,
they will do a fine job of it.

People are less willing to talk about the practices of the harming
doctors, and their craft remains largely shrouded in mystery. The
sayings of the ancestors suggest that these doctors traffic in the
murky sectors of the spirit realm that curing doctors avoid. They
use yagé in combination with the fierce red pepper; they adjust
their spiritual journeys to coincide with evil points and evil hours;
they go about doing harm instead of curing. Frequently, the harming doctors work with spirit bundles containing dirt, excrement,
stones, hair, and bones. These bundles are buried in the home or
path of the intended victim, or they are hung in a nearby tree. In
other cases, the harming doctor is said to remove the footprint of
the intended victim or to cast witchery into his or her food.

In the traditional Sibundoy worldview, the spirit realm is the
arena where human fortunes are sealed, where the many puzzling
turns of fate that afflict the human condition have their ultimate
source and explanation. The living people are not alone but rather
surrounded by meddlesome spirits of the forest and spirits of the
unquiet dead: as one Ingano informant has it, "We are full of enemies here." Contact with the spirit realm may bring positive or
negative results, depending on the circumstances. Surprise encounters with spirit presences are almost always unpleasant and
frequently lead to sickness and even death. In contrast, images
culled from dreams are a source of useful knowledge about the
spirit realm. The drug-induced visions provide further illumination
of the spiritual domain. In the hands of the spiritual experts, the
native doctors, the hallucinogenic remedies confer not only extensive vision, but also the power to modify the alignment of spiritual
forces.

One cornerstone of human interaction with the spirit realm is
the corpus of traditional sayings preserving the teachings of the
ancestors. The sayings, with roots in the primordial reality, facili-
tate a decoding of ordinary experience and a recovery of its un-

derlying spiritual import. In the light of the sayings, the spirit realm
becomes an invaluable resource, pliable to human purposes. Its
many secrets relating to the health and prosperity of individuals
and their families can be plumbed through a process of everyday
divination, and preventive or remedial strategies can be devised.
The wisdom of the sayings, confirmed through cosmos-revealing
yagé experiences, constitutes the best available means of "following in the footsteps of the ancestors," and accomplishing the Sibundoy version of the well-lived life.

6

The Cycle of Code Application

The sayings of the ancestors are imbued with the aura of ancestral times, that period of unbridled spirituality that continues to reverberate in the underlying reality of the spirit realm. In view of their continuity with the wisdom of previous generations, it might be tempting to think of the sayings as an antiquated heirloom, but nothing could be further from the truth. The sayings and the system of belief and practice surrounding them remain a vital force in the lives of the present-day generations. As one young Ingano told me, in reference to the corpus of sayings: "And so one believes in these things, they tend to come true. So we always live according to the proverbs."

In recent years, the native peoples of the Sibundoy Valley have become increasingly assimilated into the social, economic and political life of the Colombian nation. The Spanish language is sometimes heard in the veredas; new houses are often built according to the national prototypes, with cement floors and ceramic-tiled roofs; the cumbias and vallenatos of Colombian popular music, or Ecuadorian-style sanjuanitos blare from battery-operated radios, tape recorders, and record players; electricity and potable water have begun to arrive at the more accessible veredas, the ones along the national highway. But modernization in the material sphere does not necessarily entail a radical modification in worldview. The sayings appear to exercise less of an influence on those members of the native communities who achieve higher levels of education or travel to other parts of the Americas. But those who remain in the Sibundoy Valley or return to it regularly participate in the traditional folk religion and continue to guide their lives by the sayings.

The maintenance of spiritual health is surely the most serious function associated with the sayings of the ancestors. People em-

ploy a range of tactics in seeking to establish and retain this blessed
condition: they go regularly to the Catholic mass; they maintain
a home altar to the Virgin and the Saints; they have the native
doctors "cure" their homes, their persons, and their possessions;
and they consult the world of everyday experience and dreams for
clues that can be interpreted in light of the sayings of the ancestors.
The intended result of all these efforts is the resilient 'luck' that
emanates from sound spiritual health.

Even in the flush of apparent success in life, one must be on the
lookout for spiritual sickness, which results from the harmful intervention of some spirit being, either a departed soul or a spirit
of the forest. This chapter focuses on the application of the sayings
to particular life circumstances, in order to show how this interpretive code plays a part in people's calculations as they face
the pressures and problems of everyday living. The sayings possess
a logic and a frame of reference all their own, external to the human
dramas to which they are applied. These "out of context" traditional expressions must somehow be integrated into the inchoate
flow of human experience, in a manner that yields useful information. We must address each dimension of the process of code
application: the internal logic of the code, and its adaptation to
actual circumstances.

THE CODE

Each saying proposes one or more links between terms that may
be states, perceptions, actions or events. The first term, generally
expressed in the conditional mode, is presented as either a sign or
cause of the second term, which generally takes the form of an
undesirable or, occasionally, a desirable stroke of fate. The sayings
originate and terminate in the everyday world, but they incorporate
a "spiritual operator" that enriches understanding in the process
of interpretation. The spiritual operator, grounded in the ultimate
reality of the spirit realm, postulates the esoteric association between precursor experiences and subsequent events. These bonded
terms constitute the framework for all practical applications of the
code.

The sayings activate a symbolic logic binding antecedent to
consequence, and these linkages are a matter of implicit faith for
members of the native communities. People produce rationaliza-
tions—some of them quite traditional, others more improvised—

but they never question the truth of the associations between signs
and outcomes articulated in the sayings. In a sense, then, the internal logic of the code is immaterial to its application in the real
world. It doesn't really matter why a dream of chicha means rain
the following day (saying 93) whereas a dream of aguardiente foretells a day of sunshine (saying 91). To this extent the sayings resemble superstitions—that is, beliefs held in the absence of a
developed explanatory device.

However, even if the associations designated in the sayings are
in some sense independent of a supporting rationale, the Sibundoy
natives are not indifferent to the underlying conceptual foundation
of their sayings, and they produce a range of explanatory ratio-
nalizations. As already noted, they attribute the accuracy of the
sayings to God, to the ancestors, and to the spirit realm (contacted
through visionary experience). Moreover, they develop companion
rationales for specific sayings, explanatory motives that pivot on
a symbolic logic linking antecedent to consequent by virtue of
proximity or some common attribute.

Let us inspect some of these available rationales, for insight into
a native theory of the logic that binds together the terms enun-
ciated in the sayings. Consider two sayings that make recommen-
dations concerning the behavior of pregnant women. These sayings
mark a strong concern for the safe arrival of children, who are much
loved and valued within the community. Until recently, most
childbirth took place in the home, under the supervision of the
native midwives. In spite of the much-attested skills of these
women, death to the mother, the child, or both during childbirth
has been a serious problem, and a number of sayings are concerned
with the proper care of the pregnant woman.

One of these, saying 177, warns that the pregnant woman should
not eat the roasted corncob "from the nose down." The rationale
for this saying is that "if they turn the cob around, the child will
turn around in the mother's stomach." This rationale equates the
fetus and the corncob, or perhaps better, the action of reversing
the position of the corncob and the shifting of the position of the
fetus within the pregnant woman. The underlying, unstated metaphor associates the fertility of the woman with the fertility of the
earth. It is worth noting that the corncob grows on the stalk with
the "nose" at the top; this saying advocates a procedure in harmony
with natural processes that are defined by Sibundoy worldview as
especially relevant to the targeted area of human concern.

Another saying (174) states that the pregnant woman should not carry a basket on her head, lest she experience a difficult birth. The following rationale is provided: "So they say that it will be as if the baby in the mother's stomach were held in a basket." Here, the contiguity of a human artifact, rather than an action performed by the woman, creates the harmful result. The basket, like the womb, is a *container*; its property of containment may be inadvertently transferred to the mother's stomach and complicate the birth. This saying, like many others, has a subtext, instructing husbands not to demand too much labor from their pregnant wives, who must conserve some strength for giving birth.

Consideration of these sayings and their rationales points to a logic of *symbolic contamination*, allowing items that share some quality to "infect" people's fate when brought into untimely proximity. The spiritual operator active in the sayings imposes a symbolical coherence on the chaos of experience, in accordance with the constitution of the spirit realm, an ultimate reality pared down to effective forces and causes. There are two tiers in the process of symbolic contamination: the resemblence between the two terms in the sayings, which generally possess some common attribute or quality; and the fateful "drawing together" of these analogized signs in the life of some individual. This moment of proximity, the insistent presence of some dream image or wakeful observation, projects the transfer of likeness into the material circumstances of people's lives.

The native rationales assign both an indexical and causative efficacy to the associations embedded in the sayings. There are sayings that attribute a *causal* symbolic contamination: the likeness associating the two terms in the saying is automatically transferred into a person's life by virtue of the presence of its sign or portent. Feeding corn to the chicks on corn planting day might effectively "ruin the hand" of the woman who does so (saying 128). Other sayings lack this element of direct causality and merely indicate the existence of a change in condition that has occurred through a separate agency. Thus the dream of a deer does not cause spirit sickness so much as indicate the presence of spirit sickness.

The feature of structural homology underlies some of the associations between terms in the sayings. Consider a pair of sayings concerning the availability of clothing:

Dreaming the leaves of the buitsaja palm,
you are to have clothes. [saying 88]
You are made to dream squash:
you will be without clothes. [saying 89]

The native rationale defines the physical design of these two plants as the relevant feature in these associations: the squash has "a very thin skin" (similar to the 'unclothed' state), whereas the palm leaves are ample (similar to the 'clothed' state). Another consideration emerges in respect to the first of these associations: palm leaves are used for thatching the roofs of traditional houses, so that the leaves may be considered the "clothing" of these houses.

Shared patterns of usage often coexist with structural homologies in creating a perception of likeness between sign and consequence. Consider saying 85: "If you dream bread, lima beans, or corn, / money will come to you or you will find it." The three items named in the conditional proposition (corn, bread, and lima beans) are frequently associated with money. Like money, they are exchanged for goods and services; and like money, they carry connotations of prosperity and good times. The physical design of these objects, their atomistic, countable qualities, may also provide a basis for comparison.

The "dream proverbs" illustrate the indexical component of the tradition. The dreamer is a passive recipient of information originating in the spirit realm. The likenesses between dream image and personal circumstance do not infect the target but rather communicate a condition that has been independently transmitted. Sayings founded on wakeful actions often make reference to actual symbolic contamination. Consider saying 163 and its native exegesis:

If you place toasted grains of corn in your pocket,
and attempt to ford a swollen river,
you will not make it across.

The old people give this advice to their children: "I hope you aren't stuffing your pocket, if you stuff your pocket with toasted corn, when it comes time to cross a large river, if you fall, like toasted corn you will be carried off and you will die."

The notion expressed here is that the children will become as light and buoyant as the grains they carry, and so they will be swept away just as easily by the force of the moving water. At the same time, a more pragmatic purpose is evident, that of discouraging children from hoarding the succulent toasted grains of corn. In any case, the underlying logic is one of direct symbolic contamination: the contiguity of the grains is credited with the capacity to infect the children with their buoyant qualities. The outside perimeter in this chain of causality is the prevailing moral order, which calls for a life in harmony with the teachings of the ancestors.

A similar threat of direct symbolic contamination is present in a series of sayings dealing with prohibitions attaching to those who plant the corn seed. This task is reserved for women known to have a "good hand," which they acquire through curing ceremonies performed by the native doctors, and involving the use of the medicine vine. The sure sign of a good hand is the ability to plant seeds that will not be removed by the birds and other pests, seeds that will develop into sturdy, food-producing stalks. One of these sayings (129) prohibits toasting grains of corn on corn planting day. The rationale states that "you will have to stir the grains on the skillet, and that is like calling the birds." It is thought that women who toast grains of corn on corn-planting day will "ruin their hand"; that is, lose the ability to sow productive fields of corn. In this saying, the resemblance between the two actions, that of stirring the roasting grains and that of moving corn about in the hand to entice the hens, provides the thread of likeness connecting precondition to consequence; and this likeness, under the appropriate conditions of proximity, might actually produce the "ruined" hand.

In some cases, the rationales touch on a possible materialistic logic, in a manner that confounds the tidy demarcation of the spiritual and material. A number of sayings feature those still-flying creatures, the hummingbirds, that abound in the environs of the Sibundoy Valley. The hummingbird is thought to be a messenger of the native doctors (see Allen 1982), and thus occupies a position of some importance in the traditional scheme of things. One saying (123) warns against eating the eggs of the hummingbird, with this rationale: "The hummingbird is always flying about, drinking from one flower after another; you will become thirsty like the hummingbird." Here the consumption of the eggs, a material contamination, is thought to trigger the convergence in appetite.

A similar logic underlies the saying that recommends against giving the cuy's liver to children (saying 164): "They say that they will become like the cuy, so that when it is time to scold or punish them, they will just run under the benches and hide themselves." At first blush, it might appear that the eggs of the hummingbird and the liver of the cuy directly infect the person who consumes them with the qualities of the animals. But such ambiguous cases are rare, and the overwhelming majority of the native accounts focus on symbolic rather than material transference.

Most of the sayings do not carry with them standardized rationales. Generally a plausible symbolic linkage can be discerned, and this is the feature members of the community most often seize upon when they are asked to improvise an explanation of a particular saying. Consider saying 199: "It is bad to pass hot pepper in the hand. / If you receive hot pepper in the hand, / before long you will be against each other." The following rationale was provided upon request: "We are going to become just as hot as the pepper. For any little cause we are going to have problems. We are going to fight. We are going to resemble the pepper." This rationale points to a quality shared by the terms, namely the heat of the pepper and the heat of anger, which can be passed from the pepper to the relationship through the kind of proximal arrangement described in the saying.

The importance of symbolic links between preconditions and consequences in the sayings accords well with the origin of the sayings in the ancestral world, a world imbued with a highly powerful, generative symbolism. In the days of the ancestors, all action was symbolic, in the sense that whatever happened had the potential to transform material reality for all time. Symbolic logic was prevalent in those days: acquisition of the heathen's feather headdress brought with it the mind of the heathen, his powerful spiritual knowledge; the rubbing of a spirit cotton, containing a female presence, on the genital area of a man converts that man into a woman; and the actions of the shulupsi bird-woman leave their mark for all time in the appearence of that bird. The mythic narrative of the valley portrays a world constituted by the logic of symbolism.

The spirit realm, a residue of the ancestral world, is similarly arranged, and the actions of the native doctors tap into and mimic its symbolism in their efforts to influence people's destinies. The manifestations of the spirits, the forms assumed by the forest spirits and souls of the dead when they meddle in human affairs, recall the fantastic symbolism of dreams: lights that move in the darkness; formless bulks that gradually take the shape of familiar animals but change shape from moment to moment or grow rapidly larger; humanoid figures that walk without touching the ground. The expulsion of evil is made graphic as the doctor first withdraws the harmful fluids by sucking at the extremities of his patient and then walks to the door to expel the contents of his mouth; the protection of the house is symbolized by his placing a twig of sacred branches over all of its interfaces with the outside world; and the lamentable work of the harming doctor involves the deliberate planting of spirit bundles, with their cargoes of symbolic contaminants, in the paths of their intended victims.

The principle of symbolic contamination is but one statement of a "generic" human theory of magical causation, as shown by the work of Arnold van Gennep (1908), James Frazer (1922), and a host of followers. In the Sibundoy arena, it goes a long way toward explaining the logic of the associations contained in the sayings. However, native exegesis need not be exhaustive in a tradition possessing immanent truth. At a certain point, faith in the ancestors and in the God that watches over all steps in to ensure the validity of obscure concatenations. In these cases, recourse to "imported" analytical constructs can take us beyond native exegesis into a speculative "logical grounding" of the system. For instance, a number of sign-consequence pairs apparently depend upon classificatory dissonance, of the sort discussed by Mary Douglas (1966) in relation to pollution and taboo: a field animal enters the house; an Indian appears mounted on horseback or driving a car. Such sayings intimate a world in disarray, lacking the harmony and balance indicative of spiritual health.

Other sayings are best understood in reference to patterns of thought widely distributed throughout the Andes. Consider a series of sayings that associates dreams of common roots and tubers with the advent of sadness (sayings 12-16). It is reasonable to suppose that this consequence derives from the isolation of roots and tubers from Our Father the Sun and from their proximity to the underworld, a region conceived in the native myths as the abode of mulelike heathens. Or consider the series associating dreams of fat and spilt lard with sickness (sayings 34-36): this would appear to be a manifestation of the belief, well documented in the central and southern Andes, that health derives from the accumulation of bodily fat (Bastien 1978; Isbell 1978; Gose 1986). The set of sayings (71-75) revolving around an association between a dreamed river and legal difficulties presents a similar challenge: in the final chapter of this book, I explore the possible origin of these beliefs in the pan-Andean worship of a thunder deity.

IMPLEMENTATION

The process of implementing the sayings can be discussed in accordance with a sequence of phases defined by attitude and action:

1. Receptivity: people believe that ordinary experience contains veiled meaning;
2. Observation of the signs: a phenomenon is identified as spiritually significant;
3. The invocation of the saying: a particular saying is cited as relevant;
4. Adaptation of the saying: the saying is modified to suit the circumstance;
5. Retroactive affirmation: the ensuing events validate the prognostication suggested by the saying;
6. Preventive or remedial action: people respond to warnings with appropriate forms of action.

With the phase of retroactive affirmation, or preventive or remedial action, the cycle of application has run its course, and the saying of the ancestors has progressed from a condition of abstract possibility to a condition of self-evident necessity. Each cycle attends to a particular life situation while simultaneously confirming the entire interpretive system. The result is a provisional sense of mastery over circumstance, since all that happens finds its place within a coherent framework rooted in the teachings of the ancestors.

The cycle of application maps an abstract grid, determined by the internal logic of the code, onto specific life settings with all their idiosyncrasies. The entire process depends on a readiness to endow routine experience with concealed layers of meaning. This prospective readiness encourages members of the indigenous communities to scan their interactions with natural elements and their own psychical and physiological conditions for the kinds of clues named in the corpus of sayings. Children are indoctrinated into this system at an early age, as can be seen by the numerous sayings that are geared to their instruction, and individuals continue to develop expertise in this system of everyday divination throughout their lives.

The implementation process begins when someone moves beyond this state of receptivity to a perception explicitly identified as consequential. A dream image that stands out clearly in the person's mind the next morning, or notice of some striking event in wakeful experience, triggers awareness of a pertinent saying, and the "mythic consciousness" inherent in the sayings is brought to bear on the flow of real-world experience. At this juncture people will exclaim: *chi tapiami ca*, 'That is a sign'.

The fit of saying to circumstance is achieved by virtue of a certain margin of flexibility, in the content of the saying and in its application to a specific setting. The same empirical sign often has multiple interpretations, and a given eventuality may be signalled by a diversity of signs. The death of a parent, for example, is foretold by dreaming of an altar (saying 1), losing a tooth (saying 5), flying through the air (saying 6), or salt, meat, or cleaning the patio (saying 7). Likewise, the death of a parent may be foretold by the arrival of fleas (saying 98), someone covered by lice (saying 99), or ants entering the house (saying 100). Again, should the dogs howl at night (saying 109), or the owl call by the side of the house (saying 115), the same warning is conveyed. Many of these sayings leave additional room for assimilation to circumstances by stating that someone in the family, not a specific relative, is to die.

By the same token, a single empirical sign may give rise to a number of different interpretations. Consider dreaming about lice. In one saying (63), it foretells a thief from within the family. A closely related dream, of catching lice (saying 64), warns that something inside the house will be lost but does not specify the identity of the thief. Finally, dreaming of pig's lice warns of a thief from among the white people (saying 61). The consequences named in these sayings all belong to a single conceptual domain, that of loss due to thievery, but they encode a fair amount of variability, a characteristic that allows insertion into the multifaceted complexity of real-life situations.

This flexibility within the content of the traditional code favors a creative adaptation to particular circumstances. Many sayings fasten upon a sequence of cues rather than a single appearence of a particular image or sign, and these sequences lend themselves to further elaboration according to finite circumstantial factors. For example, several sayings map out the significance of dreaming a river. The basic scenario is that the dream of a river foretells an interaction with white people (saying 71). The dream of an unfordable river foretells a legal dispute in the court or cabildo (saying 72), or difficulty in any legal transactions (saying 74). Dreaming of an unfordable river that subsequently dries up and becomes fordable, still within the dream, foretells success in any encounters with whites (saying 73). The prevalence of action sequences in the traditional sayings provides a model for spontaneous elaborations of a more ad hoc character as members of the native communities seek to devise applications to their own lives.

Even more interpretive latitude derives from the license to go beyond the terms explicitly mentioned in the sayings. Frequently, the manifest content of the saying functions as a point of departure for wide-ranging idiosyncratic musings. Consider saying 94 and the commentary provided for it:

You are made to dream a person:
the next day that person will arrive.

My mother, when she dreams my sister, as soon as she awakes, she says: "I wonder what's going on with my daughter. I dreamed her like this. Is she well? Is she sick? Maybe she is going to come." There she is expecting something. It depends on the nature of the dream. Often if the dream is sad, then the person is sick. When you dream them very healthy, it means they are thinking of you, and some notice of that person will arrive.

As the commentary makes clear, the elements provided in the saying are only the beginning of the story. This saying actually authorizes a concerted search for meaning that begins with the codified association of precursor and consequent but quickly moves outward to concoct an unprecedented coincidence between dream image or sequence and real-world event. It turns out that the return of the person seen in the dream is only one possibility, perhaps the most salient, among many. One gets the idea that every additional detail contained in the dream may prove to be relevant in fashioning an improvised interpretation. As one informant stated, "Those of us who are intelligent find meaning in the dreams."

Let's consider one reported instance of this technique of dream projection. The starting point is saying 45; notice how this saying is applied to a real-world setting:

You are made to dream
that you travel mounted on horseback:
extremely strong spirit sickness.

Death came to my little brother Salvador when I dreamed like this: as he was walking down the street, a black horse came along dragging a lasso. That horse got him all tangled up in the lasso, it dragged him, carrying him along. Then he died, there was nothing we could do to cure him. A very strong spirit sickness makes you dream that.

Although the facts of this event only partially match the content
of the saying, the informant felt that the dream was close enough
to the prototype to qualify as an authentic warning of this misfortune. This application of a saying entails a number of interpo-
lations: a transfer of subject from self to younger brother; a
modification of the action sequence from riding a horse to being
caught up in the coils of a rope dragged by a horse; and the addition
of an important detail, the color black, which is generally associated with spiritual danger. Notably, the consequence mentioned
in the saying, the onset of severe spirit sickness, remains unaltered.
Even the most ingenious elaboration must preserve some con-
stancy between the surface content of the saying and the situated
interpretation as applied to someone's life circumstances.

Some sayings bring with them a fairly elaborate divinatory tem-
plate. Consider saying 101:

If the firefly should come inside
someone who built the house, the builder or a helper,
is to die before long.
Catching the firefly, they look at it:
if it is covered with hair, a woman;
otherwise, if it is without hair, a man.

This saying moves beyond the passive observation of a natural
phenomenon and implicates the person in a form of active divination. The houses of Sibundoy natives are built through collective
effort; the owner holds a *minga* (collective labor party), providing
food and chicha to all those who contribute materials or labor. As
becomes clear in additional commentary, there are other components to this interpretive scheme. For example, if the firefly moves
toward a particular corner of the house, this indicates that the
person working in that area at the time the house was built is likely
to be the one to die.

By virtue of the flexibility that resides in the sayings themselves,
as well as the interpretive procedures discussed earlier, people manage to adapt the abstract code of the sayings to the practical realities
of their lives. After concocting a plausible interpretation of the
immanent sign, people are generally on the lookout for confirmatory details. In other words, the perception of the sign, along
with the interpretation it stimulates, sets up a pattern of expectation that is fulfilled in the subsequent flow of events. In such
circumstances, members of the native communities scan the ho-
rizon of experience for confirmatory details, and all pertinent mani-

festations are assimilated to the interpretive grid. On some occasions, the true meaning of a dream or some other observed sign only becomes clear in retrospect, as the events in people's lives fall into a plausible pattern.

This pattern of expectation and fulfillment is graphically described in the anecdotes that surround and accompany the sayings of the ancestors. Consider the following instance, involving saying 92, as analyzed by an Ingano woman:

You are made to dream
that you are drinking aguardiente
when they are to give you the medicine vine.

"When I am made to dream that I am drinking aguardiente, someone might come to sell me the good vine, so I can drink it right then and there. When I am made to dream that, it is a very good dream I am having. When I dream that they are giving me aguardiente, then I think: 'Perhaps my little friend is coming, even now she is on her way to make me drink of the good vine.' "

Often the recognition and interpretation of a sign will trigger a rather intense round of anxious internal dialogue. For example, the dream of eggs warns of a fight for men (saying 81): "After having such a dream, a man will ask himself: 'I wonder who I am going to fight with. Maybe I shouldn't go to the fiesta' "; and a beating for women (saying 80): "When a woman dreams eggs then her husband is going to hit her. So they are anxious when they go to a fiesta: 'Maybe this is where he is going to hit me.' "

Warnings that relate to a person's spiritual health are regarded with special concern. The dream of a white dog foretells an encounter with a curing native doctor (saying 40), and this dream can trigger a state of curious readiness:

When you dream a white dog, they say that you are going to encounter someone who knows it properly, one who cures well. In other words, the one who has good thoughts. And so they usually say: "Who will I encounter today?" And they are anxious to find out the next day. They go out to the street and they say: "Ah, I ran into so and so. He must be the one who cures well." They are all caught up in it, you see. And usually at night they think it over: "Let's see, who did I run into? What did I do? With whom? What will he do to me?"

The expectations called forth by recognition and interpretation of the signs generally come to fruition in the unfolding events, and a great many confirmatory narratives are passed along with the traditional sayings. These stories contain a note of triumph as the forecasted consequence really comes to pass. A number of sayings predict the arrival of visitors, and social visiting is of course extremely important in a society lacking the convenience (and distraction) of the telephone. Sayings are very helpful in predicting just who will arrive and when the visit can be expected. The pattern of expectation and fulfillment is evident in the following account concerning one saying of this kind (saying 144), which associates a twitching in the toe with the proximate arrival of visitors: "It isn't natural, you know, that the toe should twitch. And so they say that someone is coming to visit, some friend. And so people are expectant: 'Who is coming to visit?' Often the visitor will arrive and they will say: 'So, such and such is the one.' He just arrives and they say: 'So that's why this was happening to me.' "

A couple of sayings that foretell visits have given rise to proverbial statements that could be classified as politeness formulas. The saying relating the dream of a person to the return of that person has given rise to the oft-heard expression: "No wonder I dreamed you last night." In a similar vein, saying 106 associates the choking or coughing of the cuy with the return of someone who had travelled far away. Visitors are not infrequently greeted with the expression: "No wonder the cuys were choking this morning!" The unwary guest to the valley may take such expressions as mere formalities, as I did at first, and miss their deeper resonance within the native worldview.

Confirmatory narratives strengthen the grip of the sayings of the ancestors on the lives of contemporary natives of the valley. They are graphic illustrations of the validity of the tradition. Taking advantage of the insights offered by retrospection, they spell out the precise implications of warning signals received in anticipation of actual events. Frequently narrators draw attention to their astute readings of the signs, while affirming the intrinsic value of the corpus of sayings. Consider the following story:

One time I dreamed the small woven belt, that I had the woven belt tied and it came undone, in that way I used to tie it to catch my hair. Mother of mine, I was working quickly like this, preparing the earth for planting. I was working along a row, grabbing the weeds with my fist, then cutting, cutting. Again, I had the grass in my hands when it rubbed me here, that rascal, the head of that damn snake. When that cold snake rubbed against me, I threw it aside, as far as I could, along with the grass and all.

This narrative touches on two important cultural domains, those of the *cuadrilla*, the roving labor crews that accomplish most heavy agricultural and other labor; and weaving, a highly skilled activity of the women, who produce belts, scarves, and ponchos that are distinctive forms of native clothing. Dreaming the woven belt warns that a snake is likely to appear at the workplace (saying 95). The association of the snake with weaving is manifested on several fronts: for example, "the belly of the snake" is one of the most popular weaving motifs; and in mythic narrative, the promiscuous bear is sometimes chased off by the use of a woven belt, which he mistakes for a snake, the one creature that he fears. The snake is a major symbol of spiritual power, associated particularly with borrachera and the work of the harming doctor. Its evocation in a dream is always a cause for concern. In this saying, the snake works as a vehicle for bridging two separate cultural domains, those of agriculture and the domestic arts. This capacity to cross intracultural (and sometimes intercultural) boundaries inheres in the symbolic logic of the sayings, as the spiritual operator tends to draw together elements that are dispersed in experience.

Another confirmatory narrative focuses on the picangui bird, a small, dark-brown bird with long legs, slightly larger than a sparrow. The picangui lives above the valley, on the wooded slopes of the surrounding hills, and only occasionally makes an appearence in the valley. Nonetheless, it enjoys a considerable presence in the traditional culture of the native peoples of the valley, appearing frequently in mythic narrative and apparently donating its name to one of the major clans, the Chicunques. According to tradition, this bird taught human beings one of the native flute melodies played at parties after mingas and at other social occasions.

The picangui's association with heat may stem from its call, "chuy, chuy," very similar in sound to the idiomatic expression common throughout the Central Andes, achuchuy, meaning 'hot!' Recall that the picangui is the bird associated with the cooking of chicha in the spiritual abode of the water birds. It is this association with heat that is featured in the saying that concerns us here, saying 187, warning against mocking the call of the picangui, lest one awake scorched by the fire. The narrative of affirmation goes like this: "One time I went into the forest with my aunt, and I started imitating the call of the picangui bird. My aunt scolded me, saying:

'Just wait and see, you are going to wake up burnt.' I don't know, since we were sleeping next to the fire, I woke up the next morning with part of my blanket burnt."

Sibundoy natives frequently modify the course of their actions in response to a perceived warning from the spirit realm. These modifications of behavior may be very slight: for example, altering one's path on the way home because of the unexpected presence of a particular bird or avoiding a party because of a dream that forecasts a possible argument. But in some cases the responses to such warnings are major in scope: for example, abandoning a plan to travel, or undertaking a costly, time-consuming series of treatments from the native doctors. Every application of the sayings is significant, a demonstration of respect for the ancestors, but those sayings that directly implicate a person's spiritual health are of special concern.

Many of the sayings point to remedial or preventive action to ward off the danger posed to one's spiritual health. The sayings are not confined to the role of divination: they carry with them, in some cases, folk medicinal prescriptions designed to adjust the person's standing in the spirit realm. These sayings encode both the warning signals and the appropriate countermeasures. Saying 170 calls for the use of ritual blowing when picking up a child who has fallen: "Picking up a child who has fallen, / if you do not blow at that time, / the child will take a fright." The commentary of an informant reinforces the importance of this remedy: "If all of a sudden a child should fall, then you have to perform the ritual blowing. Generally, as soon as the child falls, we blow on him. Otherwise, he is going to take a fright, and he will be shouting in his sleep." Saying 190 advises as follows: "When burying a deceased one, / if you fail to spit on a clod of earth / and throw it aside, / you will not forget your sadness." As these sayings indicate, the ritual blowing of the native doctor can also figure in Sibundoy "home remedies."

More often, the saying does not recommend a remedy, but the people interpreting the sign decide upon a preventive or remedial course of action. A dream of a black snake (saying 41) is especially troubling, since the snake is the familiar of the harming doctor and the color black is associated with evil. The following statement discusses a variety of responses to this dream:

Just as soon as they dream the snake, they get up and do the ritual blowing. They say that if they don't do that, they will encounter a witch who doesn't cure properly. And that one will entirely ruin your luck. And if for any reason they forget to do the ritual blowing, they say this: "Now I'll have to go see a native doctor." Others don't do this, but instead of doing the ritual blowing, they say: "Well, since I dreamed this, I am going to rub my hand with red pepper." They rub their hands and then the first person they run into, especially someone who is pretty much, well, people know which ones are the doctors and which ones aren't. And so, if that person wants to shake hands, they go ahead and shake hands. So they say: "I didn't take a fright. He took a fright himself. I returned to him that which he wanted to do to me." Because they say that the red pepper returns the intention of the other, it sends it back to him.

Some situations are so threatening that the services of the native doctor are absolutely necessary. Saying 161 warns that striking a child with the hand may cause that child to take a fright, and this condition may become quite serious if the one who strikes the child is a native doctor who has recently taken the medicine vine. The following procedure is recommended: "If you don't have them cured right away, drying up completely they will die, if you can't have them cured. The one with fright must be taken to the native doctor. The doctor will look him over and do the ritual blowing. They will cure him with the *mishachiy*, a smoke-inhalation cure. . . . Otherwise, how will they get rid of the sickness?"

With recourse to preventive measures, the cycle of code implementation has run its course, though the account of yet another successful application of the code may remain in personal and community tradition for some time. In order to underscore the pervasive role played by the sayings in people's lives, consider one final account, involving the application of two different sayings to an unfolding sequence of events. The predicament involves a disputed piece of land, which is contested in both the legal and supernatural arenas. But let's allow the participants to speak for themselves:

So my mother has a quarrel with a relative, the wife of an uncle. My mother wants to recover a piece of land that this wife of her uncle has. It is part of my mother's inheritance, and it is being contested because my mother has the title that they gave to her. And the other woman bases her case only on possession of the land. And so my mother went to Pasto to see a lawyer and prepare a complaint, but it was poorly done. And she took it to the judge's office, but it was poorly done. That complaint was claiming things that it shouldn't claim. And they would have been able to make a counterclaim against her. And so the judge nullified the complaint. And he had my mother sign a statement that she wasn't claiming all that stuff, that all she claimed was the piece of land. Because the lawyer had put in there that she was claiming a bunch of barbed wire, you know, things that shouldn't be there.

These are the machinations on the level of legal intrigue. Their spiritual counterpart (at least on this side of the issue) involves two images that come to the woman in her dreams, and the interpretation she imposes on them. The first dream image, that of jura chicha, a strong chicha prepared from sprouted grains of corn, directly activates a traditional saying (78): "There will be words, / when you are made to dream of thick, thick jura chicha." This saying is generally taken to mean that those who dream jura chicha will come across an angry discussion or find themselves subjected to a scolding.

The young man recalled that his mother spoke of her dream and was quite certain of its significance:

So my mother said: "No, I was made to dream that."
First about the chicha, my mother said: "I dreamed of a thick jura chicha. I was made to dream this, it means words. It's certain that we are going to have an argument with someone. So someone is going to pick a fight with me, or someone is going to come here to quarrel, that is certain."
She was very sure about it. Right about then the judge came by to find out what she was claiming, and she had to listen to a lot of things he was telling her: "Why did you claim that?" and things like that. She said: "You see, I dreamed what has come to pass." It really happened.

The woman's definitive interpretation of the meaning of this dream image is given after the fact, that is, after the judge has arrived to scold her. But according to her son's account, the expectation of a scolding was already in her mind even as the judge approached the house. The saying is applied prospectively to place this woman on the alert, and retrospectively to account for the unraveling of events. In this instance, the dream image and its conventional interpretation fit very neatly into the event sequence.

A second dream image associated with this situation poses more serious problems of application and allows for more creativity in matching the portent to life circumstance. Around the same time, this same woman dreams a mother duck and its ducklings walking into a fire. This dream image activates saying (70): "You are made to dream ducklings: / white people." Dreaming the ducklings puts the person on the alert for an encounter with whites, the Colombian mestizo settlers in the Sibundoy Valley. Relations between Indians and whites are problematic, and a number of sayings reflect the uneasiness with which such encounters are viewed.

In this instance, the woman extracted a great deal of meaning from this dream image, as her son explains:

And concerning the ducks, my mother said: "Surely because of that I was made to dream that. I made the complaint but at the hour of truth, it came out wrong."
She had dreamt about a duck with her ducklings, and she said that the duck stood for the judge and the ducklings stood for the police and the secretary, all those who accompany him. So she dreamed that the duck was on fire, and that the rest of the ducklings also were burned in the fire. Later, when I went to see what was going on, and when I told her that they had nullified it, then she said: "Now, so you see, that's why I was made to dream that. Didn't you just tell me that they nullified the complaint? So that's why I was made to dream that the duck was on fire." The complaint was burned and nullified.

The second saying serves as a springboard for this woman's very creative weaving of a dream interpretation that neatly fits the unfolding pattern of events. The sign here, a dream of ducks, is as specific as its consequence, an encounter with whites, is general. The saying does not state what kind of an encounter, whether friendly or otherwise, but it is usually assumed that encounters with non-Indians in the valley are fraught with uncertainty or even danger.

From this meager beginning, the woman structures an elaborate account tracing a one-to-one correspondence between elements in the dream and elements in the real world. In this account, additional components of the dream are creatively identified with aspects of the situation. The saying provides no charter for these equations, which nonetheless seem plausible enough within the framework it establishes. The main elaborations beyond the content of the saying are the equation of the judge's companions with the ducklings in the dream and the equation of the nullification of the complaint with the burning of the duck and ducklings in the dream.

Note that for all the plausibility of this interpretation, it does not adhere to a strict rationalistic logic. Rather, it follows the capricious flow of the dreamworld itself, as the duck and ducklings at one moment represent the judge and his companions and at a later moment the actual legal document that is destroyed in flames. The total interpretation fuses together three elements: the abstract code (dreaming ducklings means you will see white people); the additional details of the woman's dream (mother duck, ducklings, fire); and the present realities affecting this woman's life (the making and unmaking of a flawed legal document). Each component is essential to the elaboration of the dream interpretation.

This case study illustrates all of the major components of the cycle of code implementation. The receptivity to hidden spiritual meanings is heightened during this period of intense social intrigue, and our protagonist registers two resonant dream images: thick jura chicha and the mother duck with her ducklings. She proceeds to invoke, and in one case, to adapt, the pertinent sayings of the ancestors, bending traditional content to fit the situational moment. The confirmatory narratives we have just sampled remain behind as instructive examples, on the order of morality tales, reinforcing the value of this traditional method of everyday divination.

Daniel O'Keefe (1982: 17) has written that "divination systems mobilize all the permutations and combinations in a society's classification system to focus on and back up one . . . individual. This horoscope . . . seems magically to mobilize the whole cosmos behind him." The sayings of the ancestors routinely encode "permutations and combinations" in the Sibundoy classification system. A spiritual operator endows the commonplace with heightened significance when field animals intrude upon the domestic scene, when a dream image emerges as a metaphor of some real-world situation, or when a twitch in some part of the body brings to mind its normal mission. As noted, the process of symbolic contamination draws together terms from dispersed avenues of human experience. Those who live by the wisdom of the sayings and adapt it creatively to their own lives acquire the blessings of spiritual health, and effectively marshall "the whole cosmos" behind them to ensure health and prosperity.

The salutary effects of a completed cycle of divination can be adduced from comments of Michael Jackson (1978: 134) in reference to a system of divination practiced among the Kuranko people of Sierra Leone: "The diviner's analysis transforms uncertainty into a conditional certainty and his instructions for an appropriate sacrifice enable the consultor to move from inertia to purposeful activity (praxis). He regains his autonomy; he acts upon conditions that are acting upon him." The Sibundoy system, though practiced by nonspecialists in everyday situations, provides a similar avenue to empowerment. The application of a saying to a situation confers a provisional comprehension (and in some cases, a sense of mastery) in the face of life's many disquieting turns.

7

Sibundoy Folk Religion

Sibundoy folk religion is a nexus of popular religiosity defined by three major strands: a pan-Andean cosmological bedrock, a tropical forest ecstatic shamanism, and an overlay of folk and doctrinal Catholicism imposed by the missionaries. Over a period of several centuries, Sibundoy natives have woven these strands into a distinctive spiritual fabric with a remarkable reach among Indians and non-Indians alike throughout the northern and central Andes. Moreover, as Sibundoy migrants have carried their shamanism into the popular sectors of Bogotá, Caracas and other major cities, the impact of Sibundoy folk religion has been felt in regions even further removed from the Sibundoy Valley homeland.

Colombia's Sibundoy Valley is situated within striking distance of the Andean route connecting the great empire of the Incas with territories of the Paez, Guambiano, Muisca, and other Chibchan states to the north and midway along one of the few passable routes linking the tropical forest lowlands to the Andean highlands. We know from ethnohistorical sources that the Incas sustained hostilities with the indigenous peoples of what is now southwestern Colombia, the Pasto nation and the Quillasinga federation (with which the Sibundoy peoples were affiliated). Juan de Santacruz Pachacuti-yamqui Salcamayhua, writing a few generations after the conquest, tells us that Huayna Capac Inca engaged in hostilities with the "Quillasencas" and "advanced beyond Pasto" but quickly returned to Quito. Both Guaman Poma de Ayala (1613) and Garcilaso de la Vega (1609) speak of the Inca conquest of these neighbors to the north, though modern investigations suggest that such claims are greatly exaggerated. In the south of Colombia, at least, there is no convincing evidence that the Incas established the apparatus of colonial government (Romoli de Avery 1978, Salomon 1986a).

It is likely that the territory of the Pastos and Quillasingas, spanning the northern stretches of Ecuador and the southwestern corner of Colombia, enjoyed something of the same social and political autonomy it possesses to this day. The Spanish chronicles depict a physically isolated region intermediate between the centers of high culture to the south and a number of smaller-scale Chibchan nations to the north. The Sibundoy Valley, sequestered across the continental divide and beyond a patch of tundra-like *paramo*, is the least accessible extension of the Quillasinga federation. This difficulty of access afforded the Sibundoy peoples a degree of political independence—it is said that they "paid no tribute" (Uribe n.d.)—but it did not prevent them from participating in trade relationships with their neighbors. We know from the reports of the Spanish chroniclers that the Sibundoy peoples provided affluvial gold and agricultural products to their Pasto neighbors, and that Sibundoy curers were much respected throughout the region (Cieza de León 1883).

The Spanish conquest burst onto this scene with cataclysmic effect. In the fateful mingling of old-world and new-world peoples, the Sibundoy natives, much like their counterparts throughout the Andes, obtained the status of *indios civilisados* ('civilized Indians'), distinguishing them from the "naked savages" of the adjacent lowlands. Members of the Andean indigenous communities rapidly discovered that survival within the colonial system required conversion to Christianity and the adoption of certain aspects of the Spanish life style, especially speech and dress. No doubt many of the Andean groups already thought of themselves as culturally superior to the tropical forest peoples; with the advent of Spanish hegemony, this sense of cultural superiority became couched in terms of a Christian vs. savage dichotomy, and it came to figure as a basic element in their concept of ethnic identity.

The condition of *indio civilizado* conferred some standing within the Spanish political empire. In the early colonial period, it meant that the community was subject to coercion, often of a violent and destructive nature, rather than outright extinction. As the colony developed, it carried important legal rights, such as recognition of lands by the Spanish crown. In 1621 the Spanish *visitador* or royal envoy "sold" the lands of Sibundoy and Aponte to the Indians for 400 ounces of silver (Bonilla 1972: 24). Later, the great *cacique* or "native chieftain" of the Sibundoy Valley, Carlos Tamoabioy, left legal title to these lands to "the people of Sibundoy, Santiago, and Aponte." These transactions form the foundation for the current indigenous land claims, recognized by Colombian law in 1890 but always subject to dispute in the face of outside encroachment.

If the Sibundoy natives gained these blessings, they also surrendered much under the Spanish colonial dispensation. One eighteenth-century commentator reacted as follows to the blatant subjugation of the native population (Bonilla 1972: 35): "These Indians . . . greet travellers by kneeling before them and joining their hands together while muttering the garbled words, 'Most holy sacrament of the altar' as do the other Indians all over the country— a humiliating custom which reveals how arrogant was the religion of the conquistadors." These and other testimonies confirm the forced acquiescence of Andean natives to the newly imposed state religion, in spite of intermittent attempts to resurrect the *huacas* and return to autochthonous religious practices (Molina 1873; Ossio 1973; Lopez-Baralt 1981; Rappaport 1978).

In the face of this involuntary conversion to Christianity, many elements in the precolumbian substrate have persisted, in some cases as underground survivals, in others as components of an emergent synthetic folk religion. The Sibundoy sayings of the ancestors illustrate this second possibility: they betray the stamp of two religious orientations, the indigenous and the imposed, integrated into a syncretic system through an ongoing process of cultural accommodation.

THE ANDEAN COSMOLOGY

A great many elements in the traditional cosmology of the Sibundoy Valley are perhaps pan-human, or at least pan-Amerindian as well as pan-Andean in character. Certain fundamental themes, such as the elevation of the sun and moon to the status of principal deities, the motif of anxiously awaiting the first dawning, the layering of cosmic space, and the belief in successive creations, have their counterparts throughout the Americas and beyond (Eliade 1959; Tedlock 1982; Conrad & Demarest 1984; Bierhorst 1985). Nevertheless, there are elements in the Sibundoy mythology that are particularly evocative of the Andes: the majestic thunder deity, wielding his sling to produce bolts of lightning and thunder; the exploits of his emissary, the primary culture hero, who visits the world to establish order in nature and civilized life in society; and the feminine deities, Mama Quilla ("Our Mother the Moon") and Mama Pacha ("Mother Earth"), closely associated with the agricultural cycle throughout the Andes.

Examination of historical and contemporary sources points to the existence of a pan-Andean cosmology, launched in the civilizations of the remote past, represented in the iconography of the Tihuanaco period and elsewhere, incorporated into the state religion of the Inca empire and in the religious expression of the Chibchan peoples of the Northern Andes, and persisting in the folk religions of modern-day Andean *campesinos*. The core of this worldview—the grandiose thunder god, the worship of ancestors and earth shrines, and the recognition of the heavenly bodies as deities—composes a "theological" backdrop to the sayings of the ancestors.

Inspection of precolumbian religious systems in the Andes, as portrayed in ethnohistorical documents, affords some notion of the general distribution of key elements in Sibundoy Valley cosmology. Knowledge of religious beliefs and practices in the northern Andes is scanty but very suggestive. The culture-hero complex among the Paez, Guambiano and other Chibchan nations of central Colombia, associated with figures like Guequiau (Castillo y Orozco 1877), Bochica (Simon 1953; Triana 1951), and Juan Tama (Rappaport 1978), evinces numerous parallels to Sibundoy Valley motifs. Consider the legendary *cacique* of the Paez Indians, Juan Tama, who closely resembles the Sibundoy Wangetsmuna: "Juan Tama is said to have saved the Paez from the invading Pijao by killing them with a sling given to them by the thunder" (Rappaport 1978: 20). In one variant, the sling received from the thunder god transforms into a "long, green snake" (Rappaport 1978: 36), indicating the presence of a symbolic network that is active in the Sibundoy Valley and elsewhere in the Andes. As in the Sibundoy Valley, the Paez native doctors become the custodians of the spiritual powers acquired through the intervention of the thunder god.

Fortunately, the religious life of the Incas is comparatively well documented, making possible a more comprehensive formulation of the precolumbian substrate. Although differing in some respects from the Sibundoy case, the Incan materials portray in detail the religious outlook of Andean peoples at the time of the Spanish conquest, and thus constitute a most valuable comparative resource. The testimony of Spanish chroniclers and native commentators presents a diffuse upper pantheon that has been described as "an overarching divine complex, a multi-faceted sky god composed of myriad individual aspects" (Conrad & Demarest 1984: 100). The three central facets of this "manifold godhead" are the sky god known as Illapa to the Incas and Thunapa to the Aymaras; the creator divinity and culture hero often referred to by the name Viracocha; and the solar deity frequently subsumed under the label Inti. It appears that the Incas greatly elaborated the solar compo-

nent of this pan-Andean substrate in developing a state religion for
the expanding Incan empire (Pease 1973; Demarest 1981; Conrad
& Demarest 1984).

The Spanish chronicles contain striking portraits of the sky god,
who was primarily associated with thunder and lightning, though
his dominion extended to virtually all of the meteorological phenomena. The following citation from Bernabe Cobo (1956: 160) is
one of the fullest, most colorful of these accounts:

They imagined that he was a man who was in the sky formed
of stars, with a staff in the left hand and a sling in the right,
dressed in shining clothes, which gave that flash of lightning
when he spun about to release the sling; and that the explosion
of this caused the thunderbolt, which occurs whenever the rain
falls. . . . Since they attribute to the thunder the power over
rain and hail and everything else that has to do with clouds
and the region of the air, where these imperfect mixtures are
forged, so under the name of thunder, or as his adherents, they
adored the thunderbolt, the lightning flash, the rainbow, the
rains, the hail, and even the storms, tempests, and whirlwinds.

The thunder deity was conceived as the son, brother, servant,
or messenger of the solar deity; his staff could be represented as a
serpent, lightning bolt, or rainbow. The sling was his prized
weapon, and when he swung it around fiercely he generated the
phenomena we mortals experience as peals of thunder and bolts of
lightning. He was charged with the production of rain, a vital resource in Andean agricultural societies, and his association with
the wind is particularly suggestive in light of the Sibundoy Valley
connotations of huayra, 'wind', as 'spirit' and 'spirit sickness'. Molina (1873: 14) notes that the thunder god was the patron of the
herbal doctors known as camascas, "who declared that their grace
and virtue was derived from the thunder; saying that, when a thun-
der-bolt fell, and one of them was struck with terror, after he came
to himself he proclaimed how the thunder had revealed to him the
art of curing by herbs."

The thunder god of Sibundoy mythology, as pictured in the
Wangetsmuna cycle, appears to be cognate with this mighty pan-
Andean deity. As mentioned in an earlier chapter, the Sibundoy
thunder deity is a grandfather to the culture hero Wangetsmuna
and his older brother, the primordial miner. In the early moments
of cosmic time, the miner searches for affluvial gold at the behest
of this celestial grandfather, in order to provide his sling with balls

of shining gold. Wangetsmuna, the younger brother, accompanies the miner and keeps camp for him. After a series of episodes, the thunder deity comes to the aid of Wangetsmuna, who has outraged the heathen men; spinning about and whirling his sling, he utterly destroys the recalcitrant heathens with bolts of lightning and thunder.

The universe of the sayings is permeated with the influence of this grand celestial figure, even though he is never directly mentioned in the texts of the sayings. The thunder deity, associated with meteorological effects such as rain, sleet, thunderstorms, and wind and possessing a broad range of symbolic manifestations that includes birds, snakes, the rainbow, and the jaguar, lurks in the background throughout the greater part of the sayings corpus. All those sayings that feature the spiritual role of these sorts of physical and metaphorical manifestations derive their force ultimately from the theater of operations of this celestial deity.

Consider the series of sayings dealing with the significance of dreaming an unfordable river (sayings 71-75): the action of rain storms in the mountains causes the rivers and streams of the Sibundoy Valley to swell. When people dream that they cannot make their way across the river, they expect to encounter legal difficulties in the near future; if this same river subsides and allows the dreamer to cross, then all will go well in any legal proceedings. The thunder deity, generally portrayed as a stern authority figure holding court in the celestial reaches, appears to provide the connection between the condition of the rivers (in the dreamworld) and the dreamer's real-world experiences with secular authorities. Here as elsewhere, recourse to the underlying religious framework throws light on an otherwise obscure association preserved in the sayings.

As patron of the Sibundoy native doctors the thunder deity exercises his strongest influence in the sayings. Wangetsmuna, the first healer, received his curing powers from his grandfather, the thunder deity, and the connection between this god and the native doctors remains effective to this day. Recall that the quartz crystal used by the Sibundoy native doctors (the *huayra huahua*, 'child of the wind' or 'spirit medium') is created by the contact of lightning (hurled by the thunder deity) with the earth's surface. Those who find such objects are thought to be chosen as specialists in spiritual matters, notably in the use of the hallucinogenic medicines (Vollmer R. 1978). Particular sayings underscore the association of the thunder deity with native healers: peals of thunder announce the death of a native doctor; the chance appearance of a hummingbird (messenger of the thunder deity) signals the proximate arrival of a native doctor; and dreams of snakes (another emblem of the thunder deity) warn of harmful encounters with Sibundoy native doctors.

Finally, the thunder god, as the source of all phenomena associated with the weather, may be associated with the immense spiritual meaning attributed to the wind in Sibundoy Valley cosmology. The term *huayra* operates as a kind of cover term for the entire domain of Sibundoy spiritual belief. Although precise documentation is lacking, it is tempting to suppose that the origins of this spiritual force might be traced to the offices of this celestial deity.

In addition to descriptions of the sky god, most of the extant accounts of Incaic traditions feature the adventures of a primordial culture hero, often referred to by the name Viracocha, who visits the earth to establish precedents and pass judgments and then takes his leave. The culture hero Viracocha must be distinguished from Viracocha Pachayachachi, the creator god, and Viracocha Inca, one of the legendary Incan rulers. Viracocha in the form of the culture hero is closely associated with the thunder god and with the sun in Andean cosmology. Pedro de Cieza de León, observing and writing in the midst of the Spanish conquest, presents one of the earliest and fullest notices, identifying two Viracocha figures considerably separated in time. One of them, perhaps the creator god, appears shortly after the first dawn and is able "to change plains into mountains, and great hills into valleys, and make water flow out of stones." This earlier figure is depicted as "the Prince of all things, the Father of the Sun." He is said to perform "wonders, giving life to men and animals." Further, Cieza de León (1883: 5, 6) reports that "in many places he gave orders to men how they should live, and he spoke lovingly to them and with much gentleness, admonishing them that they should do good, and no evil or injury to another, and that they should be loving and charitable to all." In Cieza de León's account, a second, unnamed figure resembling the first appears somewhat later and goes about healing people; we are told that "where there were blind he gave them sight by only uttering words."

Statements from other early Spanish chroniclers confirm and augment this portrait of Viracocha. Juan Diez de Betanzos (1924: 85) describes a pair of Viracochas who wander about and call upon the people to "come out and populate the earth." Cristóbal de Molina (1873: 7) relates that the Creator commanded that Viracocha "should set out from this point and go by the way of the mountains and forests through all the land, giving names to the large and small trees, and to the flowers and fruits that they bear, and teaching the people which were good for food or for medicine, and which should be avoided." What emerges is a portrait of a culture hero sent out to wander the earth and establish lasting precedents in the natural and social realms. This powerful figure interacts with the ancestors of the present-day people, teaching them the names and uses of the objects and creatures in the world. In one rather fanciful account, it is said that the culture hero "rewarded and granted privileges to all the animals that gave him news that accorded with his wishes, and cursed all those whose tidings were not agreeable to him" (Avila 1966: 129).

The parallels between Viracocha of the southern Andes and the Sibundoy Wangetsmuna are unmistakable, indicating that we are dealing with manifestations of an archetypical pan-Andean culture hero complex (in evidence, as has been seen, among the Chibchan peoples of the northern Andes as well). The motifs linking Wangetsmuna and Viracocha are striking: each of them is closely related to the sun and the thunder deity, and each provides a link between the divine and mortal planes. To a degree, their activities coincide: both Viracocha and Wangetsmuna endow the animals with their voices and habits, perform healing actions such as restoring sight to the blind, grant privileges and pronounce curses, and generally teach the people the ways of civilized life. There are also regional differences: nothing in the Wangetsmuna cycle is comparable to the fireball unleashed by the besieged Viracocha nor can any equivalent be found to Viracocha's predilection to turn people into stone. By the same token, many episodes in the Wangetsmuna cycle lack any counterpart in the southern Andes materials.

The culture hero of the Sibundoy Valley, although never mentioned in the sayings, functions as a kind of ideological bedrock. As the first teacher of the Sibundoy people, Wangetsmuna is the source of all knowledge attributed to the ancestors. It is Wangetsmuna who visits the earth imparting the wisdom of his grandfather to the first ancestors of the Sibundoy native peoples. Mediating between the heavens and earth, Wangetsmuna translates the awesome power of the deities into manageable branches of human endeavor, such as planting and processing food, entering into productive social relationships, and most important, leading a life of spiritual health. The blueprint for a well-lived life presented in the sayings derives from the crucial ministry of the culture hero Wangetsmuna.

These facets of the pan-Andean "manifold godhead" pervade the mythic narrative of the Sibundoy Valley and endow it with a prominent pan-Andean aura. The Sibundoy case must be viewed as an instance of what folklorists call an *oicotype*, a regional manifestation of the general scheme, and it may well contain details that will help flesh out the existing documentary record. The relative obscurity of the third component, the solar deity, confirms suggestions that the cult of solar worship was elaborated by the Incas and never achieved much prominence in the general Andean religious substrate (Demarest 1981: 46). The sun does appear in the Wangetsmuna cycle, as father to the moon, but this deity remains largely aloof from the development of human society and peripheral in the sayings of the ancestors.

Of far greater prominence is Mama Quilla, the moon mother. She is worshiped along with the sun but as a more approachable figure, one that intervenes directly in the affairs of humankind. In the Wangetsmuna cycle the moon appears as the sun's daughter; she interacts directly with the first people, becoming the wife of the primordial miner and visiting him at night in the form of a spirit. The younger brother's curiosity about her mysterious presence sets into motion the events leading irrevocably to the founding of civilized society.

The moon remains a major figure in Sibundoy mythic consciousness to this day, though she is now most often depicted as the wife of the sun. She is perceived as a woman holding a baby, in some modern renditions as the Virgin Mary holding the infant Christ. Eclipses of the moon are viewed with great concern by Sibundoy natives, as the following testimony from an Ingano friend indicates:

When there is an eclipse of the moon, since she is the Virgin, the moon is the Virgin, you can see that it appears as if she were carrying a baby. And so they say that some animals are chasing her to steal her child. And I remember many times when I was young and there was an eclipse of the moon, it would become very dark outside, and then everyone would go out with drums, flutes, and all that. They said it was to scare off those animals so they wouldn't steal her child. And everyone went out to shout and make noise even though it wasn't carnival day. They say that this is the only way to save the child for her, by making lots of noise. They say that she is the wife of god, they say that the moon is the sun's wife.

The moon exerts a strong presence in the sayings, where she appears as a metaphor of organic growth—when she is growing (the waxing moon), the powers of humans and other living things are at their peak; when she is diminishing (the waning moon), the reverse is true. The sayings reveal a number of human activities, including the cycle of planting and harvesting, and the use of the remedies, which are timed to the phases of the moon.

One apparent point of departure between the Andean framework (as revealed in Incan materials) and Sibundoy spirituality is the relative unimportance of earth and mountains shrines in Sibundoy thought. The ethnohistorical record attests to the prominence of *huacas*, 'earth shrines', and *wamanis* and *apus*, 'mountain deities', in the central and southern Andes, and in spite of the best efforts of the missionaries such forms of worship remain prevalent in these areas (Bastien 1978; Isbell 1978). Spiritual essence floats on the wind in the Sibundoy Valley, though certain sites do exercise spiritual power. The topography of the valley contains numerous *puntos malos*, 'evil spots', that are thought to harbor spiritual malevolence. Perhaps of more relevance to the discussion of huacas are the Christian shrines and monuments constructed on previously sacred ground and sometimes accorded a spiritual efficacy comparable to the power of the earth shrines in other areas.

Some idea of the process leading to the Christianization of the native earth shrines in the Sibundoy area can be gathered from the following anecdote. The most spectacular mountain peak visible from the valley floor is Volcan Patascoy, a cone-shaped volcano lying to the south of the valley. The sayings identify this prominence as a source of power and danger: for example, a pregnant woman is warned not to stare at the volcano, lest her child emerge cross-eyed (saying 175). To this day, the people of Santiago discern a group of "doors" near the summit of the volcano, and they predict the weather according to the following belief:

Often when the volcano is shining . . . especially in the afternoon hours, it seems as if there were some doors. So we say, "Look, its going to be sunny. See, the devil's doors are open, the devil is out sunning himself." There must be some rocks or something up there, and seeing it from a distance, it looks like some doors. If there are four doors open, they say: "Look, we are going to have four days of sunshine." Or if there is nothing, they say: "This week we won't have any sunshine, its going to rain." And it usually comes true.

The concept of "the devil" is a particularly Christian, non-Andean one, so the question immediately arises whether this devil is in fact a mountain deity something on the order of the *wamanis* or *apus* in the central and southern Andes. When I asked about this belief, I received a most interesting response: "Sometimes they say that there are some aucas living up there, and they they are going to come down and feast on people. Father Bartolomé (a Capuchin missionary) used to talk like this, and they say that after the volcano erupted, Father Bartolomé went up there to place a cross, and since that time it has remained quiet."

This statement suggests that before the arrival of the Spanish, the Sibundoy natives recognized the existence of a mountain spirit that was later transmuted into a Christian devil and exorcised by the placement of that invincible Christian symbol, the cross. It may well be that whatever earth shrines previously existed in the valley experienced a comparable 'conversion' to Christianity. What is certain is that some recognition of mother earth lives on in the phrase "Our Mother on which we stand" (Bristol 1965: 25), in the worship of Christian monuments located at key points such as mountain passes and valley divides, and in the myths accounting for the earth's productivity. These myths portray the earth's fertility as a scabby girl (the scabs are a source of generative power) who comes to stay in the Sibundoy Valley; from that moment on "our little mother is quite fertile."

TROPICAL FOREST SPIRITUALITY

The Amazonian lowlands harbor indigenous populations that are strikingly different from the highland societies. As Frank Salomon (1983: 422) has it, "In both Incaic and Hispanoamerican culture, the antithesis between highland cities and lowland forests is an element of cosmology that has conditioned political relations. Highland cities are associated with centricity, culture, civility, and the power of the state, while the forest stands for the primordial, uncivilized, and centripetal powers of nature, never subdued by the state." But these contrasts should not obscure a steady pattern of interaction between highland and lowland areas. It seems certain that from time immemorial the lowland and highland peoples at all latitudes along the Andes have engaged in reciprocal forms of exchange (Flores-Ochoa 1979; Urton 1981; Masuda, Shimada & Morris 1985). If cultural innovations have found their way down the slopes of the mountains, there has also been movement of goods and knowledge in the opposite direction.

One of the most important elements in this upward drift is the

lowland shamanistic complex involving the use of visionary hallucinogenic experiences. Salomon (1983: 426) takes note of the
paradox whereby "jungle shamans, stereotyped as backward and
primitive, could at the same time appear to those in the very center
of political power as extraordinarily powerful beings." The Sibundoy native doctors are among those "jungle shamans" who have
brought lowland spirituality into the centers of highland authority.
Michael Taussig (1987: 153) discerns a general pattern to this arrangement, pointing to "an old, pan-Andean system of curing and
magical belief that credited the jungle Indians of the eastern foothills and lowlands with unique shamanic powers that could be
tapped by highlanders either directly or through the mediation of
Indians living between the highlands and the lowlands, such as the
Sibundoy." Schultes & Hofmann (1979) identify a spirituality complex associated with hunting, hallucinogens, and New World peoples. They contend that "the 'narcotic complex' preserved in the
New World in the vision quest represents a continuum of the shamanism of the mesolithic hunting societies of Euroasia" (Schultes
& Hofmann 1979: 30). These authors hold that the individual's
success in activities such as hunting and war derive from the acquisition of "outside gifts" or "medicine power," and that hallucinogenic substances often play a role in these settings (Schultes
& Hofmann 1979: 30): "American Indian religions based on the
shamanism of hunters, still actively seek the personal mystic experience, and one of the easiest and most logical ways of seeking
it is through psychoactive plants possessing supernatural forces."

What is proposed is a cultural matrix centered on hunting as the
principal means of subsistence and involving the use of hallucinogenic substances as part of an "ecstatic" shamanism, instrumental
in the process of negotiation with masters or lords of the animals
for the release of animal souls. Although not unknown in the
Andes, these elements are most intimately associated with the
tropical forest societies of the northwest Amazonian basin (Reichel-Dolmatoff 1971; Whitten 1976). Aspects of this tropical forest
cultural matrix are present in the Sibundoy Valley and enter into
the universe of the sayings.

Perhaps most resonant with Sibundoy folk religion is the ecstatic
recovery of the ancestral frame, often through the use of yagé and
other psychotropic substances, a characteristic feature of Upper
Amazonian spirituality. The Huitoto in the Colombian Amazon
provide a typical case: "the men, in a continuous return to that
atemporal existence of the ancestors, learn models of 'leadership'
and are searchers for knowledge" (Garzon y Macuritope 1987: 301).

Sibundoy native doctors specialize in the use of "medicines" capable of invoking the ancestors: *yagé* or *ayahuasca*, a powerful hallucinogen brought to the valley from the adjacent margins of the great Amazonian basin; and the even more potent *borrachera*, prepared locally from the datura trees cultivated in the valley.

"The Tale of the Shaking Lake" (see Chapter 5) indicates that in earlier times the Sibundoy native doctors made use of these medicines on occasions of public ceremony, a custom that is attested in the shamanism of the Upper Amazon. Jean Langdon (1986) reports that as recently as the 1960s the chief shaman of the Siona (a Tukanoan group resident along the Putumayo River after it descends from the Andes) conducted weekly rituals for the entire community, sometimes in relation to the hunt. Jean Jackson (1983: 195) describes ceremonies among the Tukano people of the northwest Amazon "in which the shaman transforms the longhouse and its occupants in space and time. . . . At the most sacred point in this process, the group enters ancestral time." Sibundoy native doctors use many of the same techniques as their lowland counterparts but in a practice that has become strictly private, probably in response to the concerted efforts of generations of missionaries.

The mythic narrative of the valley contains tales of shamanistic encounters with the masters of particular animal species, like the master of the wild pigs. In one story two hunters follow the herd of wild pigs into their cave and find that once inside the pigs take on human form. The formidable master of the animals scolds the hunters for taking too many animals and then provides them with a powerful drink, a hallucinogen that makes them quite "drunk" and reveals to them the secrets of the hunt. Mythic narratives of this sort are cognate to myths told among the tropical forest Tukano, where the shaman is thought to enter the spirit realm and negotiate an exchange of human and animal souls with Vai-mahse, the master of the animals (Reichel-Dolmatoff 1971: 130).

The presence of tropical forest elements in the Sibundoy folk religion is a product of the intimate association of the Sibundoy native peoples with the lowland margins of the Andes. It appears that the San Andrés Inganos entered the valley in historical times from this eastern fringe, and it is not unlikely that the Santiagueños and Kamsá migrated to the valley along the same route in prehistoric times. The lowland and highland areas have sustained a significant trade network, and some of the lowland communities, notably the Inga-speaking *amigos*, may be transplanted colonies of the highland peoples. Sibundoy natives continue to look to the peoples of the Lower Pututmayo for spiritual inspiration, and Sibundoy shamans customarily serve an apprenticeship with lowland curers.

These ties have forged a lowland calque in the Sibundoy cosmology, persisting outside of the hunting syndrome and coexisting with the pan-Andean cosmological elements already discussed. Thus the thunder deity is the patron of the native doctor, even though the chanting, dancing, and visionary experience of the native doctor derives more from tropical forest than Andean prototypes. Once again, this conceptual framework makes itself felt in the universe of the sayings. Many of the sayings deal explicitly with the visionary drug experience, and others attribute spiritual meaning to the behavior of game animals such as deer and tapir. One branch of Sibundoy spirits, the *sacha huayra*, or 'spirits of the forest', may well derive from these tropical forest antecedents. The sayings warn of encounters with forest spirits: pursuit of spiritual health entails the proper handling of these powerful spiritual forces.

ANDEAN CATHOLICISM

The Andean zone, as the seat of the most advanced indigenous societies on the South American continent, immediately came under the scrutiny of the Spaniards in their delirious search for gold. Many Andean peoples did cultivate the working of gold into ceremonial and religious objects, and the Spanish ambition was all too well rewarded, provoking further exploration, decimation and domination. The rosary and cross of the Spanish padres accompanied the sword of the conquistadores, so almost immediately upon contact the indigenous peoples were exposed to their first taste of Catholic evangelization.

Those American natives who did not perish in the initial onslaught found themselves subject to the secular authority of the Spanish *cabildos* (town councils) and *encomenderos* (Spanish lords granted provisional rights to native lands and labor by royal decree), or else they became trusts of one Catholic mission or another, charged with the redemption of their souls (and awarded the labor of their bodies). The Catholic religious orders portrayed themselves as the saviors of the Indians, and this claim has some validity in view of the harsh conditions experienced by the native peoples at the hands of the Spanish lords and settlers. Even so, the regimen imposed by the Catholic fathers could be harsh and authoritarian.

There were some nativistic movements: the tradition of Inkarrí,

the buried god regenerating in the earth (Lopez-Baralt 1979) and
the revival of the huacas in a spiritual rebellion referred to as *taqui
ongoy*, "the singing sickness" (Molina 1873; Ossio 1973) are among
the most prominent. But in many cases the native peoples of the
Andes discovered that their best option lay in conforming to Spanish expectations and asserting whatever influence they could
through the conventional political channels of the colony. This
tactic involved the adoption of Catholicism, observance of the laws
of king and cabildo, and the frequent petitioning of the crown for
relief from abuses of the system. As the colony matured, the kings
of Spain increasingly turned to the native lords, known as *caciques*,
as a counter-balance to the growing entrenchment and independence of the creole Spanish elite (Pease 1985; Salomon 1986a). By
the turn of the eighteenth century, native lords were receiving royal
confirmation of their lands, and additional guarantees from a crown
hard-pressed to maintain its authority over a Creole administrative
class born and come of age in America.

The grand colonial design just described played itself out in the
Sibundoy Valley as elsewhere in the Andes. Although the valley
was far enough removed from areas of extensive Spanish settlement
to avoid direct contact with a colonial cabildo, it fell under the
sway of Spanish encomendero and Catholic missionary. The en-
comienda system was officially abolished in 1542, but the native
peoples of the Sibundoy Valley were not entirely liberated from
this feudal system until well into the eighteenth century (Bonilla
1972: 31). The Sibundoy Valley has been the site of intermittent
but often intense Catholic missionizing for some four hundred
years and more. The valley received its first *doctrinero* or religious
instructor as early as 1547 A.D., that is, only a few decades after
the Spanish set foot on South American soil (Bonilla 1972). The
most recent mission, the Capuchin, lost its permission to mis-
sionize in the valley in 1975, after persistent winds of scandal and
some protest on the part of Sibundoy natives. In the interim, a
succession of Spanish missions, Dominican, Franciscan, and Capuchin, pursued the extirpation of idolatry and the inculcation of the
proper Catholic religious spirit.

The effect of this prolonged work of the missionaries can be
measured in the "ritual language" of the Sibundoy natives, a speech
register set aside for the accomplishment of official community
business (McDowell 1983). Discourse in this speech variety evinces
the tonality and content of Catholic litany: it is loaded with the
key words of Catholic dogma, words like *perdona* ('pardon'), *pa-
sentsia* ('forgiveness'), *lesentsia* ('permission'), *kardado* ('mercy'),

and *remidio* ('grace'). The available evidence suggests that this highly stylized speech variety emerged very early as the sign of the "civilized" Indian, and quickly became the prerequisite to social and political advancement in the indigenous community under the Spanish rule.

The Sibundoy natives converted early to Catholicism, and they remain devout Catholics to this day. In the process, the doctrines of the official church, as well as elements from a rich domain of Spanish folk Catholicism, penetrated and reshaped the religious life of Sibundoy natives. In the Sibundoy Valley very little of the precolumbian system survived the ministry of the Spanish priests intact, but it is remarkable how much of it persists to color the Catholicism of the valley and to provide a folk religious counterpart to the offical religion of the land. The persistence of the sayings of the ancestors is one of the most visible signs of this process of accommodation, carried out over a period of centuries and still in progress.

Spanish Catholicism confronted the native Sibundoy religion on two fronts: the official dogma inculcated through teachings of the priests, and a layer of folk Catholicism carried in the credulous minds of Spanish priests and settlers, who had left Spain at the height of the European witch-craze (Trevor-Roper 1978). In the Sibundoy Valley as elsewhere in the Andes, the conversion of the native peoples to the Catholic faith was perhaps deceptively successful. Conformance to the sacraments and submission to the priests masks a remarkable persistence of aboriginal patterns. Manuel Marzal (1985) has identified a number of significant deviations from orthodoxy: the failure to recognize the Holy Trinity; widespread reliance on *promesas*, a continuation of the ancient pattern of "reciprocity"; the belief that God punishes and rewards people in *this* life rather than the afterlife; and the "mythification of the saints," whose statues and relics are treated as the physical abode of living spiritual forces. The exploits of *nuestro señor de Sibundoy*, a statue of Christ on the cross that refused to be moved from the valley, demonstrate the force of this belief in the animate quality of Catholic symbols (Friede 1945; Bonilla 1972).

At the fringes of Andean Catholicism is a set of practices clearly derived from the precolumbian substrate, especially the rites of divination and propitiation centered on the traditional deities, the *apus*, *wamanis*, and *huacas*. Among these peripheral elements, two bear special relevance to the Sibundoy sayings: the belief that "death is announced by a series of omens" (Marzal 1985: 29) and the belief that "certain illnesses do not have a biological origin but are rather of another order, for example, because the sick person has suffered a shock (*mancharisca*) or an evil wind (*soqa wayra*)" (Marzal 1985: 33). These observations argue for the pan-Andean character of systems like the Sibundoy sayings of the ancestors.

The intersection of the indigenous substrate religion with Spanish Catholicism creates a remarkable tapestry revealing the interplay of five processes:

1. Equivalence: in some cases, equivalence sets were worked out so that elements in the old religion became identified with elements in the new;
2. Complementarity: aspects of the two religions persist side by side in the emergent folk religion;
3. Contradiction: elements in the two religions exist in a state of tension or hostility;
4. Substitution: an element from one religion takes the place of an element from the other;
5. Dissociation: aspects of the two religions persist but are kept separate.

Each of these processes can be charted in the evolution of contemporary Sibundoy folk religion.

The ancient religion recognized a number of celestial deities, among them Our Father the Sun and Our Mother the Moon. These two heavenly bodies became identified with the Christian God and Mother Mary, respectively. The culture hero Wangetsmuna, who is sent out "to visit the world" in behalf of his grandfather, the thunder, becomes associated with the Christian savior Jesus Christ. In some variants, Wangetsmuna returns to sit beside his grandfather in the skies; in others, he is devoured by the animals and perishes here on earth. These events correspond to aspects in the life of the Christian savior, and Wangetsmuna, like Jesus, serves as an intermediary between heaven and earth. The logic of *equivalence* allows that elements similarly placed in the two religious hierarchies can merge into a single, syncretized unit and in this manner the two religious systems persist in a state of parity.

Some comparable elements in the two religions were not assimilated into a single two-faced equivalence set but rather became incorporated as discrete entities in a relationship of *complementarity*. In such instances the similar elements stand as mute witness to the historical intersection of distinct religious systems, but they function cohesively in the emergent folk religion. The adoption of the blessed palm branches into the curing ceremony of the native doctor and the complementary role of priest and shaman are cases in point.

The blessing of the palm branches on Palm Sunday is a widespread observance among the world's Catholics. In the Sibundoy Valley as elsewhere, these branches are preserved throughout the year in people's homes, where they are thought to contribute a blessing to the members and activities of the household. These sacred branches, blessed by the priest and touched with holy water in the church, enter into the decidedly non-Christian practices of the native doctors, who use them for a number of medicinal purposes: as percussive instruments accompanying the doctor's chanting and dancing; as brushing instruments, removing harmful essences from the clothing and skin of the patient; and as an incense thought to release a cleansing and purifying smoke. In all these uses, the blessed branches commingle with the other, non-Christian resources of the native doctors.

The offices of Catholic priest and native doctor themselves stand in a relationship of complementarity, in spite of the priests' attempts to remove all traces of non-Christian spirituality. In the modern setting, the priest is recognized for one set of spiritual functions: reciting the mass, officiating at rite of passage ceremonies, and so on. The native doctor is charged with a different set of spiritual responsibilities: contacting the spirit realm to effect cures, to recover stolen property, and in some cases, to inflict harm. Lately a third professional has appeared on this medico-religious stage: the Colombian health worker, who is consulted in cases of illness that do not derive from spirit sickness (Seijas 1969).

The accommodation of elements in the two religions is not always so harmonious. Some comparable elements remain fixed in hostile relationships of mutual *contradiction*. In particular, some aspects of the pan-Andean substrate take on diabolical connotations, and these are stigmatized as negative elements in opposition to the positive forces of the Catholic church. The masters of the natural elements, a component of tropical forest shamanism, suffer this fate in the emergent Andean folk religion. They are not syncretized with the lower-echelon Catholic figures, the saints, nor do they persist in friendly, complementary relationships with their counterparts. Instead, they are viewed as demonic, diabolic enemies, to be vanquished through adherence to the Catholic rites.

This relationship obtains in a set of Sibundoy narratives depicting the power of sacred medallions, blessed in church, against the onslaught of these autochthonous nature demons. In one such story, a hunter who strays from his peers finds himself besieged by the master of the river, a dreadful being with the face of bird and the dark-draped body of a Marist monk. As the river carries its master to the edge of the hunter's refuge, a sacred medallion intervenes and forces the master of the river to retreat. Here the Christian element and the substrate element stand in opposition, and although the medallion forces a withdrawal of the river master, the frightened hunter perishes a few days later from fright.

The *substitution* of an element in the new religion for its counterpart in the old is a reflection of political realities: the Catholic faith enjoyed the absolute backing of the Spanish authorities, and it was intolerant of all other forms of religious expression. The priests labored mightily to indoctrinate native Americans in the mysteries of the Catholic mass and with equal fervor to deprive the native peoples of their "pagan idolatries." The overt forms of indigenous worship were most vulnerable to this missionary onslaught, and throughout the Andes the precolumbian rituals were firmly suppressed or assimilated to Catholic rites. In some areas, a significant portion of this ritual practice managed to survive in underground arenas (Bastien 1978). But in the Sibundoy Valley, only a few vestiges of ancestral ritual survive.

The standard Catholic rites—the weekly mass, the various rites of passage—came to replace the earlier forms of ritual observance in the Sibundoy Valley. Public worship of Jesus Christ, the Virgin Mary, and the saints replaced the previous rites directed to the celestial deities, to the masters of the natural elements, and to the first ancestors. All overt forms of religion responded to the Catholic imperative: there is one God, and Jesus Christ is His only son. Apart from the curing ceremonies of the native doctor and a few odd survivals, such as the shedding of petals at carnival season, the *boda* or ritual meal associated with the vereda-based rites of passage, and the lighting of candles to Our Father the Sun, the ritual life of the Sibundoy natives is essentially a Catholic one.

Last, some comparable elements of the two religious systems have simply persisted in separate, inviolable domains. This process of *dissociation* reveals a capacity to maintain two independent religious orientations, when forces are present to bolster each of them. The Catholic faith was imposed through coercion and enticement, whereas the weight of indigenous tradition impelled the retention of the substrate Andean faith. The process of dissociation is evident in the separate but equal status of the two religious mythologies. Sibundoy natives are well versed in the biblical story of Adam and Eve, but they are equally tuned to the adventures of Wangetsmuna and the first ancestors. They identify the first narrative cluster as "white people's things," the second as "our things." Stories from the two traditions are enjoyed on their own terms; they are carefully isolated from one another, and it is considered inept to mix them together.

The imposition of Catholicism precipitated a massive realignment of religious expression in Colombia's Sibundoy Valley and elsewhere in the Andes. In concert, the five adaptive processes provide the emergent Andean folk religion with the following traits: a predominantly Catholic public religious life; persistence of the pan-Andean cosmology in forms complementary and contradictory to the official religion; persistence of the shamanistic cults, but now at the familial rather than community level; infusion of Catholic beliefs, but in forms adapted to Andean religious sensitivity.

The sayings of the ancestors are a key element in the emergent folk religion of the valley, ensuring continuity of practice in the absence of anything resembling an organized church. This spiritual orientation has gravitated to the arena of cherished popular tradition, where it persists largely through the agency of the sayings and the companion tradition of mythic narrative. Sibundoy folk religion has proved to be a vital resource in the evolution of the indigenous peoples, and I suspect that it will continue to shape thought and action in these communities even during this period of rapid assimilation to the Western model of civilization.

Appendix:
A Note on the
Inga Language

INGA PHONOLOGY

In the absence of an official Quechua orthography, I have opted to use orthographic conventions favored by native speakers because they follow some of the methods used to represent Spanish sounds as learned in grammar schools and high schools in the valley. Some variation in the transcription of vowels in particular reflects the inherent variability of these sounds in Inga speech. For a thorough treatment of Inga phonology, including allophonic variations, see Levinsohn 1976. Inga phonemes as represented in this study are as follows:

Vowels

	Front	Central	Back
High	i		u
Low		a	

Consonants

	Labial	Dental	Palatal	Velar
Voiceless stop	p	t	ch	c
Voiced stop	b	d		g
Nasal	m	n	n	
Sibilant		s	sh	
Lateral		l	ll	
flap		r		
Semi-vowel	hu		y	

KEY TO GRAMMATICAL PARSING

Inga, like other languages in the Quechuan family, is an example of an agglutinating system, wherein "solid state" morphemes (i.e. morphemes that retain their shape) are added sequentially to a root in order to form words. In Inga, the root always precedes the morphemes, which are tacked on as suffixes. My Inga transcripts feature, perhaps to a fault, the accretion of affixes into words, in some cases recognizing affixes like -ri (inceptive/reflexive), -chi (causative), and -y (nominative) that could just as well be considered "frozen" into the roots. The ordering of words is quite flexible in Inga, although the most conventional order is verb-subject-object. The verb is the most highly elaborated part of speech, though nouns too are capable of taking on suffixes. In the table that follows, the morphemes are classified according to their association, or lack thereof, with a particular part of speech (noun, verb, or independent). This is not the time to enter into the intricacies of Inga grammar, but the reader is referred to Steven Levinsohn's comprehensive treatment of Inga grammar in *The Inga Language* (1976).

Form	*Abbreviation*	*Significance*
Nominal Suffixes		
-manda	abl	ablative ('from')
-ma	dat	dative ('to', 'towards')
-pa	poss	possessive
-pi	loc	locative
-ta	acc	accusative (focused object)
-cuna	pl	plural
-sina	comp	comparative
-hua, -huanta	inst	instrumental ('with')
-cama	rest	restrictive ('until')
-ya	verb	verbalizer
-dero, -dur	agt	agentive
-ndi	asso	associative ('together')
-pura	reci	reciprocal
-car, -cari	emp	emphasis
-aj	desp	deprecative (weak)
-nsi	desp	deprecative (strong)
-nig	pro	proximity
-quin	ref	reflexive
Verbal Suffixes		
-sca	hist	historical (past)
-ri	ref	reflexive, inceptive
-cu	prog	progressive (singular)
-nacu	prog	progressive (plural)
-mu	cis	cislocative (movement to)
-raya	sta	stative

-y	imp	imperative (singular)
-ychi	imp	imperative (plural)
-ngapa	purp	purposive
-chi	caus	causative
-spa	ger	gerundive
-pu, -pua	ben	benefactive
-g	nom	nominalizer (agent)
-gpi	cond	conditional
-gta	sub	subordinate
-glla	post	posterior
-gmanda	hab	habitual
-gri	disloc	dislocative
-hora	temp	temporal
-y	inf	infinitive
-y	nom	nominalizer

Conjugations:

-ni	1st	first person, singular,
-ngui	2nd	second person, singular
-N	3rd	third person, singular (only appears in certain environments)
-nchi	1, p	first person, plural
-nguichi	2, p	second person, plural
-ncuna	3, p	third person, plural
-rca	past	past tense marker
-rsha	past	past tense marker, 2nd person plural
-sa	1, fut	first person, singular, future
-ncangui	2, fut	second person, singular, future
-nga	3, fut	third person, singular, future
-sunchi	1, p, fut	first person, plural, future
-ncanguichi	2, p, fut	second person, plural, future
-ngacuna	2, p, fut	third person, plural, future
-qui	1 sub, 2 ob	first person subject second person object

Independent Suffixes

-mi	aff	affirmative (evidential)
-si	rep	reportative

-chu	int, neg	interrogative, negative
-ca	foc	focal
-pasi, pas	conj	conjunctive
-lla	del	delimitative ('only')
-n	conn	connective

References

Allen, Catherine. 1982. Body and soul in Quechua thought. *Journal of Latin American Lore*. 8:179-196.

Avila, Francisco de. 1966. *Dioses y hombres de Huarochirí* [ca. 1598], bilingual edition, trans. José María Arguedas. Lima: Instituto de Estudios Peruanos.

Bastien, Joseph. 1978. *Mountain of the condor: Metaphor and ritual in an Andean ayllu*. American Ethnological Society Monographs, no. 64. Minneapolis: West Publishing.

Bastien, Joseph. 1985. Qollahuaya-Andean body concepts: A topographical-hydraulic model of physiology. *American Anthropoligist* 87: 595-611.

Bennett, Wendall. 1946. The archaeology of the Central Andes. In *Handbook of South American Indians*. Vol. 2, *The Andean civilizations*. ed. Julian Steward 61-142. Bureau of American Ethonology Bulletin 143.

Juan Betanzos, Diez de. 1924. *Suma y narración de los Incas* [1551]. Coleción de Libros y Documentos Referentes a la Historia del Perú, ed. Horacio Urteaga, 2nd series, vol. 8, 75-208. Lima: Sanmartí.

Bierhorst, John. 1985. *The mythology of North America*. New York: Morrow.

Bonilla, Victor Daniel. 1972. *Servants of God or masters of men: The story of a Capuchin mission in Amazonia*. London: Penguin.

Bristol, Melvin Lee. 1965. Sibundoy ethnobotany. Ph. D. diss., Harvard University.

Bristol, Melvin Lee. 1968. Sibundoy argicultural vegetation. In *Actas y memorias, 37th Congreso Internacional de Americanistas*. Buenos Aires.

Brown, Michael. 1985. *Tsewa's Gift: Magic and meaning in an Amazonian society*. Washington, D. C.: Smithsonian.

Bruce, Robert. 1975. *Lacandon dream symbolism: Dream symbolism and interpretation among the Lacandon Mayas of Chiapas, Mexico*. México: Ediciones Euroamericanos.

Cabrera Rodriguez, Agusto. 1986. *Los Agueros en la cultura popular de Nariño.*. Pasto, Colombia: Imprenta Departamental.

Carvalho-Neto, Paulo de. 1983. Folklore according to spiritism: A new approach to inter-disciplinary folklore. *Folklore Americano* 36: 53-80.

Castillo y Orozco, Padre Eugenio del. 1877. *Vocabulario Paez-Castellano, catechismo, nociones grammaticales i dos platicas* [1755]. Collection Linguistique Americaine, vol. 2. Paris.

Cieza de León, Pedro de. 1883. *The second part of the chronicle of Peru* [1554]. Trans. and ed. Clements Markham. London: Hakluyt Society.

Cobo, Bernabe. 1956. *Historia del Nuevo Mundo* [1653]. Biblioteca de Autores Espanoles, vol. 92. Madrid.

Conrad, Geoffrey and Arthur Demarest. 1984. *Religion and empire; The dynamics of Aztec and Inca expansionism.* New York: Cambridge Univ. Press.

Demarest, Arthur. 1981. *Viracocha, the nature and antiquity of the Andean High God.* Monographs of the Peabody Museum, no. 6. Cambridge, Mass.: Peabody Museum.

Douglas, Mary. 1966. *Purity and danger: An analysis of concepts of pollution and taboo.* London: Routledge & Kegan Paul.

Eggan, Dorothy. 1966. Hopi dreams in cultural perspective. In *The dream and human societies,* ed. G. E. Grunebaum and Roger Caillois. Berkeley: Univ. of California Press.

Eliade, Mircea. 1959. *The sacred and the profane: The nature of religion.* Trans. Willard Trask. New York: Harcourt, Brace.

Flores-Ochoa, Jorge. 1979. *Pastoralists of the Andes.* Trans. Ralph Bolton. Philadelphia: ISHI.

Frazer, James. 1922. *The golden bough: A study in magic and religion.* New York: Macmillan.

Friede, Juan. 1945. Leyendas de nuestro señor de Sibundoy y el santo Carlos Tamoabioy. *Boletin de Arqueologia,* vol. 1.

Garcilaso de la Vega. 1945. *Comentarios reales de los Incas* [1609]. Buenos Aires: Emece Editores.

Garzón, Nivia Cristina y Vincente Macuritope. 1987. El chontaduro, una planta en el contexto cultural. *América Indígena* 47: 295-316.

Gose, Peter. 1986. Sacrifice and the commodity form in the Andes. *Man,* n.s. 21: 296-310.

Graham, Malbone. 1925. Some folktales of the Chibcha nation. *Publications of the Texas Folk-Lore Society* 4: 68-79.

Gregor, Thomas. 1981. "Far, far away my shadow wandered": The dream symbolism and dream theories of the Mehinaku Indians of Brazil.' *American Ethnologist* 8: 709-720.

Guaman Poma de Ayala, Felipe. 1956. *Nueva corónica y buen Gobierno.* . . . [1610-1615]. Trans. Luis Bustos Galvez. Lima: Editorial Cultura.

Harrison, Regina. 1982. The *Relación de antiguedades deste reino del Pirú* by Joan de Santacruz Pachacuti Yamqui Salcamaygua. In *From oral to written expression: Native Andean chronicles of the early colonial period,* ed. R. Adorno. Latin American Series, No. 4. Syracuse: Maxwell School of Citizenship and Public Affairs.

Hymes, Dell. 1981. *In vain I tried to tell you: Essays in native American ethnopoetics.* Philadelphia: Univ. of Pennsylvania Press.

Ibérico Mas, Luis. 1971. *El folklore majico de Cajamarca.* Trujillo, Perú: Universidad Nacional de Cajamarca.

Isbell, Billie Jean. 1978. *To defend ourselves: Ecology and ritual in an Andean village.* Austin: Univ. of Texas Press.

Jackson, Jean. 1983. *The fish people: Linguistic exogamy and Tukanoan identity in northwest Amazonia.* New York: Cambridge Univ. Press.

Juajibioy, Alberto. 1987. *Relatos y leyendas orales.* Bogotá: Servicio Colombiano de Comunicación Social.

Juajibioy, Alberto and Alvaro Wheeler. 1973. *Bosquejo ethnolinguistico del grupo Kamsá de Sibundoy, Putumayo, Colombia.* Bogotá: Imprenta Nacional.

Kroeber, Alfred. 1902. The Mohave Indians. *American Anthropologist* 4: 279-285.

Langdon, Jean. 1986. Las clasificaciones del yaje dentro del grupo Siona: etnobotánica, etnoquímica, e historia. *América Indígéna* 46: 101-116.

Lathrap, Donald. 1970. *The upper Amazon.* New York: Praeger.

Levinsohn, Stephen. 1976. *The Inga language.* The Hague: Mouton.

Levinsohn, Stephen, Antonio Maffla Bilbao, and Domingo Tandioy Chasoy. 1978. *Diccionario Inga-Español, Español-Inga.* Meta, Colombia: Editorial Townsend.

Levi-Strauss, Claude. 1978. *The origin of table manners.* London: Harper and Row.

López-Baralt, Mercedes. 1980. The Quechua elegy to the all-powerful Inca Atawallpa: a literary rendition of the Inkarrí myth. *Latin American Indian Literatures* 4: 79-86.

López-Baralt, Mercedes. 1981. Millenarism as liminality: An interpretation of the Andean myth of Inkarrí. *Punto de Contacto: Point of Contact* 6: 65-82.

López de Velazco, Juan. 1894. Geografía y descripción universal de las Indias, recopiladas por el cosmógrafo-cronista. . . . desde el año 1571 al 1574. *Boletín de la Sociedad Geográfica de Madrid.*

Lullo, Orestes di. 1944. *El folklore de Santiago de Estero: Medicina y alimentación.* Publicación Official: Santiago de Estero, Argentina.

Mannheim, Bruce. A semiotic of Andean dreams. in *Dreaming: Anthropological and psychological interpretations,* ed. Barbara Tedlock, pp. 132-53.

Marzal, Manuel. 1985. *El syncretismo Iberoamericano.* Lima: Pontificia Universidad Católica del Perú.

Masuda, Shozo, Izumi Shimada, and Craig Morris. 1985. *Andean ecology and civilization: An interdisciplinary perspective on Andean ecological complementarity.* Univ. of Tokyo Press.

McDowell, John. 1983. The semiotic constitution of Kamsá ritual language. *Language in Society* 12: 23-46.

Molina, Cristóbal de. 1873. *An account of the fables and rites of the Yncas* [1575]. Trans. Clements Markham. New York: Burt Franklin.

Morgan, William. 1932. Navajo dreams. *American Anthropologist* 34:390-405.

Myerhoff, Barbara. 1974. *Peyote hunt: The sacred journey of the Huichol Indians.* Ithaca: Cornell Univ. Press.

Niles, Susan. 1981. *South American Indian narrative: An annotated bibliography.* New York: Garland.

O'Keefe, Daniel. 1982. *Stolen lightning: The social theory of magic.* New York: Continuum.

Ossio, Juan. ed. 1973. *Ideología mesiánica del mundo andino.* Lima: Edición de Ignacio Prado Pastor.

Oviedo Zambrano, Armando. 1978. Proceso histórico de las tribus Ingas y Kamsá del Valle de Sibundoy (Putumayo). *Indigenismo: Enfoques Colombianos* 11: 113-132.

Pease, Franklin. 1973. *El dios creador Andino.* Lima: Mosca Azul Editores.

———. 1985. En busca de una imagen andina propia durante colonia. *América Indígena* 45: 309-341.

Pittier de Fábrega, Henry. 1905-07. Ethnograpic and linguistic notes on the Paez Indians of Tierra Adentro, Cauca, Colombia. *Memoirs of the American Anthropological Association* 1: 301-356.

Rappaport, Joanne. 1978. Messianic thought and the manipulation of messianic symbols in Tierradentro, Colombia. Unpublished manuscript.

Reichel-Dolmatoff, Gerardo. 1977. *Amazonian cosmos: The sexual and religious suymbolism of the Tukano Indians.* Univ. of Chicago Press.

Reichel-Dolmatoff, Gerardo. 1975. *The shaman and the jaguar: A study of narcotic drugs among the Indians of Colombia.* Philadelphia: Temple Univ. Press.

Romoli de Avery, Kathleen. 1978. Las tribus de la antigua jurisdicción de Pasto en el siglo XVI. *Revista Colombiana de Antropologia* 21: 11-56.

Rowe, John. 1946. Inca culture at the time of the Spanish conquest. In *Handbook of South American Indians.* vol. 2, *The Andean Civilizations.* ed. Julian Steward. 183-330. Bureau of American Ethnology Bulletin 143.

Salomon, Frank. 1983. Shamanism and politics in late-colonial Ecuador. *American Ethnologist* 10: 413-428.

Salomon, Frank. 1986. *Native lords of Quito in the age of the Incas.* Cambridge Univ. Press.

Salomon, Frank. 1986a. Vertical politics on the Inka frontier. In *Anthropoligical history of Andean polities.* ed. John Murra, Nathan Wachtel, and Jaques Revel. Cambridge: Cambridge Univ. Press.

Santacruz Pachacuti-yamqui Salcamayhua, Juan de. 1873. *An account of the antiquities of Peru* [1620]. Trans. Clements Markham. New York: Burt Franklin.

Santayana, George. 1906. *The life of reason; or, the phases of human progress.* vol. 3, *Reason in religion.* New York: Charles Scribner's Sons.

Sañudo, José Rafael. 1938. *Apuntes sobre la historia de Pasto.* Pasto: Imprenta Nariñense.

Schultes, Richard Evans and Albert Hofmann. 1979. *Plants of the gods: Origins of hallucinogenic use.* New York: McGraw-Hill.

Seijas, Haydee. 1969. The medical system of the Sibundoy Indians of Colombia. Ph.D. diss., Tulane University.

Seligman, C. G. 1923. Notes on dreams, *Man* 23: 186-188.

Sharon, Douglas. 1978. *Wizard of the four winds: A shaman's story.* New York: Free Press.

Sherbondy, Jeanette. 1982. *The canal systems of Hanan Cuzco.* Ph.D. diss., University of Illinois, Urbana-Champaign.

Simón, Fray Pedro de. 1953. *Noticias historiales de las conquistas de tierra firme en las Indias Occidentales* [1625]. Bogotá: Biblioteca de Autores Colombianos.

Taggart, James. 1986. "Hansel and Gretel" in Spain and Mexico. *Journal of American Folklore* 99: 435-460.

Tandioy Chasoy, Domingo, n. d. *Nugpamandacuna imasa rimascacuna: dichos, refranes y recetas de los Antiguos.* Pasto: Imprenta del Departamento.

Tandioy Jansasoy, Francisco. 1987. *Muscuycuna y tapiacuna: Sueños y agüeros en inga y castellano.* Pasto, Colombia: Comité de Educación Inga de la Organización Musu Runacuna.

Taussig, Michael. 1980. Folk healing and the structure of conquest in the southwest Colombian Andes. *Journal of Latin American Lore* (6): 217-278.

Taussig, Michael. 1987. *Shamanism, colonialism, and the wild man: A study in terror and healing.* Chicago: Univ. of Chicago Press.

Tedlock, Barbara. 1982. *Time and the highland Maya.* Albuquerque: Univ. of New Mexico Press.

————, ed. *Dreaming: anthropological and psychological interpretations.* New York: Cambridge University Press, 1987.

Tedlock, Dennis, trans. 1985. *Popol vuh.* New York: Simon and Schuster.

Thompson, Stith. 1953. The star-husband tale. *Studia Septentrionalia* 4.

————. 1966. *Tales of the North American Indians* [1929]. Bloomington: Indiana Univ. Press.

Todorov, Tzvetan. 1984. *The conquest of America.* Trans. Richard Howard. New York: Harper and Row.

Trevor-Roper, H. R. 1978. *The European witch-craze of the 16th and 17th centuries.* Harmondsworth: Penguin.

Triana, Miguel. 1951. *La civilización Chibcha.* Bogotá: Biblioteca Popular de Cultura Colombiana.

Uribe, María Victoria. n. d. *Los pasto y etnias relacionadas: Arqueología y etnohistoria.* Unpublished manuscript.

Urton, Gary. 1981. *At the crossroads of the earth and the sky: An Andean cosmology.* Austin: Univ. of Texas Press.

Van Gennep, Arnold. 1960. *The rites of passage* [1908]. Trans. Monka Vizedom and Gabrielle Caffee. Univ. of Chicago Press.

Vollmer R., Loraine. 1978. Doña Rosa. *Revista Colombiana de Antropología* 21: 315-374.

Wallace, Anthony F. C. 1958. Dreams and the wishes of the soul: A type of psychoanalytic theory among the 17th-century Iroquois. *American Anthropologist* 60: 234-248.

Whitten, Norman. 1976. *Sacha runa: Ethnicity and adaptation of Ecuadorian jungle Quichua.* Urbana: Univ. of Illinois Press.

Yoder, Don. 1974. Toward a definition of folk religion. *Western Folklore* 33: 2-15.

Index

www.ingramcontent.com/pod-product-compliance
Lightning Source LLC
Chambersburg PA
CBHW020610270326
41927CB00005B/256